BEST EVIDENCE

BEST EVIDENCE

2ND EDITION

An Investigative Reporter's Three Year Quest to Uncover the Best Scientific Evidence for ESP, Psychokinesis, Mental Healing, Ghosts and Poltergeists, Dowsing, Mediums, Near Death Experiences, Reincarnation and Other Impossible Phenomena That Refuse to Disappear

Michael Schmicker

Writers Club Press
San Jose   New York   Lincoln   Shanghai

Best Evidence
2nd Edition

Writers Club Press
an imprint of iUniverse, Inc.

For information address:
iUniverse, Inc.
5220 S. 16th St., Suite 200
Lincoln, NE 68512
www.iuniverse.com

Cover photo: Digital Imagery copyright 2000 Photo Disc Inc.

ISBN: 0-595-21906-3

Printed in the United States of America

To Patricia, Christopher and, most of all, my brother John who kept the project alive when I had given up on it.

Epigraph

"I shall not commit the fashionable stupidity of regarding everything I cannot explain as a fraud."

Dr. Carl Jung in a 1919 speech to the Society for Psychical Research

Contents

Preface

We've all got our own standard of proof. What's yours? What would it take to make you believe in ESP? Ghosts? The survival of consciousness after death? Choose the description below that best matches you.

Debunker: You are 100 percent certain that all paranormal phenomena are false because they violate the proven, immutable Laws of Science. No evidence could convince you otherwise.

Comfortable Disbeliever: You're convinced that most—if not all—paranormal claims are false, based on everything you have learned in school, and conversations with persons you respect. It would require extraordinary evidence to make you believe and, given the slim odds of finding it, not worth searching for. So you're not going to go looking for it. If someone wants to bring you evidence, you'll give it a quick look. However, if any conventional explanation is available at all, you'll automatically choose it first.

Skeptic: You don't know whether paranormal phenomena exist or not, but you're always ready to look at repeatable, tightly controlled laboratory experiments. However, you find anecdotal, human testimony hard to swallow.

Cautious Believer: You suspect paranormal phenomena exist, based on how often people have reported them throughout human history. But you want to see some scientific evidence before you commit. You prefer laboratory demonstrations of psychic phenomena. But you'll also consider high quality human testimony—i.e. multiple reports over a period of time describing essentially the same phenomenon; from multiple witnesses who are reliable, credible and have no known reason to fabricate a story. Ideally, a written record of their observations will have been made immediately or shortly after the event, allowing subsequent independent follow-up analysis, testing and verification of those claims. Like a juror, you're prepared to carefully weigh less than perfect evidence and reach a decision based on it.

True Believer: You already believe paranormal phenomena exist. Your belief is based on one of the following: personal experience, intuition, philosophy, religion or simply the verbal testimony of some person you trust.

Done? Good. I don't want to waste your time or money. This book has nothing to offer the " Debunker" whose mind is already made up. If you're one, save your money. "Comfortable Disbelievers" should also beware. This book offers no evidence so extraordinary that some kind of alternative, conventional explanation—however weak—can't be found. If, for you, the worst conventional explanation will always trump the best paranormal explanation, go no further. If you're a "Skeptic," I believe you'll find some compelling scientific evidence to your liking (repeatable laboratory experiments). But not all "best evidence" presented in this book comes from a laboratory. You'll have to settle at times for high quality human testimony, offered without apology. If you're a "True Believer" you won't find a book filled with anecdotes and heart-warming human stories (though it includes some). Nor is it based on the author's personal epiphany with the paranormal. You may find this heavily-footnoted book a hard slog, even unnecessarily academic for your needs. But persevere, and you'll have the tools to talk with those of us (the majority) who require some evidence before we'll accept your claims.

And if you're a "Cautious Believer"? Buy two. This book's for you.

Acknowledgements

All opinions, and any mistakes, are mine alone. For providing me material to ponder, my thanks go out to the hundreds of inquisitive and often courageous scientists, researchers, university professors and others who, sometimes at great risk to their professional and personal reputations, produced the many books, papers, monographs, case studies and laboratory experiments described in this book. Their labors deserve a wider audience. My hope? That readers will be sufficiently intrigued by my layman's overview to seek out and read the original materials cited in the book. For their kind comments and encouragement, my special thanks to Larry Dossey MD, John Alexander, Edgar Mitchell, Fred Alan Wolf, Dean Radin, Stephen Braude, Henry Bauer, Stanley Krippner, Marcello Truzzi, Richard Broughton, Jon Klimo, Bruce Greyson, William Roll, Daryl Bem, Dan Cavicchio, Patrick Huyghe, Arthur Hastings, Bob Hieronimus, Anita McCormick, William Rauscher, Peter Sturrock, Dennis Stillings, Janet Cunningham, Jody Jovanovich, Cynthia Larson, Dick Allgire, Mike Tymn and John Ball. Last but not least, my thanks to Jack Houck for a mind-bending spoon-bending PK party in Mesquite, Nevada. I kept the spoon, Jack.

Part I: PSIentific Facts

1.

Nobody Really Believes This Stuff, Right?

"Assertions of impossibility are based on the
metaphysical creeds of the scientists of the day."
C.J. Ducasse

Feeling embarrassed or apologetic about believing in ESP, mind over matter, the possibility of ghosts, life after death, or a world beyond the five senses? Don't. Most Americans share your belief in paranormal phenomena. In fact, you're part of the majority, not the minority. Modern science may have a problem with the paranormal but millions of Americans don't. Major national polls, done by research firms of unquestioned integrity such as Gallup, Roper and Yankelovich repeatedly confirm significant and widespread belief in a world beyond what our five senses present to us.

Take for example the1990 Gallup public opinion poll[1] that found a whopping 93 percent of Americans polled believed in one or more of 18 paranormal phenomena offered for consideration. Half believed in five or more. And three out of four had actually experienced at least one of these paranormal phenomena, with half having experienced more than three. The list included many phenomena now being seriously studied by reputable scientists, including ESP, mental telepathy and clairvoyance; psychokinesis (PK); mental healing; ghosts; communications with the dead; near death experiences (NDE); life after death; reincarnation and UFOs. (It also included a half-dozen popular folk beliefs scientists aren't seriously studying).

In May 2001, Gallup did a follow-up poll called "Psychic and Paranormal Phenomena."[2] It found that belief had actually increased in twelve out of thirteen phenomena measured in both the 1990 and 2001 polls—and increased significantly (5 percent or more) in seven of them (today, for example, more American *believe* in ESP, telepathy, mental and faith healing and haunted houses than disbelieve). Belief in a world beyond the five senses, then, is American as apple pie. Just about all of us believe in something science says doesn't exist (people in Western nations outside the U.S. share this belief,[3] but we will focus on Americans).

Understandably, not every American believes in every paranormal phenomenon. We all have our own list of beliefs, and assign different levels of probability to different phenomena. You may believe in ESP and psychokinesis but not dowsing or out-of-body experiences; or you may accept the possibility of intelligent life elsewhere in the universe, but reject UFOs. Each of us has our own list.

How do your personal views match the average American's view as measured by the May 2001 Gallup Poll on psychic and paranormal phenomena? Let's take a look.

ESP: 1 out of 2 Americans (50%)

Mental Telepathy: 1 out of 3 Americans (36%)

Among the public at large, ESP believers far outnumber skeptics: the 2001 Gallup Poll found that 50 percent of Americans believe in "*ESP or extrasensory perception,*" while only 27 percent don't believe (the rest are undecided). And more than one in three Americans (36 percent) believe in "*telepathy, or communication between minds without using the traditional five senses.*" Interestingly enough, other, earlier polls I uncovered also show that anywhere from 67 to 75 percent of the American scientific and academic community believe that ESP is either "an established fact" or a "likely possibility"[4]

Clairvoyance: 1 out of 3 Americans (32%)

How about clairvoyance? Some 32 percent of Americans polled in May 2001 accept the *"power of the mind to know the past and/or predict the future."* One in three may be a minority, but based on a 2001 national population of 285 million people, it's a sizable minority of more than 90 million Americans.

Psychokinesis: 1 out of 5 Americans (17%)

How do you feel about psychokinesis—the ability to move or affect objects without physically touching them (sometimes called telekinesis and often abbreviated as "PK"?). While the May 2001 Gallup Poll didn't measure it, the earlier 1990 Gallup Poll discovered that 17 percent of Americans believed in *"the ability of the mind to move or bend objects just using mental energy."* Incidentally, if your knowledge of PK is limited to the famous but controversial feats of Israeli spoon-bender Uri Geller in the '70s and early '80s, you're in for a surprise. Later on in this book, I'll introduce you to the extensive and exciting PK research now being done at prestigious Princeton University, former home of Albert Einstein, where Princeton Engineering Anomalies Research (PEAR) laboratory scientists have conducted breakthrough research in psychokinesis.

Mental and Spiritual Healing: 1 out of 2 Americans (54%)

When you were sick, did you ever try "mind over matter," prayer, visualization, or other unconventional healing techniques? If you did, you weren't alone. The May 2001 Gallup Poll found that most Americans—54 percent—believe in *"psychic or spiritual healing, or the power of the human mind to heal the body."* Skeptics are again a distinct minority: only 26 percent don't believe. Indeed, belief has significantly increased (up 8 percent) between 1990 and 2001. Interestingly enough, as education increases, belief increases. The May 2001 Gallup Poll discovered that "Americans with the highest levels of education are more likely to believe in the power of the mind to heal the body." (The same is true for ESP and telepathy, according to the poll).

If your physician chides you for such medieval thinking, tell him or her that a growing number of Americans not only believe in mental healing but are also actively trying mind-body healing techniques that are not accepted by the AMA and the modern medical establishment. If he doesn't believe you, tell him to look it up: According to a now-famous survey published in 1993 in the *New England Journal of Medicine,*[5] 34 percent of adult Americans reported using at least one unconventional therapy in the past year. An unconventional therapy was defined in the survey as "medical interventions not taught widely at U.S. medical schools or generally available at U.S. hospitals"—including mental healing techniques such as guided imagery (visualization techniques), energy healing, spiritual healing and prayer, biofeedback and hypnosis."

Americans exhibit a strong belief in the power of prayer to heal. According to a *Newsweek* poll appearing in a cover story on "The Mystery of Prayer" in the March 31, 1997 issue, 87 percent agreed with the statement "God answers prayers"; and 79 percent believe "God answers prayers for healing someone with an incurable disease."

Ghosts: 4 out of 10 Americans (38%)

Haunted Houses: 4 out of 10 Americans (42%)

When it comes to ghosts, haunted houses and communication with the dead, the May 2001 Gallup Poll found a very significant increase in belief over the last decade. Today almost four out of ten Americans believe in ghosts (*"that spirits of dead people can come back in certain places and situations"*), up 13 percent in the last decade; similarly, more than four out of ten (42 percent) Americans believe *"that houses can be haunted,"* a belief also up 13 percent in the last decade.

Communication with the Dead: 3 out of 10 Americans (28%)

Channeling: More than 1 in 10 Americans (15%)

The 2001 Gallup Poll found nearly one in three Americans (28%) believe "*that people can hear from or communicate mentally with someone who has died*," a sharp 10 percent increase in belief in the last decade. Other national polls provide additional evidence of Americans' belief in communication with the dead. For example, the University of Chicago's National Opinion Research Center found that 42 percent of Americans say they have been in contact with someone who has died; and among widows and widowers, the rate of contact with the deceased rises to almost two-thirds.[6]

The 2001 poll also surveyed Americans' belief in channeling ("*allowing a 'spirit-being' to temporarily assume control of a human body during a trance*"). While belief in mental communication with the deceased is significant, a distinct minority—only 15 percent—believe in the form of communication called channeling, or trance mediumship. Belief in channeling did however see a 4 percent rise over the last decade.

Intelligent Life Elsewhere in Universe: 1 out of 2 Americans (46%)

Although the 2001 Gallup Poll didn't include the question, it's worth noting that the 1990 Gallup Poll found 46 percent of Americans believe intelligent life exists elsewhere in the universe. ("*Do you think there are people somewhat like ourselves living on other planets in the universe, or not?*") Incidentally, the same poll found that 90 percent of us have heard or read about Unidentified Flying Objects; 47 percent, or almost one in two Americans, believe UFOs are something real and not just people's imagination; and 14 percent of Americans had themselves seen something they thought was a UFO. I also uncovered an interesting, earlier 1977 poll of members of the American Astronomical Society, done by Stanford University astrophysicist Peter Sturrock, which found that 53 percent of those polled felt the problem "certainly" or "probably" deserved scientific study, 27 percent replied "possibly," 17 percent "probably not" and only three percent replied "certainly not." The survey also found that 75 percent of the respondents would like to obtain more information on the subject, and some 62 respondents (about 5 percent of the total 1,356 who returned the questionnaire) had "witnessed or obtained an instrumental record of an event which they could not identify and which they thought might be related to the UFO phenomenon."[7]

Life After Death: 2 out of 3 Americans (65%)

When we come to the biggest human mystery of all—the question of life after death—Science can't prove or disprove it. But while some scientists believe in an afterlife, it's fair to say that modern science itself has difficulty fitting it into its materialistic world view. Most Americans, by contrast, find a place for it in their lives. A separate Gallup Poll done in 1991 on "Fear of Dying" found that almost two out of three Americans believed in an afterlife.[8] And modern science is having a hell of a time— pun intended—stamping out what many scientists see as a particularly stubborn form of primitive, unscientific thinking. This 65 percent figure has been relatively stable over the last 50 years: Gallup Poll data since 1944 show a range of 65 to 77 percent belief in life after death. Believers can even be found within the scientific community. Gallup polls, for example, show that among top scientists in the U.S., one in six (16%) believe in life after death.[9] Interestingly enough, this number doubles for the field of medicine, where scientists work more closely with life and death questions: one in three (32%) leading scientists (defined as persons listed in Marquis's *Who's Who in America*) in this field believe in an afterlife.

What happens when you die? Maybe you believe when you die you will meet your previously deceased relatives and friends again in a heavenly paradise, or stand before God who will review your life with you. Surprise! Both are described in some Near Death Experiences (NDE) suffered by people who almost die and are revived again by modern medical science. These mystical encounters with an afterlife apparently aren't that isolated or rare. The 1991 "Fear of Dying" Gallup Poll found 12 percent of Americans had such experiences when they were on the verge of death or had a close call with death. (*"Have you yourself ever been on the verge of death or had a close call which involved any unusual experience at that time?"*) Further, according to several national polls conducted by NDE researchers, approximately 98 percent of all NDE experiencers end up with an unshakable belief in the afterlife.[10]

Reincarnation: 1 out of 4 Americans (25%)

Of course, not everyone believes in an eternal afterlife. Millions of people around the world believe that after you die you are later reborn again back on earth. It was Voltaire who declared "It is not more surprising to be born twice than once." Do you believe in previous lives here on earth? If you do, you're part of a sizable crowd. What used to be seen as an exotic Asian belief, espoused in the West only by assorted Hare Krishna oddballs, is gaining in popularity. According to the May 2001 Gallup Poll, one in four Americans now believes in reincarnation. That means over 70 million Americans share your belief. You're not a majority yet but, who knows, someday you might be. The poll reconfirms an earlier 1982 Gallup poll that showed 23 percent of American adults believed in reincarnation, including one in four Catholics and one in four Protestants. And a 1981 Gallup "Survey of Beliefs of Leading Scientists About Life After Death" found one in ten (9 percent) of their exclusive fraternity also believed in reincarnation.[11] Incidentally, many other Westerners besides Americans believe in reincarnation: 26 percent of Canadians and 18 percent of Western Europeans, according to Gallup polls.[12] One *Times* poll in London found 29 percent of Britons believed in reincarnation.[13]

Meeting God in the Afterlife: 1 out of 2 Americans (54%)

In a separate poll, Gallup asked Americans the following question: *Tell me which of these words or terms apply to your beliefs about life after death or heaven?"* One of the choices was *"One will be in the presence of God or Jesus Christ."* A majority (54%) of those polled who expressed a belief in an afterlife also agreed with this statement.[14]

Despite the ridicule their unorthodox beliefs often generate, why do so many Americans continue to believe in a world beyond the five senses?

One reason may be because they themselves have personally experienced that world. The same 1990 Gallup Poll that asked Americans about their beliefs in psychic and paranormal phenomena also asked them if they had had first-hand experience with one of these phenomena. Again, the results may surprise you as much as they did me when I first came across them. It discovered that:

- 25 percent had experienced telepathy
- 25 percent had success with mental healing
- 17 percent had communicated with the deceased
- 14 percent had been in a haunted house
- 9 percent had seen or felt a ghost
- 8 percent had experienced reincarnation
- 7 percent had personally seen a psychokinesis display

Other professional surveys show anywhere from 50 to 75 percent of Americans believe they have had one or more psychic experiences.[15] With this level of personal experience, it's no wonder that many Americans have a problem swallowing a scientific world view that tells them that such a world doesn't exist. Could they be right?

2.

Yeah, But I'll Bet They're All Wierdos and Nut Cases

"To doubt everything or to believe everything are two equally conven-ient solutions; both dispense with the necessity of reflection."
French mathematician and physicist H. Poincare

Faced with the results of these Gallup Polls, skeptics will grudgingly concede that millions of Americans believe in phenomena they con-sider unscientific and non-existent. It makes them mad that such dis-graceful "medieval thinking" (to their mind) persists in the 21st century. Still, their consolation is the knowledge that at least they aren't part of this credulous herd of uneducated, low-class, social misfits who believe in ESP, ghosts, an afterlife and other nonsense.

Is this popular image of the typical believer as a gullible, mentally-unbalanced person of low social, educational and economic status real-ly accurate? Among believers, there are undoubtedly some social mis-fits, or unintelligent, credulous and psychologically troubled people (you can say the same, of course, about skeptics or scientists as a group). But the evidence doesn't justify that label for the majority of believers.

Indeed, many intelligent, well-known business people, astronauts, scientists, psychologists, military leaders, philosophers, authors, and even former U.S. presidents have expressed their belief in phenomena science says don't exist, and some have even personally experienced these phenomena.

Thomas Edison, America's most famous inventor, also tried to invent a machine to communicate with spirits,[1] and conducted experiments in psychokinesis.[2] He had several shelves of books devoted to psychic powers and reincarnation in his library in West Orange, N.J. laboratory complex. According to biographer Neil Baldwin, despite the fact that Edison's psychic explorations jeopardized his scientific credibility, Edison continued his investigations right up to his death.

Albert Einstein, the 20th century's most brilliant scientific mind, wrote favorably of mental telepathy research in a preface he penned to a German edition[3] of Upton Sinclair's book *Mental Radio*. Published in 1930, Sinclair's best seller described telepathic experiments the American novelist conducted with his wife.

Sigmund Freud was a pioneer in dream research who also accepted the possibility of mental telepathy, particularly during sleep.[4] Freud realized that his belief in ESP would perhaps hurt psychoanalysis by associating it with the paranormal, but he felt it was important to proclaim his own belief. [5] He did however agree to not publish his essay "Psychoanalysis and Telepathy," originally prepared for the International Psychoanalytic Congress in 1922, until after his death.[6] Freud was also a member of both the American Society for Psychical Research and its British counterpart, the Society for Psychical Research.[7] Though hardly a wide-eyed believer, Freud found their work quite interesting. In a letter to a friend, he once declared that if he had his life to live over again, he would pursue psychic research.[8]

Carl Jung, Freud's most well-known disciple, was familiar with near-death experiences (NDE) and describes them in his monograph on synchronicity, and in his autobiography *Memories, Dreams, Reflections.*

Jung himself did his M.D. degree dissertation on the topic of occult phenomena; believed in the reality of ESP and psychokinesis (PK); and developed a paranormal theory (synchronicity) to explain how meaningful coincidences might be more than chance.[9] He also experimented with mediums, and apparently met a ghost in an English country house.[10]

Alfred Russell Wallace, who co-founded the theory of evolution with Charles Darwin, was a pioneer in psychic research and a confirmed spiritualist who believed in survival of the soul after death.[11]

Edgar Mitchell, former Apollo astronaut, has a significant interest in the paranormal. He conducted ESP experiments on a trip to the moon,[12] and also introduced Israeli psychokinesis practitioner Uri Geller to Stanford Research Institute researchers for PK and ESP testing. He describes his involvement in paranormal research in his 1996 book *The Way of the Explorer: An Apollo Astronaut's Journey Through the Material and Mystical Worlds*. He also helped found the Institute of Noetic Sciences (www.noetic.org) in Sausalito, California which does research on the mind-body connection, holistic health, spirituality, and consciousness studies.

Chester Carlson, Xerox inventor and physicist, helped the American Society for Psychical Research acquire their New York headquarters building, and endowed a chair at the University of Virginia to study reincarnation.

James S. McDonnell, aircraft industry pioneer (McDonnell Douglas planes), helped fund paranormal research at the Psychophysical Research Lab in Princeton, N.J.[13]

Laurence S. Rockefeller, wealthy businessman and philanthropist, teamed with the McDonnell Foundation to help fund psychokinesis and precognition research at Princeton University's PEAR laboratory.[14]

Many famous authors have also devoted significant time or effort to exploring the world beyond the five senses.

Michael Crichton, Harvard Medical School-trained doctor and author of *Jurassic Park* and other blockbusters, describes in his book *Travels*[15] his personal experiences with spoon-bending psychokinesis and altered states of consciousness, and accepts the validity of some psychic phenomena. He ends his book with an intelligent and witty speech in defense of paranormal exploration which he planned, but never had the opportunity to deliver, to a skeptics club at CalTech.

Sir Arthur Conan Doyle, creator of that world-famous detective and model of deductive reasoning Sherlock Holmes, was a strong believer in Spiritualism, a philosophy that accepts the reality of discarnate spirits and mediums able to communicate with them. He went on speaking tours of Europe and the U.S. promoting psychic research and his strong belief in the evidence for an afterlife.[16] A detailed account of his interest in psi phenomena is found in the book he authored, *Wanderings of a Spiritualist.* [17]

Charles Dickens, 19th century English author of *Oliver Twist, David Copperfield, Tale of Two Cities, Great Expectations,* and many other well-known novels was a member of England's venerable Ghost Club, whose members investigate hauntings and poltergeist activities in Great Britain. Of course, Dickens himself created three of the most famous ghosts in the world, found in his Christmas classic *A Christmas Carol.*

Arthur Koestler, English author of *Darkness at Noon* and many other novels and philosophical essays, used some of the proceeds from his writings to endow a parapsychology lab at the University of Edinburgh, Scotland in 1983. Today it attracts students from around the world to do scientific research on paranormal phenomena.

Margaret Mead, renowned anthropologist, publicly supported the vote by the American Association for the Advancement of Science, the nation's top science organization, to allow the Parapsychological Association to affiliate with them in 1969. The Parapsychological Association studies such phenomena as ESP and psychokinesis (PK). When opponents attacked parapsychology as a "pathological science," and called for its rejection, she pointed out in her speech that the Parapsychological Association used statistics, double blinds and other standard scientific methodologies in their research. The history of scientific advance, noted Mead, was full of scientists investigating phenomena that the scientific establishment didn't believe existed. She urged the Association to admit the Parapsychological Association, which they did.[18]

Abraham Lincoln, arguably America's greatest president, participated in séances in the White House, and believed strongly in precognition. In fact, he foretold his own death to his closest colleagues in the Cabinet, based on a dream he had shortly before he was assassinated by John Wilkes Booth. Lincoln's own ghost has reportedly been seen or sensed in the White House by many famous persons, including presidents Franklin Roosevelt and Dwight Eisenhower, and by former British Prime Minister Winston Churchill.[19] Besides seeing the ghost of Lincoln, Churchill reported that, once while in the process of painting a picture of his deceased father, he had seen his father's apparition—and had conversed with him about politics at some length before his ghost vanished.[20] President Warren Harding's wife had a clairvoyant visit the White House for séances,[21] and Teddy Roosevelt, yet another American president, was among the founding members of the American Society for Psychical Research.

Can sober, sane, intelligent people believe in reincarnation? Despite the snickers of skeptics, belief in reincarnation is not restricted to Hollywood actresses like Shirley MacLaine. The May 2001 Gallup Poll found over 70 million Americans accept the reality of reincarnation. Their ranks have historically included some pretty impressive people.

Benjamin Franklin, signer of the Declaration of Independence, statesman, author, inventor and rationalist, apparently believed in reincarnation.[22]

Henry Ford, industrialist, business leader and creator of the modern automobile industry, accepted the theory of reincarnation at age 26 and it put his mind at ease, providing him with the assurance that he would have several lifetimes to spend developing all the ideas and projects he wanted to do.[23]

General George "Blood and Guts" Patton, America's irascible hero of World War II, strongly believed in reincarnation. During World War II in the town of Langres, France, he declined the offer of a French liaison officer to show him around the town's Roman ruins. Instead, he conducted the French officer on a tour. Although he had never been in the town before, he accurately identified the old amphitheater, and various temples, forums and a Roman army drill ground. His explanation? He himself had in a previous life fought with Caesar's legions.[24]

Being famous, like being in the majority, doesn't mean you're right. Famous people can be as foolish and wrong in their beliefs as anyone else. But since skeptics of a world beyond the five senses like to play "guilt by association"—some uneducated, irrational, low-class people believe in ghosts; you believe in ghosts; therefore, you're an uneducated, irrational, low-class person—it's important to balance the picture. The ranks of America's business, political and military elite include believers in paranormal phenomena.

And how about us ordinary folks? Scientific studies have confirmed that, taken as a group, believers in a world beyond the five senses are not significantly different from non-believers. Skeptics sometimes assert that people most susceptible to paranormal beliefs are usually the poorly educated, the unemployed, etc. (in psychological terms, the "Social Marginality" hypothesis). They also commonly argue that believers in the paranormal tend variously to be illogical, irrational, credulous, uncritical and foolish (the "Cognitive Defects" hypothesis).

How much truth is there to these claims? Psychologist Harvey J. Irwin sat down and did an exhaustive review of more than 150 scientific studies done over the last 60 years on people who believe in the paranormal. His comprehensive paper, entitled *Belief in the*

Paranormal: A Review of Empirical Literature,[25] found little support for either accusation.

Regarding the social marginality charge, Irwin found no consistent pattern showing that paranormal believers were uneducated, unemployed persons of low social status. The cognitive defects argument (the typical believer is stupid and credulous) also failed the test of consistency. For example, one major study done in 1977 found a positive correlation between intelligence and paranormal belief (i.e., the more intelligent you were, the more you believed in a world beyond the five senses).[26] Another 1984 study, a sample of high school students, found higher grade point averages correlated positively with belief in psi.[27] Yet another study yielded the unanticipated result that students enrolled in the natural or biological sciences had greater belief in the paranormal than did students of the humanities.[28] (Skeptical scientists expect those who major in arts and literature to be less scientifically literate and thus gullible, but they don't expect their own to embrace superstition).

Other published polls support Irwin's conclusion. A June 1984 poll of *Psychology Today* magazine readers found that 90 percent of the 600 poll respondents believed in the authenticity of paranormal phenomena; 83 percent accepted the validity of ESP; more than 50 percent accepted the reality of UFOs, faith healing and ghosts; and 47 percent accepted reincarnation.[29] Who reads *Psychology Today?* Based on a 1992 readership profile[30] I found, they're not the socially marginal or cognitively defective. In fact, 56 percent were in management or the professions, over 60 percent had a college education, and their median household income was $53,000.

The 1993 *New England Journal of Medicine* survey cited in Chapter 1 found that alternative medicine—a category which includes mind-body healing, energy healing and spiritual healing—is most likely to be practiced not by the socially marginal or the cognitively defective but by affluent (incomes above $35,000), college-educated people between the ages of 25 to 49. And as we saw in the same chapter, the May 2001 Gallup Poll reported that the higher the level of education, the more likely you were to believe in mental and faith healing, additional support for Irwin's conclusions.

The 1989 CBS television poll done in conjunction with "48 Hours" (see footnote Chapter 1), found that 64 percent of respondents believed in the existence of paranormal phenomena. But the poll also uncovered another interesting fact among those polled—75 percent of persons with a college degree believed in paranormal phenomena, while only 36 percent of people with less than a high school degree believed in these phenomena. In short, as education increased, so did belief.[31]

The too-easy stereotype of paranormal believers as uneducated, low-class, *National Enquirer* kooks and social misfits simply doesn't fit the facts. Their profile basically matches that of the average American—you and I—and their ranks include a fair share of brilliant, famous and respected business, political and military leaders. If we have a problem with the paranormal, we need to move beyond criticizing the believers to criticizing the evidence.

3.

OK, But Do Any Scientists Take This Stuff Seriously?

"The whole history of scientific advance is full of scientists investigating phenomena that the establishment did not believe were there."
Anthropologist Margaret Mead

Many scientists today refuse to even examine the evidence for ESP, out-of-body experiences, life after death or a world beyond the five senses, afraid that they will dignify superstition and encourage unwarranted credulity, thus sending science back to the Dark Ages.

But a significant and growing group of "heretics" within the scientific community—attached to reputable universities, laboratories, non-profit foundations and private industry—argue that science is more threatened by a close-minded dogmatism that declares the current materialist world view to be the only measure of truth. As a result, they're ignoring ridicule and examining with an open mind all evidence available for the phenomena, including evidence collected outside the laboratory from humans who have experienced or witnessed the phenomena. In terms of career advancement and professional reputation, they sometimes pay a price for their heresy. But they operate squarely in the finest tradition of science "by investigating phenomena that the establishment did not believe were there," as anthropologist Margaret Mead has noted.

Dr. Peter Sturrock, Emeritus Professor of Applied Physics at Stanford University, is a good example of this kind of open-minded investigator. He explores puzzling anomalies science can't explain and skeptics dismiss out-of-hand. And he publicly encourages other scientists to do the same.

As mentioned in Chapter 1, the intellectually curious Sturrock in 1977 polled members of the American Astronomical Society about their opinion on the UFO phenomenon. Many scientists would think twice before doing that. If your colleagues get the idea you "believe in little green men from Mars"—or even accept the theoretical possibility of UFOs—your career could be seriously hurt. Scientists are supposed to automatically reject such preposterous ideas, no evidence examined, no questions asked. But Sturrock went ahead anyway, and discovered a majority of his fellow astronomers actually viewed it as a legitimate question for science to investigate.

Sturrock can get away with asking the question because he has unassailable professional credentials and standing within the scientific community. Skeptics have a tough time trashing Sturrock's reputation. He has a doctorate from Cambridge University, and worked closely with world-famous cosmologist Sir Fred Hoyle. He has authored over 150 scientific papers during his distinguished career at Stanford University where he served as the Deputy Director of the Center for Space Sciences and Astrophysics. He has a bookshelf full of scientific awards—the annual prize from the Gravity Research Foundation in 1967; the Hale Prize in Solar Physics in 1986 from the American Astronomical Society; the Arctowski Medal in 1990 from the National Academy of Sciences; and the Space Sciences Award in 1992 from the American Institute for Aeronautics and Astronautics (former recipients of this award include James Van Allen, discoverer of the radiation belt, rocket pioneer

Herbert Friedman, and X-ray astronomer Riccardo Giacconi, director of the Hubble Space Telescope Science Institute).

How do you call Sturrock a kook? You can't. So if he suggests further scientific investigation of the UFO phenomena, at least some people listen.

Sturrock is also emeritus president and founder of the Society for Scientific Exploration (www.scientificexploration.org). The SSE was founded in 1982 as a forum for scientific research on anomalies currently outside the pale of Establishment science. The SSE, which has grown from 95 members and associates in 1983 to over 700 in 45 countries today, doesn't endorse the existence or non-existence of paranormal phenomena; it simply offers a place where scientific evidence can be presented and debated without fear of ridicule or prejudgment. This doesn't sound like much—isn't that how science is supposed to work?—but it's a major breakthrough within the scientific community.

The association's quarterly *Journal of Scientific Exploration* tackles a fascinating range of anomalies. Articles have dealt with various intriguing aspects of ESP, clairvoyance and psychokinesis (PK); death bed visions and near death experiences (NDE); the analysis of alleged UFO photos; reincarnation claims; trends in the study of out-of-body experiences (OBE); mental healing and the effect of prayer on disease and illnesses; the nature of time; and even the Loch Ness monster.

In fact, the Loch Ness monster is sort of a symbol for the SSE. Each year, the society awards a Dinsdale Prize to the member who has contributed the most to push scientific knowledge beyond its present confines. It's named for Nessie's most dogged pursuer, Tim Dinsdale. The Society bestowed its first annual Dinsdale Prize on physicist and SSE member Dr. Helmut Schmidt, a former Boeing Scientific Research Laboratory scientist who invented the atomic random number generator (RNG) device that helped to establish the reality of the psychokinesis phenomenon. Before he bestowed the award on Schmidt, SSE vice president Henry Bauer, at that time a professor of chemistry and science studies at Virginia Polytechnic, paid tribute to Dinsdale as a "worthy model for serious anomalists." (An anomalist is someone who studies things that don't fit into current scientific theories of reality). Does the Loch Ness monster exist? Some famous photos purporting to be of the monster were later discovered to be fakes, and any evidence is very limited. But at Loch Ness in 1960, Tim Dinsdale personally filmed something he couldn't explain and decided to pursue the mystery, quitting his job as an aerospace engineer to visit Loch Ness 50 times, sometimes for months, out in a small boat on the lake, looking for the creature he had filmed.

Bauer noted that many people considered Dinsdale misguided, even crazy, out on a wild goose chase. But Dinsdale eventually earned people's respect for the quiet honesty and dignity he demonstrated in his pursuit of the truth, making him a worthy model for SSE members exploring scientific anomalies.[1]

If you attended an SSE annual meeting, what kind of scientists would you rub elbows with? You'd find a group of sober, responsible academics distinguished enough to make even most skeptics feel comfortable.

In addition to Sturrock and Bauer, they include such well-known scientists as Prof. Robert Jahn, Dean Emeritus of the School of Engineering and Applied Sciences, Princeton University. Jahn and his research colleagues conducted breakthrough psychokinesis, precognition and remote viewing (clairvoyance) research at the Princeton Engineering Anomalies Research (PEAR) laboratory (www.princeton.edu/~pear/). The PEAR program, founded by Jahn, has been doing pioneering research in PK since its inception in 1979[2] and has produced strong, classic experimental data to support the existence of these phenomena. Jahn, a professor of aerospace science and an authority on aerospace engineering, has worked on many NASA and Dept. of Defense projects. He and Dunne co-authored *Margins of Reality* [3]which describes the first decade of PEAR research and examines the apparent role of consciousness in the establishment of physical reality.

Another SSE member, Dr. Ian Stevenson, M.D., Carlson Professor of Psychiatry at the University of Virginia Health System, is perhaps the world's foremost authority on reincarnation research. He works at the Division of Personality Studies, a unit of the university's Dept. of Psychiatric Medicine. The Division studies how mind and brain relate, and the question of post-mortem survival, including reincarnation, near death experiences, out-of-body experiences, deathbed visions and spirit apparitions (http://hsc.virginia.edu/personality-studies). Stevenson was born in Canada and received his M.D. degree from McGill University in Montreal. He was trained in psychosomatic medicine at Cornell University Medical College and in psychoanalysis at the New Orleans and Washington Psychoanalytic Institutes. His many books include the classic *Twenty Cases Suggestive of Reincarnation* (his work is discussed later in this book). His impeccable scientific credentials include membership in the American Association for the Advancement of Science, the American Psychiatric Association, and the American Medical Association. *Washington Post* reporter Tom Shroder traveled with Stevenson on several of Stevenson's reincarnation investigations and describes them in his 1999 book *Old Souls: The Scientific Evidence for Past Lives.* [4]

Dr. Dean Radin is an engineer, psychologist and parapsychologist who early in his career worked at AT&T Bell Laboratories and GTE Laboratories, and in 1992 received a grant from the Richard Hodgson Memorial Fund at Harvard University to conduct a meta-analysis of experiments involving direct mental healing. He later went on to found the Consciousness Research Division of the Harry Reid Center, University of Nevada, conducting ground-breaking ESP and PK experiments. He is currently Senior Scientist at the Institute for Noetic Sciences (www.noetic.org). Radin has researched the potential for humans to use PK to disrupt computer systems, and the possibility of creating "psibots"—his term for robots that can respond to mind commands. His book *The Conscious Universe: The Scientific Truth of Psychic*

Phenomena, won Amazon.com's 1998 Category Bestseller Award for parapsychology, is in its fourth printing, and has been translated into French, Korean and Chinese. A past president of the Parapsychological Association, Radin is open-minded about paranormal claims but is not reluctant to test and expose false claims.[5]

Dr. Jacques Vallee is an astrophysicist, computer scientist, author and UFO researcher. Vallee, a former principal investigator on Department of Defense computer networking projects, received his doctorate in computer science from Northwestern University in 1967. He became interested in the UFO phenomenon when he witnessed the destruction of tracking tapes of unknown objects at a Paris observatory. He has spent several decades investigating UFO sightings and was the real-life model for the French scientist portrayed by Francois Truffaut in Steven Spielberg's film *Close Encounters of the Third Kind*. He is the author of a half-dozen books on the UFO phenomenon.

Dr. Harold Puthoff is a physicist who holds patents in the laser, communications and energy fields; co-authored the standard physics textbook *Fundamentals of Quantum Electronics*; and currently serves as Director of the Institute for Advanced Studies at Austin, Texas, where he conducts theoretical studies in gravitation, energy generation and space propulsion. Puthoff pioneered "remote viewing" (clairvoyance) studies and directed a now- famous CIA-funded ESP research program (see Chapter 6). Remote-viewing and other forms of ESP have obvious military applications if they can be harnessed, and the U.S government has over the years spent millions on unclassified and classified parapsychology research.[6] The Army funded ESP experiments as far back as 1952; and the Air Force conducted automated ESP testing in the early 1960s.[7] Puthoff was co-author with Russell Targ of the remote viewing classic *Mind Reach: Scientists Look at Psychic Ability*.[8]

Dr. Larry Dossey, M.D. is a practicing physician, former chief of staff of Medical City Dallas Hospital, and a leading researcher in the field of mental and faith healing (www.dosseydossey.com) He served as the co-chair of the Panel on Mind/Body Interventions in the Office of Alternative Medicine within the National Institutes of Health. He has authored many influential books in the field, including the *New York Times* bestseller *Healing Words: the Power of Prayer and the Practice of Medicine* (1993), and *Reinventing Medicine: Beyond Mind-Body to a New Era of Healing* (1999).

Dr. Stanley Krippner is currently professor of psychology at the Saybrook Graduate School in San Francisco (www.saybrook.edu). Krippner's interest in parapsychology began when he was a 14-year old boy in Wisconsin. One day, he was startled by the sudden thought that his uncle Max was dead, and a moment later his mother received a telephone call informing her that Max had indeed died suddenly and without warning.[9] Krippner earned his doctorate in education at Northwestern University, and later became director of the Dream Laboratory at Maimonides Medical Center in Brooklyn, N.Y. where he pioneered experiments in telepathic dreaming. He is the editor in chief of an ongoing series of parapsychology papers entitled *Advances in Parapsychological Research*. He is also very active in forging links between American and foreign parapsychologists.

In short, SSE boasts highly-qualified, mainstream scientists working at respected universities, institutes and corporations in the United States (as well as foreign countries). But the SSE isn't the only place you'll find reputable scientists and academics investigating a world beyond the five senses. The Parapsychological Association (PA), so eloquently championed by Mead in her 1969 speech to the AAAS, includes several hundred more scientists and academics interested in examining the evidence for these claims.

The Parapsychological Association (www.parapsych.org) was founded in 1957 "to advance parapsychology as a science, to disseminate knowledge of the field, and to integrate the findings with those of other branches of science." Full membership is restricted to persons who hold an advanced degree, are active in the parapsychology field, and have published high-quality parapsychology papers. The PA's distinguished roster includes university professors, physicists, psychologists and psychiatrists, biologists, medical doctors, anthropologists, philosophers and other scientists and academics from around the world. You'll find PA members on the faculties of some of the best universities in America, like Princeton, Yale, Cornell and Stanford. Within the PA, a small group of full-time, experimental parapsychologists currently make their living studying psi phenomena—primarily ESP and PK. They conduct laboratory experiments on these phenomena and publish their research in refereed journals like the *Journal of Parapsychology, Journal of the American Society for Psychical Research, European Journal of Parapsychology*, and the *Journal of the Society for Psychical Research.* They employ the same familiar experimental controls used by their physical and social sciences colleagues, including statistical analysis, blinds and placebos. They hold advanced degrees in the physical and social sciences.

A good example of these psychic sleuths is Dr. Richard Broughton, former director of Research at the Institute for Parapsychology at the Rhine Research Center (www.rhine.org) in Durham, North Carolina. Broughton (who is also an SSE member like some other paranormal researchers) earned his Ph.D. in psychology from the University of Edinburgh, Scotland (writer Arthur Koestler would later endow a parapsychology lab there). His 1978 Ph.D. dissertation was on "Brain Hemisphere Differences in Paranormal Abilities With Special Reference to Experimenter Expectancies." After graduating, he worked several years in Europe at Holland's state-supported parapsychology lab at the University of Utrecht; returned to the U.S. and became a research associate at the Dept. of Behavioral Sciences, State University of New York; and in 1981 joined the Institute of Parapsychology where he spent almost 20 years investigating all aspects of psi anomalies, including psi in animals, and investigations of ESP and its relationship to the brain's two hemispheres.

The Institute he headed until recently is perhaps the most famous parapsychology lab in the world. It is the successor to the Duke University Parapsychology Laboratory where Dr. J.B. Rhine and his wife Dr. Louisa Rhine pioneered ESP research using a specially designed deck of cards with five symbols—a star, circle, square, cross and wavy line. Rhine's research was repeatable, based on probability statistics accepted by science, and involved many standard, experimental controls. Because of this, his ESP experiments in the 1930s and 1940s earned grudging respect from skeptics in the science community and laid the foundation for modern, lab-based parapsychology research.

Broughton himself is the author of *Parapsychology: The Controversial Science*, an excellent overview of parapsychology for anyone seriously interested the subject. In the introduction to his book, he recounts how a reporter asked him whether he believed in "this ESP and psychokinesis stuff." He answered "No, I don't believe in it." After leaving the reporter in shock for a second, he explained that "belief" was more appropriate to matters of faith, not science. For himself, he preferred to rely on evidence—and there existed a tremendous amount of evidence for such psychic abilities. Broughton currently heads Intuition Laboratories Inc., a non-profit company (www.intuitionlabs.com) whose goal is to develop methods of identifying "intuitively advantaged individuals" for business and other professions.

In addition to the Parapsychological Association and the SSE, the American Society for Psychical Research (www.aspr.com), America's oldest paranormal research society, is another home for serious scientific investigation of the afterlife and a world beyond the five senses. Founded in 1885, its purpose and scope is described as: "the investigation of telepathy, clairvoyance, precognition, veridical hallucinations and dreams, psychometry, and other forms of paranormal cognition; of phenomena bearing upon the hypothesis of survival of bodily death; of claims of paranormal physical phenomena such as psychokinesis and poltergeists; the study of automatic writing, trance speech, alterations of personality and other subconscious processes insofar as they may be related to paranormal processes; in short, all types of phenomena called parapsychological or paranormal."

At the ASPR, where the blockbuster film *Ghostbusters* was researched, you'll also find a number of distinguished scientists (again, some of whom also hold membership in the PA and SSE as well).

A good example is C. Bruce Greyson, M.D. a psychiatrist and Bonner-Lowry Professor of Personality Studies at the U. of Virginia where he works with Stevenson. For almost two decades now, Greyson has served as Director of Research for the International Association of Near Death Studies (www.iands.org/), conducting ground-breaking investigations of near death experiences as well as research on other phenomena suggestive of postmortem survival including death bed visions and spirit apparitions.[10] He edits the *Journal of Near Death Studies*.

Interesting to note, the ASPR's first president was an astronomer, Simon Newcombe, and a number of well-known scientists have helped the society grow over the years. Physicists Sir William Barrett and Sir Oliver Lodge (who pioneered the study of radio waves) helped launch the Society for Psychical Research in England (the ASPR started out as an American branch of the SPR) and physicists continue today to remain at the forefront of anomalies thinking. Within the scientific community, quantum physicists are among the most open to the possibility of a world beyond the traditional five senses.[11] They're more comfortable than most scientists with the idea of rewriting the "basic laws" of the universe—time, space, causality—to incorporate new discoveries. Classical physics was extensively revised early in the 20th century because Einstein's Theory of Relativity and new quantum physics theories better explained serious anomalies unexplainable by the old paradigm. Most scientists remain mentally wedded to the classic physics and associated materialist philosophy under whose rules psi (paranormal) phenomena are difficult to conceive of. But a number of well-known physicists see nothing in quantum physics that forbid psi phenomena.[12] They include Henry Margenau, Professor Emeritus of Physics at Yale University; the late David Bohm, a University of London Professor of Physics who was a co-worker of Einstein's at Princeton U. and author of *Quantum Theory* (written in 1951 and the standard textbook on quantum physics for several decades); and physicist O. Costa de Beauregard of the Poincare Institute in France. Indeed, both Bohm and de Beauregard argue that certain axioms of quantum physics almost require the existence of psi phenomena.[13] Parapsychologist Lawrence LeShan notes that statements made by many modern physicists sound like they came from the mouths of mystics instead of scientists.[14] Margenau, for instance, has declared, "To put it bluntly, science no longer contains absolute truths...the old distinction between the natural and the supernatural has become spurious."[15]

A fourth notable institution conducting serious scientific investigation of anomalies is the National Institute of Discovery Science (www.nidsci.org), a privately-funded organization founded by multimillionaire developer Robert Bigelow. The NIDS scientific advisory board is stocked with well-respected physicists, astronauts, medical doctors, aerospace scientists, biologists and other Ph.D-credentialed scientists and academics (along with experts trained in police work who do field investigations on anomalies). NIDS personnel routinely call in help from nationally accredited laboratories in the biological, chemical and materials sciences to help them analyze anomalous evidence. Chairman of the NIDS Science Advisory Board is Dr. Hal Puthoff, the SSE member we profiled above. His colleagues on the 12-person board include UFO expert Dr. Jacques Vallee; Apollo 14 astronaut Edgar Mitchell; Dr. Melvin Morse, M.D. who pioneered investigations of the near death experiences of children; and Dr. Jessica Utts, a statistics professor at the University of California, Davis who helped the CIA evaluate the famous government-funded "Star Gate" psychic spy program described in Chapter 6 (NIDS staffer Dr. John Alexander, a

32-year career veteran with the U.S. Army, helped run that psychic spy program).

The scientific community, then, is not uniformly hostile to the possibility of a world beyond the five senses, skeptics claims not withstanding. The open-mindedness of a Stanford astrophysicist like Dr. Peter Sturrock, a Princeton engineer like Dr. Robert Jahn, a University of California statistics professor like Dr. Jessica Utts, or a Yale physicist like Dr. Henry Margenau is in the grand tradition of Thomas Edison, Albert Einstein, Carl Jung and other scientific pioneers who pondered these intriguing questions before them. If they're willing to risk reputation and ridicule to examine the evidence, shouldn't we?

4.

But Science Says...

"He ought not to risk his reputation by presenting to the learned body anything which appears so much at variance with established knowledge, and withal so incredible."
England's Royal Society rejecting Jenner's smallpox vaccine

Although scientists and other learned men in the 1790s had heard many reports of stones falling out of a clear, blue, sky, the most eminent remained skeptical. One who did accept the evidence was German lawyer, E.F.F. Chladni, who in 1794 published a study of some of the stones, one of which observers had connected to an earlier fireball sighting. Chladni carefully and thoughtfully examined the evidence, and correctly inferred that they were extra-terrestrial objects that had been heated in their plunge through the atmosphere. But his explanation was widely rejected despite the evidence he offered, notes William Hartman in his textbook *Moons and Planets: An Introduction to Planetary Science.* His contemporaries were simply "loathe to accept the idea that extra-terrestrial stones could fall from the sky."[1]

Today, a similar situation often faces investigators of paranormal phenomena which fall outside the framework of materialism, the currently dominant, Western philosophy of reality. Since the phenomena don't fit the philosophy, many scientists refuse to even examine the evidence. Ironically, they act exactly like the fundamentalist religious believer. Both claim allegiance to a higher power than empirical evidence.

Yet the history of science itself demonstrates how often yesterday's heresies turn into today's orthodoxy:[2]

- When English physician William Harvey (1578-1657) first offered his new theory of blood circulation, he was called "crack-brained" by his fellow scientists.
- When Dr. Edward Jenner (1749-1823) came up with the smallpox vaccination, the Royal Society rejected his paper, and his work was attacked and discredited.
- French chemist Louis Pasteur (1822-1895), founder of both the modern science of microbiology and a cure for rabies, met the same hostility from conservative scientists who preferred their theories to the evidence. Pasteur, on the other hand, maintained that scientific facts stemmed from observation, not merely hypotheses or preconceived ideas.
- British surgeon Joseph Lister (1827-1912), who introduced antiseptics into the operating room, thereby saving millions of lives, was ignored at first by an unimpressed medical establishment. Why? Because Lister's theory of infection by germs conflicted with science's belief at that time that festering was caused by "bad air." Some doctors went so far as to throw their surgical tools on the ground, step on them and rub them in the dirt in order to prove that they could operate with dirty instruments and nothing would happen to their patients.
- Lord Kelvin (1824-1907), British mathematician and physicist world-renowned for his work on heat and electricity, confidently declared that X-rays would prove to be a hoax. He wasn't alone. Many scientists thought X-rays were a hoax when they first heard about them.[3] Kelvin, president of the prestigious Royal Society, England's top scientific group, is famous for

another piece of scientific arrogance. In 1895 he confidently declared, "Heavier-than-air machines are impossible." He wasn't alone. The Chief Engineer of the U.S. Navy, Rear Admiral George Melville, called human flight "absurd." And the *Scientific American* in its Jan. 13, 1906 issue branded the Wright Brothers a pair of hoaxers.[4] Kelvin is also famous for yet a third piece of scientific arrogance. In 1897, he confidently declared, "Radio has no future."[5]

- When the phonograph of Thomas Edison was first demonstrated at the French Academy of Science, one scientist leapt up and grabbed the exhibitor in anger, saying "I won't be taken in by your ventriloquist."

- Edison's incandescent light bulb invention was ruled preposterous by Sir William Preece, the Chief Engineer of England's Post Office Dept. "Edison's electric lamp is a completely idiotic idea," he declared to the Royal Society, England's highest scientific body. Preece at least could be partially excused for his arrogance because he lived thousands of miles away from Menlo Park where Edison's bulbs were lighting up the sky in a public nighttime display. But Professor Henry Morton, who lived nearby, didn't even deign to pop over for a look himself. Instead, he declared the need "to protest in behalf of true science" that Edison's experiments were a "fraud upon the public."[6]

- German geologist and meteorologist Alfred Wegener (1880-1930), developer of the theory of "continental drift," was derided and the butt of ridicule during his lifetime by his geologist colleagues.[7]

- When physicist Dr. Albert Einstein (1879-1955) in 1915 first published his General Theory of Relativity—the greatest revolution in scientific thinking since Isaac Newton—the new theory created a violent controversy. Most scientists found the whole idea incomprehensible, and even those few who could follow the math rejected it as being contradictory to common sense.

- British physicist Ernest Rutherford (1871-1937), knighted for his great contributions to the study of radioactivity and atomic structure, in 1933 dismissed the idea of atomic power as "moonshine." Maybe as a scientist he was simply deferring to the brightest scientific mind of the 20th century—a year earlier, in 1932, Einstein had confidently declared, "There is not the slightest indication that (nuclear energy) will ever be obtainable. It would mean that the atom would have to be shattered at will." A little over a decade later, the atom was shattered at will, despite Einstein's dogmatic pronouncement.

- Great Britain's Astronomer Royal (top astronomer), Richard van der Riet Wooley, when asked in 1936 about sending a rocket into space, declared, "The whole procedure presents difficulties of such a fundamental nature that we are forced to dismiss the notion as essentially impractical." Two decades later, rockets were launching satellites into space. In 1956, he confidently declared, "Space travel is utter bilge." A little more than a decade later, astronaut Neil Armstrong was walking on the moon.

Science, then, is not a set of immutable truths but rather a method of inquiry. Scientific theories and hypotheses change as new evidence appears to challenge existing views of reality (as it always does).

Unfortunately, even scientists can be reluctant to give up cherished old ideas faced with evidence to the contrary. The public regards scientists as paragons of rationality and objectivity, notes sociologist Marcello Truzzi. But studies show scientists as a group are just as dogmatic and authoritarian, foolish and illogical as the general public, even when they're practicing science.[8] British psychologist and parapsychology critic C.E.M. Hansel, for instance, started his "scientific" evaluation of ESP by stating, "In view of the apriori arguments against it, we know in advance that telepathy cannot occur."[9] Another skeptic was consulted by a journal editor reviewing a paper describing scientific ESP (remote viewing) experiments submitted by (then) Stanford Research Institute researchers Dr. Hal Puthoff and Russell Targ. Even though the paper, submitted to the *Proceedings of the IEEE* (Institute of Electrical and Electronics Engineers) met all requirements for a standard, professional journal submission, the skeptic's comment was simply "This is the kind of thing I would not believe even if it existed."[10]

SSE founder Peter Sturrock has publicly decried the tendency by some scientists to view certain anomalies as "heresies" for sociopolitical reasons, rather than objective reasons.[11] Sturrock notes that organized science had something akin to an inquisition. If the Loch Ness monster were to turn out to be real, zoologists would lose face. Thus it isn't surprising that such claims are sometimes treated as heresies. Instead, he argues, scientists should honestly and fairly examine the evidence, review any investigations undertaken, evaluate the properties of the phenomenon, and then come up with possible explanations. Unfortunately, such responses aren't typical from scientists faced with anomalies.

One of the best summaries of the difficulty scientists have in dealing with anomalies outside the current scientific paradigm is found in Thomas Kuhn's classic book *The Structure of Scientific Revolution*.[12] Kuhn noted that initially "only the anticipated and usual are experienced" even when an anomaly is observed. In short, most people, including scientists, tend to see or find what they *expect* to see or find. Scientific "truths" thus reflect the current, majority consensus view of the scientific community, not necessarily immutable truth.[13]

In addition to a prejudicial philosophy of reality (materialism) and the reluctance of all human beings, including scientists, to have their beliefs or life's work challenged by contrary evidence, established science offers up a third formidable roadblock to a fair evaluation of the evidence for paranormal phenomena—the current emphasis on the experimental method in a controlled laboratory setting almost exclusively over other methods of investigation (for example, the collection and evaluation of reports of human witnesses to paranormal events).

Unfortunately, most paranormal mysteries can't be easily studied and automatically replicated in a laboratory setting, including near death experiences, death bed visions, ghosts and poltergeists, and reincarnation claims. Other phenomena, like ESP and psychokinesis can be studied in a lab, but also happen spontaneously outside the lab in more dramatic form. If the experimental method won't allow them to be studied when and where they occur, should we simply throw away the evidence? Or do we investigate them with other tools in the toolbox of science?

The famous psychiatrist Dr. Carl Jung voiced objections to a science that focused solely on experiments that are repeatable in a lab. Such a method automatically rules out real but unique or rare events, he argued, thus imposing artificial limits on nature. The resulting "scientific worldview" was nothing more than a "psychologically-biased partial view," missing everything that couldn't be grasped statistically.[14] Scientists can sometimes forget that reality exists outside the laboratory as well as inside; further, that double-blind lab experiments aren't a requirement for reality (for example, both penicillin and aspirin—two modern miracle drugs widely and successfully used by the medical community—were accepted and deployed without any double-blind studies. Not understanding how something works doesn't mean it isn't real).

Many scientists rejecting evidence for a world beyond the five senses say, "Bring the phenomenon into the lab and prove it there. We don't believe eye-witness reports." But Dr. Stephen Braude of the University of Maryland argues that the authenticity of eyewitness, anecdotal reports regarding ESP, PK and some afterlife-suggestive claims (e.g. near death experiences, reincarnation cases, etc.) are often of excellent quality. He confronts the standard arguments against human testimony raised by skeptics with some interesting counter-arguments of his own.[15]

Skeptics point to the possibility of errors in observation, but Braude notes that the best paranormal cases involve multiple, independent witnesses whose testimony agrees.

Skeptics warn that some people who report paranormal events may be biased towards belief in their reality. Braude notes many skeptics bring an equally unscientific bias towards disbelief to their investigations—a prejudice so strong that they won't accept a phenomenon even if they personally witness or experience it. He quotes C.J. Ducasse: "There is likely to be just as much wishful thinking, prejudice, emotion, snap judgment, naiveté and intellectual dishonesty on the side of orthodoxy, of skepticism, and of conservatism, as on the side of hunger for and of belief in the marvelous."[16]

Skeptics claim that reporters of paranormal events are publicity-seekers, looking for excitement and notoriety. Braude counters that most eyewitnesses of a strange, paranormal event have little to gain and much to lose by reporting them. They're usually branded as wackos and nut cases. In fact, research shows that many people who see a ghost or poltergeist, or have a near death experience or experience a dramatic precognitive dream that later comes true, will avoid talking about it publicly for fear of facing scorn and ridicule. It's just not socially acceptable to profess a belief in a non-material world beyond the five senses. As a result, *under*-reporting of these phenomena is more likely than over-reporting.

Truzzi notes that some anecdotal reports are better than others. Courts don't rule out all human testimony; science could do the same, giving eyewitness testimony more weight than hearsay; expert witnesses more credibility than ordinary witnesses, etc. "Anecdotes are not all scientifically equal, and certainly not equally dismissable."

Braude, Truzzi and Sturrock, then, are squarely in the corner of science when it comes to investigating the world beyond the five senses.

They aren't looking to junk modern science, or do away with the experimental method. They are simply encouraging the use of *all* available scientific methodologies and tools to study the phenomena, along with a firm commitment on the part of the scientists who use them to pursue knowledge without bias or prejudgment, wherever it leads.

Pioneering psychologist Dr. Charles Tart, professor emeritus of psychology at the University of California at Davis, draws an interesting and important philosophical distinction between Science and "Scientism."[17] Many scientists, and the general public as well, often confuse the two. "Science" is essentially a *process* used to find the truth, he argues. In contrast, "Scientism" is a *philosophy* of materialism, masquerading as scientific truth. Paranormal research, he argues, has used the process of science to prove the existence of a variety of phenomena, including ESP and psychokinesis, that simply don't fit within Scientism's philosophy of materialism. If evidence conflicts with philosophy, the evidence shouldn't be dismissed; instead, the philosophy should be revised.

Tart notes that Freud was among the first to recognize the mistaken human tendency to believe that science consists of nothing but proved propositions. Such a belief best suited people who craved authority and "the need to replace religious catechism with a scientific one."[18]

Like ordinary people, scientists themselves can—and do—have paranormal or psychic experiences. Dr. Tart has created TASTE (The Archives of Scientists' Transcendent Experiences), an online (http://issc-taste.org) journal offering accounts of transcendent experiences voluntarily reported by scientists. The goals of this unique database are to give scientists a safe place to report these experiences without embarrassment; to debunk the stereotype that real scientists don't have psychic or mystic experiences; and to build a database to help scientists further understand the powers of the mind. The reports themselves are fascinating reading, reinforcing the universality of these phenomena.

Yet scientists who investigate or offer evidence challenging the prevailing scientific materialism can sometimes pay a steep price, one of the reasons Tart created his TASTE "safe space" where scientists can admit to these experiences. They become the attacked, harassed and pilloried targets of dishonest skeptics and professional debunkers.

Honest, honorable skeptics restrict their criticism to the evidence. Instead of saying, "That's impossible!," they say "Show me what you've got to support your argument." In the process, they perform a valuable service, challenging sloppy research, fuzzy reasoning and wishful thinking. In contrast, the closed-minded debunker knows the answer before the question is asked. Such self-appointed guardians of scientific truth share many of the traits of religious fanatics—sincerity poisoned by an unshakable belief in an immutable orthodoxy; extreme zealousness in the hot pursuit and punishment of deviant thought and behavior; and an atrophied sense of humor.

The church of these true believers is the Committee for the Scientific Investigation of Claims of the Paranormal (www.csicop.org). Their bible is the *Skeptical Inquirer*, a magazine you can find in most big bookstores such as Barnes & Noble or Borders. CSICOP apparently started off with honest intentions: to submit a burgeoning number of psychic phenomena claims—many rising out of the counter-culture 60s and 70s, and rapidly spreading into mainstream American life—to scientific investigation.[19] It was, and still is, a worthy goal.

CSICOP co-founders in 1976 included two academics: Paul Kurtz and Marcello Truzzi. Kurtz was a professor of philosophy at the State University of New York at Buffalo, and editor of *The Humanist*, published by the American Humanist Association. Truzzi, a sociologist of science who had earned his doctorate in sociology at Cornell University, was better equipped to investigate paranormal claims than the average person. He grew up around circuses, learned magic and ventriloquism from side show performers by age 7, and was active as a magician and member of the Psychic Entertainers Association. He was interested in anomalies and familiar with tricks performers used to fake anomalies.

Unfortunately, CSICOP appears to have been dominated from the beginning by anti-paranormal crusaders with a less than complete commitment to even-handed, unbiased scientific investigation of the claims of the paranormal.[20] Within a year, Truzzi had resigned and CSICOP soon became known for its harassment of unorthodox scientific thought.

CSICOP's first attempts at scientific investigation turned out to be somewhat embarrassing. CSICOP conducted a formal investigation of a paranormal claim made by a French psychologist who offered statistics implying that more world-class athletes were born when the planet Mars was rising or transiting, in essence an astrological theory. CSICOP ended up being accused of deliberate fraud. CSICOP reported in the *Skeptical Inquirer* that their research showed no proof of the claim. In fact, the opposite was true, according to Dennis Rawlins, a CSICOP founding member and executive council member who quit the organization in 1979. According to Rawlins, leading CSICOP debunkers knew their data was being manipulated and hushed it up.[21]

Their investigation created a major PR problem for CSICOP. Several members quit CSICOP in protest after Rawlins revealed the fraud. After leaving CSICOP, Truzzi became editor of the *Zetetic Scholar* which published independent investigator Patrick Curry's epitaph on the scandal: CSICOP's work could well serve as a "model and a warning of how to *not* conduct such investigations."[22]

Members of the many skeptics clubs modeled after CSICOP are usually available to provide a reporter with a witty put-down of some *National Enquirer* story on Elvis' ghost (while too often avoiding serious investigation, analysis and comment on the best research and evidence); or a handy generic attack on all paranormal phenomena complete with just the right touch of world-weary sophistication.

Occasionally, some CSICOP members, like respected University of Oregon psychologist Ray Hyman, raise a scolding voice, accusing some skeptics of employing more emotion than logic, or making sweeping, unsubstantiated assertions and challenges to paranormal claims.[23] Hyman, a trained psychologist, statistician, mentalist and magician, has produced many intelligent and well-framed critiques of parapsychology in the last three decades and, ironically, is partly responsible for the evidence getting better. Now in his seventies, Hyman is eager to turn the task of devil's advocate over to someone else but worries about finding a worthy successor. In a July 2000 interview carried on the CSICOP website, Hyman noted that most of the popular critics of parapsychology can't meet the challenge of critiquing today's sophisticated parapsychology research. "Most of the criticism of the field is of straw people. The criticism has been very bad," he declares, adding later in the interview "Most of the criticisms of parapsychology are unfair."[24]

Another skeptic concerned about the increasingly bitter clash between skeptics and paranormal investigators is Brian Siano, Contributing Editor at *Skeptic* magazine, a publication of the Skeptics Society. He authored a thoughtful article entitled "Culture Wars: Skeptics, Parapsychologists and New Agers: Has the 'Good Guys Vs Bad Guys' Rhetoric Hindered the Quest for Truth?"[25] CSICOP, Siano says, is less of a scientific organization than a "science club." Siano notes that skeptics have done valuable and respectable work in challenging paranormal claims, but he warns against skeptics who portray believers and opponents as not merely wrong, but "deluded, credulous, 'religious' in a pejorative sense, or dangerously irrational" and view themselves as being in an apocalyptic battle against enemies of civilization and enlightenment. Such an approach, says Siano, will only "serve to encourage distrust of the skeptics."

By definition, a true skeptic is someone who raises doubts, says ex-CSICOP co-founder Marcello Truzzi. A true skeptic begins with uncertainty or doubt—*non belief* rather than *disbelief*. In contrast, too many skeptics and debunkers are disbelievers, offering answers rather than questions.[26] Truzzi, now a member of the Society for Scientific Exploration, continues to remain open-minded about the existence of the paranormal. His classic book *The Blue Sense: Psychic Detectives and Crime*, examining the uses of psychics in police work, demonstrates the honest form of skepticism he espouses.[27] Truzzi's Center for Scientific Anomalies Research (Ann Arbor, Michigan) began collecting data and case histories on the "blue sense" in 1980. Today its Psychic Sleuths project files are the most comprehensive database in the U.S. on the use of ESP and clairvoyance in the service of criminal justice.

Britain's equivalent of CSICOP is COPUS—the Committee On the Public Understanding of Science, founded in 1986 and run by England's most exalted scientific institutions, including the Royal Society so repeatedly embarrassed in the past by its dogmatic pronouncements. COPUS chairman and biology professor Dr. Lewis Wolpert is on record as declaring "Open minds are empty minds." [28]

The contrast between CSICOP/COPUS and SSE in regards to examining scientific anomalies is significant. CSICOP/COPUS looks at a paranormal claim and tends to ask, "Where's the trick?" The Society for Scientific Exploration looks at a paranormal claim and tends to ask, "Where's the evidence?" The SSE's publicly-stated position on anomalies is clear: it's not a pro-paranormal lobbying group. "The Society has no intention of endorsing the reality or significance of any particular topic." But it also does not regard current scientific knowledge as immutable, and "no subject will be prohibited from discussion or publication simply because it is not now an accepted part of scientific or scholarly knowledge."

What honest science says about the paranormal, then, is simply this: Examine, without prejudice or preconceptions, all available evidence, using all available scientific tools. And as we will discover later in this book, the best evidence is interesting indeed.

5.

The Times They Are A-Changing

"To put it bluntly, science no longer contains absolute truths...the old distinction between the natural and the supernatural has become spurious."
Yale physicist Henry Margenau

Back in 1940, to the anger of skeptics, Dr. J.B. Rhine's *Extra-Sensory Perception After Sixty Years* became assigned reading for the introductory psychology classes at Harvard.[1] The book summarized a decade of experimental lab work on ESP and backed up its conclusions with extensive statistics. It reviewed the thirty-two principal criticisms skeptics had leveled against the experiments over the years, and showed how they couldn't account for all the results. It forced the scientific Establishment to take the subject seriously. In the process, it secured a scientific beach-head for a world beyond the five senses. By 1973, a scientific survey of its readers done by *New Scientist* showed that 67 percent of scientists believed that ESP was either "an established fact" or a "likely possibility," with only 3 percent believing it was an "impossibility."[2] A later, large-scale (2,000 people) poll of university academics in the U.S. found 66 percent agreeing that ESP was either established fact or a likely possibility, with "hard" scientists, notably physicists, most in agreement.[3] By 1990, the widely used college text-book *Introduction to Psychology* (10th Ed.) included a small section entitled "Psi Phenomena." [4]

Today, the classic Western, mechanistic, reductionist, materialistic world view remains dominant, but no longer goes unquestioned. Unprecedented discoveries in quantum physics, astronomy, mind-body medicine and consciousness research suggest possibilities undreamed of when Issac Newton described reality. New scientific theories of space, time and causality are being hypothesized and debated, some of which are surprisingly compatible with the idea of the paranormal. Quantum physics, for example, can allow for the same object to be in two places at the same time, or effects to precede their causes. Indeed, science and the paranormal may be headed towards a reconciliation in the new millennium.[5]

This gradual shift in scientific opinion regarding ESP mirrors a larger shift in the general public's opinion regarding the paranormal. The gulf between science's definition of acceptable reality and the average person's personal beliefs and experiences accelerated in the 1960s and 1970s. A generation of middle-class Americans discovered Eastern philosophy, and thought-provoking alternative views of reality possessing their own defendable, internal logic found in cultures and traditions not dominated by Western, left-brain thinking. Some young people experimented with reality-altering drugs like LSD or devoted themselves to spiritual and meditation practices which provided them with direct, personal experience of altered states of consciousness. Psychologists and psychiatrists began seriously questioning the cultural basis of Western society's consensus reality. Claiming a paranormal experience in the 1950s could get you locked away; by the 1970s, tolerance was becoming common. As long as you weren't a danger to yourself or others, your personal view of reality might be ridiculed, questioned or rejected but you were free to believe it without fear of being committed to a nuthouse. The Seventies also saw the publication (1975) of Dr. Raymond Moody's best-seller *Life After Life*, a small but powerful collection of near death experiences compiled by this medical doctor. Soon after (1978), an International Association of Near Death Studies (IANDS) was formed to promote serious, scientific research on this phenomenon. By the 1980s, the New Age was in full bloom, reintroducing Americans to mediums (renamed channelers); scientific evidence suggestive of reincarnation from Dr. Ian Stevenson at the U. of Virginia; and breakthrough, Princeton University-based psychokinesis research. The '90s reinforced this culture shift towards openmindedness through national radio shows like *Art Bell* and major Hollywood box office hits like *Sixth Sense, Contact, Michael, Ghost,* and *What Dreams May Come.* The award-winning TV program *X-Files* was notable for sympathetically presenting paranormal themes and claims—ghosts, poltergeists, ESP, life after death, parallel universes, psychokinesis, out-of-body adventures, intelligent life elsewhere in the universe and altered states of consciousness. The '90s also saw encyclopedias starting to treat psi phenomena seriously[6] and objectively, including the *Colliers, Americana,* and *Britannica* editions. Indeed, disappointed skeptics accused the *Americana* encyclopedia of being too pro-paranormal.[7] Only the *Comptons* encyclopedia remained clearly biased against parapsychology, including it under the pejorative term "pseudo-science."

A quick look back at the last decade offers some surprising examples of how far we have come as we start the 21st century.

According to a story in the Sept./Oct. 1992 issue of *John Harvard's Journal*, the alumni magazine published by America's oldest university, the Facilities Maintenance Dept. at Harvard used dowsing before construction began at the Law School site on campus to locate underground electrical and water lines that weren't on the ground plans.[8] The electrician who did the dowsing learned it from a senior electrician and had been dowsing since 1969. The story in the alumni magazine generated little controversy and just a few angry letters denouncing the practice as "unscientific." Meanwhile, mainstream media are beginning to carry informative stories on dowsing as well. *Science News* published a cover story on dowsing in its Aug. 5, 1995 issue,[9] objectively presenting the results of some interesting scientific dowsing experiments in Germany. *National Geographic Explorer*, a national TV program produced by *National Geographic* magazine which runs on TBS, in April 1994 featured its own story on dowsers and the dowsing art.

In December 1993, *National Geographic World*, a young reader's monthly magazine published by the prestigious National Geographic Society, featured an illustrated, three-page story on the history of the UFO phenomenon, including tips on how to categorize distant sightings (nocturnal lights, daylight discs and radar-visual) and how to classify sightings themselves (Close Encounters of the first to fourth kind). The well-balanced article explained that most UFOs later turn out to be *Identified* Flying Objects; some UFOs are miss-identifications of planets like Venus, or deliberate hoaxes; and its easy to fake a UFO photograph. But they also noted that the argument "Only crackpots have seen UFOs" is a myth, and point out that airplane pilots, policemen, teachers and even U.S. presidents have seen UFOs.

In 1994, Sony Corp. had a research team studying the power and effects of *ki*, the "life force" or energy field that acupuncturists believe flows through the body and can be manipulated by needles (an energy force Science rejects). That year, more than 10 Japanese companies were sponsoring *ki* research at a Tokyo University, and senior executives from Mitsubishi, Casio, NEC and Sony were regularly training themselves in developing their *ki*.[10]

In November 1995, the U.S. Central Intelligence Agency publicly confirmed that, for the previous 20 years, it had been employing psychics with ESP talents in a spying operation eventually known as "Star Gate." The secret "remote viewing" program (see Chapter 6), which spent $20 million over two decades, was reportedly used to penetrate super-secret Russian weapons facilities, locate the place where Italy's terrorist Red Brigade was holding American Brig. General James Dozier hostage, track Libyan leader Moammar Gadhafi and help drug enforcement agencies in their work.[11]

In 1997, a physicist and a biologist from Brown University used a magnetic field at MIT's Francis Bitter National Magnet Laboratory and successfully levitated frog embryos for several minutes—the first reported experiment in which living creatures were levitated in a magnetic field. A short while later, a British team of scientists reported being able to levitate an adult frog, using a magnetic field 1 million times as strong as that of the earth. The article reporting the event concluded, "With an even more powerful field, humans could also float on air, the scientists say."[12]

In October 1998, physicists at Caltech University produced the first bonafide teleportation of matter.[13] They took a beam of light in one place and instantly materialized it in another place some distance away. The same teleportation process applies in principle not just to a bunch of photons but to other particles as well. Researchers are already looking to teleport atoms, or collections of atoms (like us). According to scientists, the immediate use of the technology is for super-fast, ultra-powerful "quantum computers." But some scientists believe the technology could also someday be used for something like *Star Trek*-style, human transporters. "Beam me up, Scotty."

In November 1998, the U.S. Patent Office issued the first U.S. patent for a psi (ESP/psychokinesis) effect. Mindsong Inc. received patent No. 5830064 for an "apparatus and method for distinguishing events which collectively exceed chance expectations and thereby controlling an output." Dr. Robert Jahn and some of his colleagues from the Princeton University PEAR laboratory (see Chapter 7) are among the inventors listed on the patent.

As we saw earlier, in May 2001, the Gallup Poll found that Americans' belief in the paranormal had significantly increased, almost across the board, in the last decade of the 20th century. Today Americans who believe in the reality of ESP and mental/faith healing outnumber skeptics 2 to 1. They're the majority, not the minority. Americans who believe that houses can be haunted, and mental telepathy is a fact are also now a majority, not a minority. A rapidly growing minority of one in three American (up 10% in the last decade) now accept as fact that people can hear from of communicate mentally with someone who has died. A quarter of a century ago, reincarnation was a fringe belief held by 9 percent of Americans.[14] Today 25 percent of Americans accept the idea.

Paranormal claims are no longer an automatic ticket to the funny farm. The current edition of the *Diagnostic and Statistical Manual of Mental Disorders* (4th Ed., released in 1994), used by the American Psychiatric Association, includes a new category titled "Religious or Spiritual Problem" which parapsychologist and psychologist Stanley Krippner has called a major step towards recognizing "alternative models of psychotherapy and medicine with parapsychological components."[15] Such unusual, reality-challenging human experiences as near death experiences, out-of-body experiences and past life experiences can now be approached under this non-pathological diagnostic category rather than be treated automatically as mental disorders as they have in the past. Krippner himself is co-editor of the recent book *Varieties of Anomalous Experience: Examining the Scientific Evidence*,[16] published in 2000 by the American Psychological Association. The book fairly and honestly examines evidence for a wide range of anomalous experiences, including some examined in this book—ESP, anomalous healing, near death and out-of-body experiences, and past life claims.

Meanwhile, the impact on the material body of intention, will, focus, thought, emotion and other non-physical expressions of consciousness (mind over matter) is gaining serious recognition—particularly as applied to healing. Mind-body interactions once considered impossible or ridiculous by mainstream medical science are today being seriously studied in laboratories, employed in treatments and reimbursed by insurance. In 1992, the U.S. Congress created an Office of Alternative Medicine within the National Institutes of Health, charged with evaluating alternative or unconventional medical treatments. In 1998, the Office was upgraded to become the National Center for Complementary and Alternative Medicine (http://nccam.nih.gov). The alternative medical treatments being formally studied include a multitude of mind/body interventions like hypnosis, meditation and biofeedback as well as scientific paradigm-challengers like prayer healing, psychic healing and Therapeutic Touch. (Therapeutic Touch, which involves a modern version of the Biblical "laying on of hands," is now being practiced by over 18,000 nurses, physicians and other health professionals in the U.S. It involves rebalancing the body's energy field and is being used in the management of pain, anxiety, tension and stress, and to accelerate wound healing and promote a sense of well-being).[17] Incidentally, the venerable American Society for Psychical Research is among those groups providing the NIH with information and recommendations for funding future research programs. The Society's century-long investigation into the area of exceptional human experiences includes significant reports and observations on the topic of mental and faith healing.

In July 1993, Mutual of Omaha insurance company, the nation's largest provider of health insurance for individuals, announced that it would start paying insurance benefits for meditation exercises designed to reverse heart disease. (Excessive blood cholesterol is one of the major factors for heart disease. Meditation has been scientifically shown to be capable of lowering blood cholesterol by one-third, is cost-free, and is virtually free of side effects, a claim few drugs can make).[18] The meditation exercises are part of an alternative treatment regimen that also includes diet, exercise and support groups. The program has been proven just as effective as conventional coronary care but costs only one-tenth the price. The breakthrough program, developed by Dr. Dean Ornish, Director of the Preventive Medicine Research Institute in

Sausalito, California, was the first non-surgical, non-pharmaceutical therapy for heart disease to be accepted by the insurance industry.[19] The Maharishi must be smiling.

That same year (1993), a book on the effect of prayer on health became a New York Times bestseller. The book *Healing Words: The Power of Prayer and the Practice of Medicine* was written by Larry Dossey, M.D., former chief of staff of Humana Medical City in Dallas and co-chairman of the Panel on Mind/Body Interventions at the Office of Alternative Medicine, National Institutes of Health.

In 1997, the federal government's National Institutes of Health formally endorsed acupuncture as effective for a wide range of illnesses, including nausea, pain, stroke rehabilitation and asthma, among other conditions.[20] Acupuncture is now widely used and accepted in the U.S. Some nine to twelve million Americans use acupuncture every year. It is being taught in mainline medical and dental schools like UCLA, New York University and St. Louis University, and an estimated 3,000 conventionally trained physicians now offer it as a treatment mode.[21] (Incidentally, here's a fun fact: more Americans (6 million) practice yoga than do cross-country skiing or skateboarding.) [22]

In the half century after Harvard put Rhine's ESP book on an assigned reading list, some 40 universities in the U.S. awarded 57 master's degrees and over 115 doctorate degrees to students who wrote their theses and dissertations on some aspect of the paranormal.[23] These universities include Harvard, Yale, Stanford, Berkeley, USC, UCLA, Ohio State, Michigan, Wisconsin, Minnesota, Missouri, Oklahoma, Arkansas, Texas, LSU, North Carolina, Duke, Brown, Boston University, New York University, Columbia, Purdue and Penn State.

Paranormal topics treated in these university theses and dissertations have included the use of psychics by police as an investigative aid (California State University, Long Beach); archeology and parapsychology (California State University, Fullerton); a history of spiritualism (U. of Wisconsin); correlated hemispheric asymmetry in the sensory and ESP processing of emotional and non-emotional videotapes (City University of New York); telepathy between mothers and daughters (New York University); a comparative study of medieval, Christian and contemporary accounts of near death experiences (Harvard); faith healing (U. of North Carolina); the psychology of people who report having seen a UFO (Carleton University, Ottawa); the psychic reader as shaman and psychotherapist (UCLA); ESP and mediums (Boston University); psychic readers and human auras (Berkeley); the Kirilian effect (Columbia); the seer Edgar Cayce (U. of Chicago); the effects of the drugs amytal and dexadrine on ESP (Yale); meditation and psi performance (Northern Illinois University); psychokinesis and the mind-over-matter concept (Adelphi University); possession trances (Berkeley); hypnotizability, creativity and psi in the Ganzfield (City University of New York); testing for a psychokinetic effect on plants: the effect of "laying on of hands" on germinating corn seeds (West Georgia College); philosophical implications of psi phenomena leading to a reconciliation of science and religion (U. of Oklahoma); clairvoyance and creativity (U. of Georgia); and lucid dreaming (Stanford University).

It's doubtful researchers will ever run out of intriguing anomalies to study. Unexplainable phenomena suggesting a world beyond the current limits of scientific theory continue to occur with unrelenting regularly as they have for thousands of years.

One of the first people to systematically catalogue these phenomena that don't fit established scientific theory was American iconoclast Charles Fort (1874-1932). Born in Albany, N.Y., he worked as a journalist and writer before coming into a small inheritance at the age of 42. Thereafter, he spent his days in the New York Public Library, culling stories of the unexplained from various newspapers and magazines. His first collection of anomalies appeared in *Book of the Damned,* printed in 1919 by the company that published his friend and fellow novelist Theodore Dreiser. The "damned" was Fort's term for data that science had excluded from consideration because they didn't fit into the prevailing orthodoxy. He later moved to London, and spent his days in the British Museum, collecting more news accounts of the unexplainable—UFOs, poltergeists, levitating stones, footprints of giants, mysterious lights, and strange things that continue to fall out of the sky to confound scientists like meteorites did to European scientists in the 18th century. Fort's research turned up a bizarre list of falling objects that included fish, frogs, turtles, snails, ants, worms, jellyfish, spiders, snakes, lumps of coal and stones of every size, grain, iron objects, blood, and waterfalls from a clear sky. For good measure, he also collected stories of mysterious radio and telephone transmissions, odd sightings by astronomers, spontaneous explosions, and sudden, unexplainable darkness that sometimes settled over cities and towns from Memphis, Tennessee to London, England. He eventually returned to New York and in 1931 published another puzzling collection of strange phenomena under the title *Lo!*. When he died in 1932, he left a pile of 60,000 notes, now found in the New York Public Library. Incidentally, Fort coined the term "teleportation" used by the media 66 years later to describe Caltech's 1998 scientific feat.[24]

Today, several Fortean societies continue his work of cataloguing and reporting anomalies that challenge current scientific theory. One Fort devotee, researcher William Corliss, has produced a multi-volume catalog (www.science-frontiers.com) of "all phenomena that cannot readily be explained by prevailing scientific theories." In his compendium, each anomaly is briefly but clearly described, classified, the source (primarily scientific journals) carefully cited, and in some cases "scores" for reliability and degree of anomalousness added. Another good contribution to anomalies research is Jerome Clark's 443-page compendium entitled *Unexplained!: 347 Strange Sightings,Incredible Occurrences and Puzzling Physical Phenomena*.[25]

Belief in the paranormal, then, doesn't continue to exist simply because people are ignorant, credulous or uneducated. Belief continues because paranormal phenomena—phenomena that violate known laws of science—continue to occur. They continue to be seen, felt, experienced and reported, by people of all ages, races, cultures, and socioeconomic backgrounds; in every country on earth; often in forms and manifestations unchanged since mankind started recording them four thousand years ago. Ridicule doesn't make them disappear; education doesn't make them disappear; the immense technological achievements and intellectual prestige of modern science cannot eradicate belief in them. Perhaps it's time to sit down and honestly examine the best evidence believers and experiencers can offer for the existence of these science-challenging phenomena.

Part II: Best Evidence

6.

Extra-Sensory Perception (ESP)

"The greatest skeptic concerning paranormal phenomena
is invariably the man who knows the least about them."
H.H. Price

One of my relatives, Fr. E.J. Weibel, was a Swiss-born Catholic priest working in Arkansas in the early 1900s. Not too long ago, my mother received a copy of his memoirs, published by a press in Indiana.[1] In passing, he recounts several fascinating ESP incidents which happened to him during his life. They're typical of the kind of personal stories I heard from other people when researching this phenomenon. Because they were stories from my own family, I found them particularly fascinating.

"In early November of the scholastic year 1870," Fr. Weibel recounts, "the thought pursued me that my stepmother, Katherine Weibel, whom I dearly loved, would die. I dreamed of it. Day and night she seemed to hover before me. I could no longer take part in games. During recess, I entered chapel to pray for her. Finally, I could no longer endure my painful uncertainty. I accosted the Prefect, Father Bernard Benziger, and requested permission to go home, giving as excuse that my mother must be dying. I could, however, give no satisfactory reason or proof of my contention." (In 1870, the telephone was still six years in the future so Fr. Weibel couldn't simply call home to check up on his mother's health.)

The Prefect, who ran the school, laughed at him and told him he would be terribly embarrassed if he got home and his mother were fine. Permission was denied. So Fr. Weibel returned to class, "staring blankly, for my spirit was far removed from my surroundings." Finally, he couldn't stand it and asked the Prefect again. The Prefect sent Fr. Weibel to his brother, Fr. Roman Weibel, also living at the monastery. His brother "feared that I might have a nervous breakdown and contended that it was better to let me go home than to be obliged to place me in the insane asylum of St. Urban in Canton Lucerne. His remarks didn't intimidate me," wrote Fr. Weibel in his memoirs. The Prefect reluctantly agreed.

So Fr. Weibel happily set out on foot in deep snow, crossed the mountains, caught a train, and at eleven o'clock the next night arrived in his home town. For a second, he panicked. "Suddenly my mood changed and scales seemed to drop from my eyes. I said to myself, 'What will I say if I find everyone asleep peacefully at home?'" But he went ahead. "As I neared the house, I saw no light. My fears mounted with each step, and with palpitating heart I knocked. My oldest brother opened and inquired, 'Why are you here?' I related my experiences. While mounting the stairs, I obtained the following account from him: 'Our mother died at five o'clock this evening. She became ill yesterday. Today, three doctors were with her and declared her condition much improved. Half an hour after their departure, she was dead.' "

I am impressed that Fr. Weibel had enough confidence in his premonition to risk such potentially heavy ridicule and embarrassment.

It wasn't the only time he experienced ESP. Another time, an "inner voice" as he describes it, announced to Fr. Weibel the death of his own father. Father Weibel was in Arkansas at the time, and announced his father's death to the church congregation before he had received the official death notice from Europe. A few weeks later, official notice of his death arrived in the form of a letter. A third incident happened when he was ill in bed in Arkansas. "A pupil from the local school came into my room to stoke the fire. I thought I heard a knock and sent him to the door. He reported that no one was there. Involuntarily I exclaimed, 'Then Sister Angelina Willimann has died in Eschenbach.' (The nun had been his former art teacher and lived in Eschenbach, Switzerland.) The youth relayed the supposed message to his teacher who later chided me for my superstition. Two weeks later, the death notice of sister arrived. The nun had died at about the exact time when I had made the statement regarding her death," notes Fr. Weibel in his journals.

Extra-sensory perception, ESP, a "sixth sense"—call it what you will, it's an odd phenomenon familiar to most of us. Scientists define it as the ability to obtain knowledge without the use of the five senses (sight, hearing, touch, taste, smell). Science says it's impossible. My relative, Father Weibel, would beg to disagree.

Parapsychologists, aware of the many, different ways ESP can manifest itself, have special names for each type of ESP.

"Precognition," also called "premonition," is one type. It involves the ability to somehow see a future event; or get knowledge of the future before it happens. My relative, Fr. Weibel, had a premonition wherein he saw a future event—the death of his mother and father—before it happened.

"Retrocognition" is the ability to see events in the opposite direction, backwards in time.

"Telepathy" refers to direct communication between two minds, without the use of words, gestures, touch or any of the five senses. Telepathy is the perception of thoughts, not objects. In experiments, it usually involves a "sender" who knows a message and tries to mentally communicate it to a "receiver" who doesn't know the message. The term was coined in the late 1800s by Frederic Myers, one of the co-founders of the Society for Psychical Research. This same group, which conducted the first modern, scientific studies of ghosts and apparitions, also conducted the first modern, scientific ESP experiments.

"Clairvoyance" is often referred to today as "remote viewing." It involves the ability to see objects at a distance using something besides the five senses.

Perhaps the most famous name in ESP research history is Dr. J.B. Rhine who did his most interesting psi research at Duke University in the 1930s and 1940s. The Ohio-born Rhine and his wife Louisa originally planned to be professional foresters, and both earned doctorates in biology from the University of Chicago. But after hearing a lecture on psychical research by Spiritualist and author Sir Arthur Conan Doyle (the creator of Sherlock Holmes), both dropped the pursuit of plant mysteries for the pursuit of paranormal mysteries.

Rhine started his paranormal research career with a Hodgson fellowship at the psychology department at Harvard University in 1926-1927 (the fellowship was created in honor of Richard Hodgson, a researcher in mediumistic communications, or communications with the spirits of deceased individuals by means of a medium or human message channeler). He worked under department head William McDougall, himself an accomplished psychical researcher. And when McDougall moved to Duke in 1927 to head the psychology department there, he secured a position on his faculty for Rhine.

From 1928 until his retirement in 1965, Rhine conducted paranormal research at Duke. In the beginning, he focused his efforts on collecting and analyzing evidence for postmortem survival, and he earned a doctorate in psychology from Duke in 1933 on the subject—the first doctorate in psychical research ever give by an American university. But he concluded in the end that anecdotal research on postmortem survival would always be open to scientific challenge and ambiguity. The only way one could really prove the paranormal to a skeptical scientific community, he decided, was to demonstrate it in the laboratory, using experimental controls. It was a fateful decision for psychical research, setting the course for the next 40 years.[2]

What Rhine set out to do was demonstrate ESP as well as psychokinesis in a controlled, laboratory experiment. Proving the reality of either one had the potential of shaking the foundations of the mechanistic materialism underlying modern Science. Both are considered impossible. But Rhine was not daunted by the task. Over the next three decades, he conducted hundreds of controlled laboratory experiments on mental telepathy, clairvoyance and precognition.

Rhine suspected that ESP was not a supernatural phenomenon, but rather an unknown but natural phenomenon ultimately understandable under the laws of classical physics. Consequently, it could be studied in the laboratory like any other natural phenomenon. It was also not a gift limited to a few exceptional individuals or the product of an abnormal mind or a mind in an altered state. Instead, Rhine believed that all of us have the ability to perform ESP at some level. Because of this, Rhine used as his test subjects not famous psychics but average people off the street—or in his case, off the Duke campus.

Rhine started with telepathy. To test the ability of one person to mentally send information to another person without the use of the five senses, he had the "sender" turn over a card from a special deck, note the symbol printed on the face of the card, then concentrate on the symbol while a "receiver" tried to guess what he was thinking. His special Zener card deck had 25 cards with five cards each of five symbols (a circle, star, square, cross and wavy line). By the statistical laws of chance, the receiver should be able to guess five cards correctly on average. If he correctly guessed 6 or more, something other than chance was possible. The higher the number of correct guesses, the higher the probability of it being true ESP and not luck. Of course the receiver would have to repeat the feat over many runs; doing it once might itself have been just a fluke.

Fortunately for Rhine, the science of probability statistics was coming into its own just about the time Rhine began his experiments. Statisticians could now provide Rhine with a yardstick to measure just how significant various experiment results were in terms of decisively eliminating chance as an explanation. With the help of statistics, Rhine was confident he could demonstrate repeatability in the lab, as physical scientists did with their experiments. He hoped to establish its reality, and understand its workings. His goal was to tame and control a psychic ability which to that point had been considered spontaneous, unpredictable and maddeningly inconsistent—if not outright impossible.

Psychical researchers had conducted similar card-guessing experiments as far back as the late 1800s, but Rhine systematized the experiments. He used the special Zener cards. And to satisfy skeptical colleagues in the scientific community, he tried to reduce or eliminate the possibility of fraud or cheating. He established experimental controls to keep the sender and receiver from accidentally or deliberately communicating with each other, placing them in different rooms during the experiments so they couldn't see or hear each other. His controls weren't airtight, but they were better than most earlier ESP experiments.

His first telepathy experiments produced promising results, including several spectacular series of successive hits. Rhine's best sender-receiver team recorded 26 straight hits in a row.[3]

Rhine next turned to the possibility of clairvoyance. Could the need for a sender be eliminated and the receiver get information directly from the cards (clairvoyance)? To tests this, cards were simply dealt face down on the table without the dealer seeing the faces of the cards, and the receiver—usually located in another building—had to guess what they were. His experiments in clairvoyance proved equally successful. Rhine considered his "Pearce-Pratt" series as the most convincing of all his clairvoyance experiments. J. Gaither Pratt, Rhine's assistant, sat at a table in the physics building at Duke and dealt a card a minute face down, without looking at it, until he had run the whole deck. Hubert Pearce, a Duke divinity school student, sat in a room a hundred yards away and every minute recorded a guess. At the end of the session, Pearce's guesses were compared to the actual cards dealt by Pratt and the results compared to chance expectations. Four experiments ultimately were conducted, with this dynamic duo separated in some trials in buildings 250 yards apart. Out of 1,850 cards guessed in these trials, the laws of chance would expect 370 correct hits. Pearce and Pratt recorded 558 correct hits. [4] The odds against guessing that many right cards was an astronomical 22 billion-to-one. Even more spectacular—though less important from a scientific proof standpoint because it was only accomplished once—was Pearce succeeding on one occasion in getting 25 straight hits in a row. The odds against such a feat? One in 300 quadrillion. [5]

Rhine also established that increasing the distance between the receiver and the target in telepathy and clairvoyance tests did not result in diminished performance, unlike our usual five senses. Senses like sight and hearing, for instance, fade with distance. A bird ten feet away can be seen by the naked eye; a bird five miles away cannot. Same for hearing. If I'm in my back yard and my mother opens the back door and calls for me, I have no trouble hearing her. But if I'm in another town, I can't. Rhine conducted one clairvoyance experiment where the receiver was able to "see" a target 4,000 miles away.[6]

Besides telepathy and clairvoyance, Rhine also conducted experiments in precognition, where the receiver in the Pearce-Pratt experiments made his guess *before* the card was dealt from the deck. Eventually, Rhine concluded that precognition and clairvoyance were somehow two aspects of the same phenomenon. In clairvoyance, you see the target as it is now; in precognition, you see the target as it will be in the future. Eventually, Rhine would conclude that psychokinesis (PK) operated similarly to ESP.[7] Today, many parapsychology researchers agree with Rhine, studying ESP and PK under the common name of "psi" phenomenon.

Like distance with clairvoyance, time did not seem to be a barrier to precognition. One could see far into the future, not just the next hour, day or week. In one experiment, a Duke University college coed who had previously served as a test subject for Rhine took a year abroad to study in France. While there, she did some more clairvoyance tests and sent her answers back to Rhine who kept them unopened. A year later, Rhine created a target list, then opened the coed's answers and matched them to the targets. The results beat chance odds, even though she had made her guesses a year before the actual target list was even created. One year ahead was the longest time interval for any formal precognition test conducted by J.B. Rhine, but anecdotal stories of spontaneous precognitive dreams collected by Louisa Rhine included people seeing years and even decades into the future.[8] (A half-century later, scientists would finally have enough precognition studies—309 experiments involving 50,000+ people and 2 million sessions conducted between 1935-1987—to conclusively eliminate the skeptics' favorite explanation for precognition, the "chance" hypothesis.)[9]

Rhine's research encountered some surprises, difficulties and experiment design challenges along the way. For instance, Rhine confirmed what common sense could expect in ESP experiments where people being tested had to repeat the same boring experiment over and over again to build up enough results to be statistically significant and eliminate chance as an explanation—they got bored, lost interest, and their scores dropped. Rhine dubbed this the "decline effect." Unfortunately, the "decline effect" made impossible Rhine's goal of a repeatable experiment that automatically produced ESP. Physical scientists can heat fresh water at sea level and it will boil at 212 degrees Fahrenheit a million experiments in a row. It never shows a "decline effect." Human beings were different. They clearly couldn't produce ESP each time, every time, a million experiments in a row. Thus Rhine faced a dilemma.

If he wanted to combat the "decline effect" and have his test subjects perform their best, he had to drop the classical scientist's neutral, objective, emotionally uninvolved attitude towards the experiment and its outcome. It helped to become a cheerleader, encouraging and emotionally supporting the efforts of his test subjects, psyching them up, varying routines, making the environment comfortable and pleasant. But if he got too involved, he opened himself up to charges of experimenter bias, or weak controls against fraud or trickery. Skeptics could argue that positive encouragement could easily turn into interference or unconscious collusion.

Rhine had also hoped to show that ESP was a normal human ability, not a special gift reserved to the exceptional, abnormal or entranced person. His research did suggest that the average person off the street could perform ESP; but it also showed that some people were clearly better than others. ESP talent was not spread equally among humans. Strong ESP ability was more an unusual talent than an ordinary one. Rhine also discovered the importance motivation played in achieving success, a discovery he considered among the most important made about ESP.[10] Highly motivated people had a better chance of producing ESP than someone off the street who didn't care about the results. Some years later, Dr. Gertrude Schmeidler demonstrated that believers also tend to score higher than skeptics in psychic experiments. Skepticism, doubt and unemotional neutrality apparently work to decrease or eliminate psychic abilities.

Rhine had designed his experiments with the hope that any scientist repeating his experiment using the same protocols (rules for how to run the experiment) could produce the same results. It didn't work out that way. Sometimes skeptics, and even researchers open to the possibility of ESP, were unable to produce the same results Rhine reported. To make matters worse, though his statistical methods were accepted,[11] Rhine himself was sometimes careless in his work and his experimental controls inadequate, providing skeptics with ammunition to challenge his results.[12] Last but not least, Rhine never succeeded in firmly determining how and why and when ESP operated. For all his research, ESP remained a quirky, paranormal phenomenon.

In the end, however, even though his findings violated many laws of classical physics, Rhine believed he had collected enough solid, scientific evidence to prove to any open-minded person the reality of ESP and PK.

In 1934, a half-decade after starting his research, he published a monograph entitled *Extra-Sensory Perception*, detailing his experimental methods and results. In it, he argued that ESP had not yet been explained, but it certainly existed, "puzzling as its explanation may be."[13] ESP was a fact. What was left to do was to explain how it worked. *Extra-Sensory Perception* earned favorable reviews from a number of influential persons, including *New York Times* science editor Waldeman Kampffert. Within the scientific community, psychologists showed the most interest in his research. Articles on Rhine's research also began to appear with some frequency in the media, including *Time, Reader's Digest, Scientific American* and *Harper's*.

In September 1937, Zenith Radio Corporation produced a series of weekly national broadcasts that allowed listeners to participate in ESP experiments using decks of cards Zenith provided with its logo on the back. A month later, Rhine came out with *New Frontiers of the Mind*, a book on ESP aimed at the general public. It was a Book-of-the-Month Club Selection in an era before television existed for the general public. It's impact on the public was substantial. In that same year, Rhine and other ESP researchers got a scientific publication of their own, the *Journal of Parapsychology*, where they could present the results of their work to other researchers and academics.

In 1940, Rhine produced *Extra-Sensory Perception After Sixty Years* (the book's title referred to six decades of research on ESP by the parapsychological community since the SPR's founding in 1882). It became assigned reading for the 1940-41 school year for students in the introductory psychology classes at Harvard University, perhaps the pinnacle of academic respectability.

Meanwhile, Rhine's wife Louisa, had also been busy researching ESP and PK. Some of her most important insights, however, came not from laboratory experiments but from collecting and analyzing anecdotal stories of spontaneous psychic experiences. People from all over America who heard about their ESP research at Duke sent letters telling them of their own strange experiences.

In 1948, Louisa Rhine began systematically studying these anecdotal reports which grew to almost 14,000 cases by the time she retired three decades later.[14] Based on this impressive database of 14,000 cases, Louisa reached some interesting conclusions about spontaneous ESP experiences.

For instance, she discovered that nearly 60 percent of these reported ESP experiences occurred during dreams. Our dreaming state of consciousness, then, is very conducive to psychic experiences. Louisa further classified these ESP dreams into two types—realistic dreams, which made up about two-thirds of the ESP dreams; and symbolic dreams which accounted for the remainder. Broughton provides good examples of both types in his book *Parapsychology: The Controversial Science*.

In one typical *realistic* dream, a grandmother dreamed she saw her baby grandson struggling against being smothered under his blankets. She awoke at 3:45 in the morning, wondering whether to awake her daughter at such an ungodly hour over such a bizarre nightmare. In the end, she decided it was better to be embarrassed if she were wrong than to ignore the dream and possibly regret it the rest of her life. When she called her daughter, her son-in-law was already up. The baby had indeed been smothering in the blankets. They had heard him and had reached him in time.

A typical *symbolic* dream resembles a normal dream except that the dreamer awakens convinced that this dream is special and important. He or she intuitively senses that it is not just another strange dream. Broughton cites the case of a California mother during World War II who dreamed one night that her sailor son came to her and handed her his uniform, all dripping wet, saying "Oh mom, it's all so terrible!" She held her sobbing son in her arms and suddenly he became an infant again. As she rocked him in her arms, he stopped crying and she awoke. She was convinced the dream had some special meaning for her—and it did. A week later, the U.S. Navy informed her that her son's ship had been torpedoed and gone down on the night she had her precognitive dream. He was missing and presumed dead.

ESP during waking hours accounted for most of the remaining 40 percent of the ESP cases Rhine logged. Unlike dreams, waking ESP normally involves little imagery, just a direct, immediate knowledge of some fact. In one typical case involving ESP during waking hours, a divorced woman was chatting with her daughter when suddenly and without warning in the middle of the conversation her expression changed to astonishment. When her surprised daughter asked her what had happened, she told her that her father was getting married again. Her daughter, who was close to her father and spoke regularly with him, pooh-poohed the idea. She had just received a letter from her father and he had mentioned nothing about a marriage. But the mother, who had viewed her divorce as a matter of shame and sorrow, insisted. A short while later, the daughter received a letter from her father. He had indeed remarried on the evening of the day the mother had received her sudden ESP knowledge.

The majority of Rhine's ESP cases involved receiving important, even life-or-death information. Interestingly enough, however, many reported ESP insights brought unessential or insignificant information. The ESP recipient might get information on the shirt a friend would wear at their next meeting, the outcome of a Little League game, or advance notice of an unexpected visit from his favorite Aunt Jody.

According to Broughton, more than 50 percent of all ESP experiences are precognitive—they foresee the future.[15] If you know about it in advance, can you prevent something from happening?

In an attempt to find out, Louisa Rhine conducted an analysis on 191 carefully selected precognitive cases to determine if the ESP recipient was able to affect the foreseen outcome. In almost 70 percent (131) of the cases, they were able to take action to avoid the undesirable event. [16]

One of those 131 cases involved a streetcar operator in Los Angeles. He dreamed one night he was operating a tram through the busy intersection. A big, red truck, making an illegal turn, was unable to see his tram because another passing streetcar blocked his view. In the following crash, two men in the car died and a woman passenger was injured. In his dream, the injured woman, who had large blue eyes, repeatedly shouted at him, "You could have avoided this." He awoke sweating and scared, but managed to put the dream out of his mind. That day, as he pulled up to the intersection, he suddenly felt sick to his stomach. When he saw the other streetcar appear, the dream came back to him. He cut the engine and applied the brakes just in time—a small truck with bright red advertising on the side barreled through the intersection. Three people were in the truck, as his ESP dream had foretold: two men and a woman with blue eyes. As they passed by the streetcar motorman, the startled woman gave him an "A-OK" sign with her thumb and forefinger, thanking him for stopping. The motorman was so upset he had to be taken off the job.[17]

Louisa Rhine's collection and analysis of spontaneous ESP case histories provided a number of other important and interesting insights into the ESP phenomenon, but it was her husband's laboratory experiments that forced the scientific establishment to deal with ESP. His ESP experiments were far from perfect, and not all scientists today accept his conclusions, but he spoke a language they understood. He used the same statistical methods they used. He successfully wrapped ESP in the cloak of modern, scientific respectability.

Rhine's contribution to making paranormal research respectable to open-minded members of the scientific community was significant. By the 1970s, as we noted in Chapter 5, anywhere from 67 to 75 percent of scientists and college professors believed ESP was either "an established fact" or a "likely possibility." Believers included 55 percent of natural scientists, 66 percent of social scientists (excluding psychologists) and 77 percent of academics in education, arts and humanities.[18] Rhine's influence on the public was equally important. Of all paranormal phenomena, ESP has the second highest belief rate based on the May 2001 Gallup poll, with one in two (50%) Americans accepting extra-sensory perception as a fact.

But diehard skeptics in academia, particularly in psychology departments, continued to find fault with ESP research. At Rhine's death in 1980, psychology textbook publishers were still refusing to provide legitimacy to ESP experiments by including the subject in their college textbooks. Indeed, psychologists as a group had turned out to be the most resistant to ESP among all academics and scientists. A 1979 survey of 1,100 U.S. college professors found only 34 percent of psychologists believed ESP was an "established fact" or a "likely possibility." Further, another 34 percent declared ESP was an impossibility (in contrast, only 2 percent of other professors felt ESP was impossible).[19]

The late professor Charles Honorton of the University of Edinburgh in Scotland can be credited as the ESP researcher who finally forced many hold-out skeptics to face the evidence for ESP, and in the process convince at least one popular psychology textbook publisher to include a section on psi phenomena. He did it in two ways. First he developed an improved version of the "Ganzfield " procedure which met reasonable demands by open-minded skeptics for a tightly-controlled, repeatable scientific experiment. Honorton even called in Dr. Daryl Bem, a

Cornell University psychology professor who is also a "mentalist"—a magician who performs mental tricks, including ESP—to examine his Ganzfield research protocol for possible flaws. Second, he applied an accepted analytical method, meta-analysis, [20] to his Ganzfield experiments to establish that ESP was the best explanation for the data rather than some error in statistics or flaw in the design of the experiments.

Honorton's version of the Ganzfield technique (the procedure itself originated in the 1930s) basically involves putting the person trying to achieve ESP into a mild state of sensory deprivation by reducing distracting sounds and sights. When I was a kid, I and my five brothers and sisters used to make so much noise and commotion that my mom would often say, "Stop it! I can't hear myself think." Indeed, try any mental activity—reading a book, praying, daydreaming, meditating or even intensely focusing on a difficult task—with a lot of noise, things happening, and people coming and going all around you. It's hard to concentrate. Honorton theorized that ESP messages were subtle communications easily drowned out by the cacophony of sights, sounds, tastes, smell and touch information flooding our brains during normal waking consciousness. Honorton knew that many mystics and psychics throughout the ages taught that the door to the infinite and the paranormal was an undistracted, inwardly-focused, ego-less state of mind. ESP experiments conducted in a relaxed, quiet state of mind would perhaps produce better results than those conducted under normal waking consciousness (like Rhine attempted). His Ganzfield procedure was designed to induce that potentially favorable state.

During a typical Ganzfield session, half ping-pong balls were taped over the ESP receiver's eyes to eliminate visual distractions. All the subject saw was a diffuse, soft red light. To eliminate unwanted sounds, earphones played "white noise," a pattern-less, low-level, background hiss, giving the subject nothing to focus aural attention on. To reduce touch sensations, the test subject was invited to sink down in a soft, reclining chair where he lay comfortably cradled and motionless during the experiment. Tight clothing was loosened, shoes and glasses were taken off. The room itself was acoustically isolated to keep out extraneous sounds. As the receiver lay there, he was given quiet relaxation suggestions through the earphones that could go on for ten or fifteen minutes. Finally, when the receiver's mind was relaxed, free of sensory distractions, and no longer thinking about the daily worries of life ("Was that dinner tomorrow at 7:00 PM or 8:00 PM?...I gotta remember to buy milk after this session is over...."), the actual ESP test began. His Ganzfield experiments also had a variety of special safeguards built into the testing protocol to guard against inadvertent information leakage to the test subject, or even outright fraud.

Usually, two experimenters worked together to conduct the experiment. A distinct, dramatic image (photo, drawing. cartoon, video or film clip) with a strong visual or emotional impact was randomly selected from a group of images to serve as the target of the ESP test. For the next 30 minutes, one experimenter acted as the "sender" concentrating on the picture, trying to "send" the image to the now-relaxed test subject "receiver" in another room. While this was going on, the "receiver" was being encouraged to describe whatever images popped into his or her mind to another experimenter who recorded those images. The receiver is usually told to not try and actively work at seeking out images; he or she is told to simply sit back and let them come naturally. After a half-hour or so, the ping-pong balls were removed, the white noise stopped, and the test subject was "awoken." The test subject then had a chance to choose from a set of four pictures the one he or she felt was closest to the image received during the experiment Since there is a one-in-four chance of choosing the correct one by pure luck, the hit rate expected by chance is 25 percent. Any hit rate over this begins to suggest something other than chance—true ESP being one possibility.

In one typical Ganzfield experiment described by Broughton,[21] the test subject received mental images of riding in a car on a pebbly road out in the country. The four pictures she ended up choosing from were 1) a painting of a Chinese nobleman in exotic clothes; 2) a still life with flowers; 3) cars in a parking lot buried in snow; and 4) a *National Geographic* photo of a rural countryside like Kentucky or Tennessee with a country road running through the scene and a lone pick up truck cruising down the road. Number 4 was obviously the closest to the ESP images she received during the experiment, and she chose it. She was correct.

Honorton determined that certain persons typically will do better in a Ganzfield experiment than others. The people most likely to succeed at ESP include people who are artistic and creative; people who have personally experienced a psychic event in their lives; people who believe in the reality of ESP; people who regularly practice meditation, relaxation or biofeedback; extroverts and intuitive personalities; and people who had earlier participated in other psi experiments.

Researchers also have learned that dynamic visual images (video clips with motion and sound) are easier to communicate via ESP than static images (still photo or drawing); that friends make better "senders" to receivers than strangers; that a warm, friendly laboratory ambiance was more conducive to ESP than a cold, clinical, unemotional laboratory setting (further confirming Rhine's earlier work which stressed the importance of the right "psychological atmosphere of testing").[22]

Honorton's rigorously designed and executed Ganzfield ESP experiments offer some of the best scientific evidence ever produced for the reality of ESP.

In 1990, a historical event in modern parapsychology happened. That year, one of the most widely-used American college psychology textbooks, *Introduction to Psychology*, included for the first time a small section entitled "Psi Phenomenon," featuring a discussion of current ESP research [23] and calling the Ganzfield procedure "worthy of careful consideration."

But while most parapsychologists continue their controlled, laboratory experiments in ESP, some researchers today are increasingly uncomfortable with what they perceive as an overemphasis on reductionist, laboratory-oriented psi research and the application of existing behaviorist methods and theories of psychology to psi phenomena.[24] They argue for an approach that recognizes the equal importance and value of studying spontaneous psi events, and for remaining open to a model of reality much broader than the mechanistic materialism Science embraces today. The problem, declared psychologist and parapsychologist Keith Harary, was that much post-Rhine parapsychology embodied a reductionistic approach towards psi phenomena more typical of classical behaviorism than the emerging psychology of the 21st century.[25] ESP happens more frequently outside than inside the laboratory, they remind us. A successful Ganzfield-ESP test, valuable as it is, is like capturing a firefly in a bottle for observation while ignoring an evening sky all around us filled with thousands of tiny, blinking lights.

Meanwhile, unbeknownst to most academics squabbling over Honorton's Ganzfield research and the reality of ESP, the U.S. government had already secretly tested ESP, concluded it was real, taken it out of the lab—and was applying it in real life situations with some surprising successes. In 1972, the U.S. government had launched a research program later to become famous under the name "Star Gate. " The research effort quickly spawned a secret, classified program to employ psychics with ESP in the service of their country. This intelligence gathering part of the research program wasn't publicly confirmed until 1995, when the government admitted that for over 20 years the CIA and many other government agencies had used specially-trained clairvoyants (called "remote viewers" by the program) in a variety of operational missions—to penetrate secret Soviet military installations; hunt down Libyan leader Moammar Gadhafi; locate a downed Soviet Tupolev-22 bomber lost in the jungles of Zaire; look for American general kidnapped by Italian terrorists; and other missions still classified.

The list of government agencies using the services of psychic spies apparently included the CIA, the Pentagon, the U.S. Army, the U.S. Air Force, the National Security Council, NASA, the NSA and the DIA. [26]

Some $20 million was spent on the remote viewing ESP program before it was terminated in 1995.Like Honorton's Ganzfield studies, the Star Gate program results (together with the non-classified research programs which sparked the covert operational efforts) provide us with some of the best scientific evidence available for the reality of ESP. One of the best scientific summaries of Star Gate's ESP research effort, written by the scientists who actually ran the program and/or later evaluated its results in terms of evidence for ESP, can be found in the Spring 1996 edition of *Journal of Scientific Exploration*.[27] A year later, science writer Jim Schnabel came out with *Remote Viewers: The Secret History of America's Psychic Spies*,[28] a less technical, more accessible, but well-documented account of the whole ESP spying effort.

The research was funded at the height of the Cold War by a U.S. government which feared the Russians had developed and were using psychic weapons against the U.S. Many of the spying activities (and accomplishments) conducted under this secret ESP program reportedly remain classified to this day.[29] Most of the scientific experiments up to 1989 were conducted at Stanford Research Institute (now SRI International), then at Science Applications International Corp. (SAIC) in 1990.The ESP scientific research was spearheaded by a small team of scientists. Their ranks included physicist and former National Security Agency employee Dr. Harold Puthoff (who we met in Chapter 3), who served as the program's founder and first director (1973-1985); physicist Dr. Russell Targ; and physicist Dr. Edwin May who ran the program from 1985 until its closure in 1995.

The remote viewing technique borrowed from earlier ESP research but various researchers added new twists over the 20-year period the program operated. Techniques also varied depending on whether the assignment was simply research or an actual spying assignment. One of its most interesting, and successful, approaches was to use geographical coordinates (latitude and longitude expressed in degrees, minutes and seconds) to identify targets to be remote-viewed.

The first experiments achieved some stunning successes which soon caught the eye of the CIA. In one now unclassified, double-blind test in mid-1973, two remote viewers in California were able to direct their clairvoyant vision to a specific latitude and longitude in West Virginia and describe details of a hidden, underground government facility 3,000 miles away. The two remote viewers, a New York artist named Ingo Swann and a California ex-police commissioner named Pat Price, did more than simply draw a detailed map of the building and grounds of the target, the National Security Agency's secret listening post at Sugar Grove West Virginia; Price was also somehow able to get inside the super-secure building with his mind and read the names of facility personnel off desk placards, read the titles of documents on desks, and labels off folders inside locked cabinets at the site—a feat that understandably set alarm bells ringing at the government agency responsible for security of the site. The information they provided was later verified as accurate by the government agency that had sponsored the test. [30]

In another early test, Price remote-viewed the other side of the globe for a target that later turned out to be a radio listening post in the Ural mountains of the Soviet Union. He located the target and, as often happened, described it in surprising detail: "Elevation 6200 ft. Scrubby brush, tundra-type ground hummocks, rocky outcroppings, mountains with very steep slopes...Area site underground, reinforced concrete, doorways steel of the roll-up type. Unusually high ratio of women to men, at least at night. I see some helipads, concrete. Light rail tracks run from pads to another set of rails that parallel the doors into the mountain. Thirty miles north (5 degrees west of north) of the site is a radar installation with one large (165 foot) dish and two small, fast-track dishes." His description of the Urals mountain site was substantially correct, as verified by other sources.[31]

In July 1974, Price performed yet another amazing feat of remote viewing ESP. After being given a set of geographical coordinates, and told that the site was an R&D test facility, Price sent his mind to what turned out to be a very secret Soviet atomic bomb laboratory in Semipalatinsk in the Soviet Union. Once there, he described and drew a picture of an unusual multi-story, industrial crane, among other things. His drawing almost exactly matched the crane seen in classified satellite photos of the site taken by the U.S. military.[32] Impressed by Price's ability, the CIA let him continue his spy effort at Semipalatinsk. Price managed to mentally slip inside a closed building at the site (which U.S. satellite photography obviously couldn't penetrate), and describe a large room where people were assembling a giant metal sphere of some sort, which he drew. Price reported his impression that the people in the building were having trouble welding the object together. After the session, the CIA left Price and Targ without any feedback on how Price had done, and returned to Washington. Three years later, *Aviation Week* magazine essentially confirmed Price's mental observations inside the building. It carried a story on operations at Semipalatinsk, describing how Russian scientists there were trying to build a giant metal sphere which could be used for nuclear weapons testing. It also mentioned that U.S. physicists doubted whether the Russians could create a strong enough weld to make it work.[33]

These early experiments provided a number of interesting insights, some of which reconfirmed Rhine's earlier clairvoyance experiments: 1) Distance didn't affect results. A superstar remote viewer like Price could see a target ten thousand miles away as easily as he could view a target a mile away. 2) Information received by remote viewers wasn't perfect. It often had inaccurate details and information mixed in with the accurate, Price included. But sometimes, remote viewers could achieve "blueprint accuracy" and reliability as high as 80 percent. [34] 3) Though it can be improved by training, remote viewing is not a common, natural skill. Only one out of a hundred persons who volunteered to attempt remote viewing proved consistently successful. 4) Some people are natural superstars at remote viewing. Ingo Swann and Pat Price were Michael Jordans compared to most other remote viewers recruited during the life of the program. In 1977, CIA chief Adm. Stanfield Turner described a person Targ believes was Pat Price in a *Chicago Tribune* interview. Turner declared that the Agency had found someone who could use his psychic powers to "see" what was going on anywhere in the world.[35] Another top remote viewer, Joseph McMoneagle, evidently did well enough to earn a National Legion of Merit Award for his ESP skills on more than 200 missions, bringing back intelligence information not attainable through any other source. According to McMoneagle, one of his notable feats was pinpointing the location of U.S. Army Brig. General James Dozier, kidnapped in Italy in 1981 by the Red Brigades terrorist organization.[36] He described the hideout as the second floor of a house in Padua, Italy and drew a picture of the distinctive storefront of the shop below the house. He also drew a street map. In the end, the Italian police didn't use McMoneagle's information; they had learned Dozier's whereabouts from confessions made by other terrorists in the gang they had caught. But when they finally stormed the house, it apparently matched the location and description produced by McMoneagle.[37] 5) Remote viewers can sometimes sense the past and future at a target site as well as the present. Price did just that in one remote viewing experiment. He accurately described a swimming pool complex in Palo Alto, but included two water tanks that weren't there. Twenty years later, Targ received a centennial annual report for Palo Alto. It included a picture of the swimming pool site Price remote viewed as it looked in 1913. The photo included two water tanks, just like Price had drawn. The site had once hosted the municipal waterworks.[38] 6) But perhaps because the experiments were less repetitive and boring, remote viewers didn't always suffer Rhine's old "decline effect" in their work.

From a strictly scientific, laboratory experiment point of view (controlled tests to prove the existence of ESP), the group's early operating protocols weren't perfect in design. But as the work proceeded, the testing protocols became tighter and the results less subject to challenge. In 1988, a detailed analysis was done on all 154 experiments conducted at SRI from 1973-1988.[39] The conclusion? Remote viewing (clairvoyance) was quirky but real. Some human beings, using only their minds, could on occasion see and describe with some accuracy distant target places and objects.

In 1990, the government-sponsored program moved from SRI to SAIC. There, under the direction of Ed May (who moved over to SAIC with the program), six more remote viewing experiments were conducted. These later SAIC remote viewing experiments were not designed to prove the existence of clairvoyance/remote viewing—May and his team felt that had already been established. Instead, they were designed to further understand *how* ESP works. Different types of targets were tested as well as variations in the size of the pool of potential targets. Out of these experiments came several testable hypotheses for how ESP may work.[40]

May's SAIC team also conducted four additional, non-remote viewing experiments, including a fascinating "remote staring" experiment which suggests that people can sense when someone is staring at them, even when the person is behind them.[41] The same experiment also concluded that the effect was stronger when the people involved were of the opposite sex.

Best Scientific Evidence

1988-1989 Honorton Ganzfield ESP Studies

In 1985, Honorton and a well-known ESP skeptic, psychologist Ray Hyman of the University of Oregon, were challenged to apply the relatively new research technique called "meta-analysis" to evaluate the growing database of successful Ganzfield studies. Some 55 percent of 42 ESP Ganzfield studies done between 1974-1981 had produced significant indications of ESP. Were these positive results because of sloppy research, or was ESP really happening? The host for their "debate" was the *Journal of Parapsychology* which printed the results of their analyses in 1986. In the end, Hyman was forced to accept that something other than sloppy research was causing the positive results that a number of ESP investigators had produced, but he and Honorton both agreed that the final verdict awaited more experiments conducted under more stringent standards. [42]

Honorton accepted the challenge. Three years later, in 1989, Honorton had eleven new Ganzfield studies, conducted under strict guidelines recommended by critic Hyman. Because skeptics often argue that any good magician can produce amazing "psychic" results, Honorton even had two "mentalist" magicians who specialize in simulating ESP, Daryl Bem and Ford Kross, sign off on the test procedures before he conducted the tests. The experimental protocols, wrote Kross, an officer in the Psychic Entertainers Association, "provide excellent security against deception by subjects." The experiments themselves were "autoganzfield" experiments because a computer controlled the selection of the target images to be sent by the sender to the receiver, eliminating potential biases discovered in the earlier, human-controlled Ganzfield experiments, but they incorporated the basic Ganzfield technique. The results? Ten of Honorton's eleven studies produced positive results. The overall success rate was 34 percent (vs. an expected 25 percent if chance alone were at work). The odds against this positive result being due just to chance?—20,000-to-one.[43]

In 1991, Hyman agreed that Honorton's experiments had produced "intriguing results" and that if others could use the same rigorous methods and produce the same results, then " parapsychology may indeed have captured its elusive quarry." [44] Since then, some (though not all [45]) laboratories have independently replicated Honorton's

Ganzfield ESP results. They include researchers at the University of Amsterdam, Netherlands; and the University of Edinburgh, Scotland.[46] In May 1993, the prestigious but traditionally skeptical scientific journal *New Scientist*, describing Ganzfield research conducted at Edinburgh, declared, "Psychical research has long been written off as the stuff of cranks and frauds. But now there's one telepathy experiment that leaves even the skeptics scratching their heads."[47] Broughton, like many parapsychologists, feels that a competent experimenter can produce Ganzfield ESP, making it "the key to the repeatable ESP experiment" parapsychologists have sought for so long.[48]

1972-1995 Government-Sponsored Remote Viewing Program

On November 28, 1995, the Central Intelligence Agency released an official report on the Dept. of Defense's remote viewing program and its achievements.[49] The report commissioned by the CIA was entitled "The American Institutes for Research Review of the Department of Defense's Star Gate Program," and evaluated both a) the laboratory research experiments in remote viewing as well as b) intelligence operations employing the remote viewing techniques. Two university professors were recruited to help American Institutes for Research in-house staff to evaluate the project: Dr. Jessica Utts of the University of California, Davis; and Dr. Ray Hyman of the University of Oregon (the well-known skeptic of paranormal phenomena who challenged Honorton and is closely and publicly affiliated with the skeptic group CSICOP described in Chapter 4).

The American Institutes for Research final report concluded that the laboratory ESP experiments were statistically significant. [50] For her part, program reviewer Dr. Jessica Utts agreed. Their success was not due to chance, methodological flaws in the experiments, or fraud. From here on, she recommended, researchers should focus on how the phenomenon worked, not on proving whether it existed "since there is little more to be offered to anyone who does not accept the current collection of data."[51] Her counterpart, Dr. Ray Hyman focused his attention on the later SAIC experiments. He agreed that the SAIC experiments were well-designed and the results not dismissable as statistical flukes, but didn't agree that the experiments conclusively proved the reality of psychic functioning. He would admit, however that "the case for psychic functioning seems better than it ever has been," and that "I do not have a ready explanation for these observed effects."[52] Puthoff and Targ's SRI clairvoyance/remote viewing experiments have essentially been replicated by the Princeton Engineering Anomalies Research (PEAR) program, further establishing the reality of this form of ESP.

Regarding the operational use of remote viewing (as opposed to experimental proof for its existence) the AIR Report declared that in no case had the remote viewing information been used to guide actual intelligence operations. Dr. Ed May, who had worked on the project from the mid-1970s and had served as Project Director from 1986 until its closure, vehemently disagreed and wrote his own report.[53] He noted, like Hal Puthoff, that much information remains classified to this day. Interestingly enough, in a speech in Sept. 1995, President Jimmy Carter confirmed that the CIA has successfully used a remote viewer to find a downed plane that had crashed the jungle in Zaire, Africa that American spy satellites tried and couldn't find.[54] Though Carter didn't go into details, according to one account[55] the plane was a Soviet Tupolev-22 bomber which the Americans wanted to find before the Soviets did in order to examine the Russian plane's communications technology. The Pentagon turned to Hal Puthoff's remote viewers. One of them, Gary Langford, "saw a river in the jungle with the tail of the aircraft sticking out" and described the roads and topography of the area in detail. A second remote viewer, a woman named Frances Bryan, subsequently produced a sketch that closely matched what Langford had described. Their work was so specific that the CIA was able to actually locate on a terrain map the site they had described. The CIA eventually found the plane "within barely 5 kilometers of the spot Langford and Bryan had described." A photo was taken of the site and later circulated around Puthoff's SRI office. "Langford's sketch agreed with the picture so completely that he might have copied it."

Louisa Rhine Database

Louisa Rhine's database of 14,000 ESP cases (on file at the Institute for Parapsychology in Durham, North Carolina) provides excellent, anecdotal evidence for the existence of ESP. Though Rhine did maintain standards for accepting cases, few were personally investigated or authenticated by Rhine. Their scientific value, then, is primarily in the clues the raw reports provide about patterns of human ESP experiences, and the testable hypotheses they suggest.[56] The database demonstrates that ESP is not a rare anomaly, but rather a fairly common human experience; and not something experienced just by uneducated or lower class people but by people of all educational levels, social classes, ages and both genders. The sheer number of reports—14,000—should also make any reasonable, open-minded person willing to seriously consider the possible reality of ESP. Can each and every one of the 14,000 claims be the result of a hoax, mental illness, poor memory, or wishful thinking? This would seem to be more of a miracle than ESP itself.

Highly Recommended Reading:

Radin, Dean. *The Conscious Universe: The Scientific Truth of Psychic Phenomena*. San Francisco: HarperEdge, 1997. An excellent, general audience book on ESP and PK research. Radin's book won Amazon.com's 1998 Category Bestseller Award for parapsychology, is in its fourth printing, and has been translated into French, Korean and Chinese. Radin knows what he writes about: in 1996, he won parapsychology's Alexander Imich Prize, given to the scientist who make the most important experimental contributions to parapsychology during the preceding five years.

Journal of Scientific Exploration (Vol. 10, No. 1, Spring 1996). This issue contains an excellent discussion of the 24-year long government sponsored STAR GATE remote viewing experiments at SAIC and SRI, along with the in-depth comments of former program founder and first director Dr. Hal Puthoff, who ran the program from 1972-1985 ; his colleague Dr. Russell Targ; Dr. Ed May, who ran the program from 1985 until its closure in 1995; and papers by Dr. Jessica Utts and Dr. Ray Hyman who were tasked by the government to assess the evidence for psychic functioning (ESP) arising from the program.

Broughton, Richard. *Parapsychology: The Controversial Science.* New York: Ballantine Books, 1991. Broughton's book provides an excellent history of ESP research, including detailed accounts of Honorton's historic Ganzfield experiments and Louisa Rhine's ESP research.

7.

Psychokinesis (PK)

*"I have seen what I would not have believed on your testimony,
and what I cannot therefore expect you to believe on mine."*
Dr. Treviranus to Coleridge

On May 26, 2000, in a large conference room at the Oasis Resort an hour outside Las Vegas, Nevada, I and my brother John finally got to participate in one of Jack Houck's famous "PK parties."

A systems engineer with a large southern California aerospace corporation, Jack has been involved in ESP (remote viewing) and PK research since the mid-1970s. Based on this research, Jack had developed his own conceptual model for paranormal phenomena,[1] concluding that the best way to produce a paranormal phenomenon like psychokinesis was to create a very emotional event. Challenged by other researchers to test his theory, in January 1981 he held his first PK party. He rounded up 21 friends and associates, created a party-like atmosphere, supplied everyone with silverware, gave his "instructions," and 19 out of the 21 attendees produced macro-PK in the form of spoon-bending. He went on to hold hundreds of PK parties for everyone from army generals at the Pentagon to famous writers like *Jurassic* Park author Michael Crichton (who describes his party with Houck in his 1988 book *Travels*).

Almost 20 years later, he's still showing average Joes off the street (like my brother John and me) how to bend spoons with their mind. John and I were among several hundred excited, expectant people gathered in the ballroom in a large circle around Jack that Memorial Day weekend to hear his instructions. You can bring your own silverware if you want, or you can pick a fork or spoon from the big box of cutlery Jack carries to each event (he buys the silverware at garage sales and flea markets). There is no mumbo-jumbo, no New Age incantations, no dimmed lights, no elaborate formalities. Jack gives a brief history of his PK research, shows samples of spoons and forks bent by people in earlier PK parties (our party was his 340th), goes over his theory of how he thinks PK is produced, and leads us through the three steps we will follow to hopefully produce bent spoons: 1) Make a mental connection with what you want to affect, focus your attention and concentration on the spoon 2) Command what you want to happen by shouting "Bend! Bend! Bend!" and 3) Release, let go mentally, let it happen.

The crowd was large, vocal and into it, creating the very emotional event Jack's model required for producing PK. Within 20-30 seconds of shouting our commands, people were bending spoons. Jack encourages people to scream and get excited when their spoons bend because it helps intensify the emotion and helps other people let go too. My brother John and I quickly mastered "kindergarten" level spoon bending—waiting till we felt the spoon go warm and soft, then twirling and bending the handle in tight circles. Typically, 85 percent of PK party attendees can achieve this PK feat—not surprising since an average person can do this by simple, non-paranormal, physical force. But within minutes, a middle-aged woman a few seats in front of us had progressed to "high school" bending—buckling the bowl of a silver-plated spoon. If you think that's easy, try it. The shape of the spoon bowl makes it virtually impossible for someone to do it by human physical force alone. A while later, Chuck, a young lawyer from D.C. with whom we had earlier eaten dinner, also bent the bowl of a spoon right in front of us. In

Jack's experience about one in three (33%) people can achieve this feat ((he passes out questionnaires after each party). Other "high school" feats were also performed. A 13-year old boy a few seats to our right bent an aluminum rod by simply stroking it. Kids often perform better than adults, perhaps because they are more open to these experiences than adults. Both John and I later tried to physically bend a similar aluminum bar and couldn't do it.

The party ended with everyone trying "graduate school" bending, the real test of PK powers. Everyone simply holds a fork in their hand by the handle, raises it up high, and commands it to bend. You don't stroke it, or try to physically manipulate it. You simply hold it. I had already dropped out after the "kindergarten" level, and didn't expect anything to happen for me. And it didn't. But the guy right next to me, literally a foot away, suddenly shouted out, "Look, it's moving!" I watched in disbelief with my own eyes as the tines on the fork began to slowly spread apart. A few seconds later, several other people in the room also started shouting excitedly as their forks started spontaneously bending—a feat achieved on average by 11% of PK party attendees.

But the best performance of the night was by a young man who looked to be in his 30s who apparently managed to bend with his mind an inch-thick steel bar. The bar wasn't bent in a complete circle, or even a half-moon, just a modest but very visible curve. I later examined the bar and talked to him. He was both excited and stunned by what he had accomplished, and planned on bringing the bar back home with him.

John and I ended the night getting a photo of ourselves with Jack, who took all the cheers, whoops, shouts and amazed looks of the participants in stride. Just another party, another night of normal, average human beings producing an effect Science says doesn't exist. One of the spoons with a buckled bowl from that party now sits on my desk at work.

Skeptics says PK is impossible. The forks and spoons, aluminum rods and steel bars bent at Jack Houck's PK party were pre-stressed or rigged;

or all the benders were liars; or their eyes tricked them; or they were bent using force, or everyone in the room was suffering from a mass hallucination; or Houck had somehow hypnotized everyone. Physical action requires a physical force. There is no such thing as "mind over matter." You can't bend a spoon, or stop a clock, or lift a table or chair simply by using the mind.

Anyone who attended Jack Houck's PK party and witnessed or experienced a "graduate school level" spoon or fork bend would obviously disagree. And believers are slowly gathering support from scientists, academics and parapsychologists who say both laboratory and anecdotal evidence exists for a phenomenon called psychokinesis. They define PK as the ability of humans to influence objects or processes outside themselves without the use of known physical energies or forces. In layman's terms, we refer to it as "mind over matter."

What kinds of psychokinesis manifestations have humans described and experienced? The long list of observed PK phenomena can be divided up into micro-PK (small scale) and macro-PK (large-scale) phenomena.

Spoon-bending is a large-scale PK effect. You can see it with your own eyes as it happens. Examples of recorded, large-scale PK effects include levitating heavy furniture or people; making objects appear or disappear (materialization or de-materialization); making various objects move, jump or fly across a room; bending metal objects (like Jack Houck trains people to do); or even using the mind to print an image directly on the film without using a camera. This dramatic macro-PK is the average layman's image of psychokinesis. A table slowly rises into the air; a key turns by itself in a lock without anyone touching it. Poltergeist effects, however they're produced (by the human mind or by spirits) are typically also large scale PK—strange raps, bangs and other noises; phantom music, interference with electrical equipment like TVs, telephones and radios; starting fires, and creating ghostly phantasms and apparitions.

Small-scale PK effects, in contrast, are deliberately produced by parapsychologists in an experimental laboratory setting under controlled conditions. This is the most common form of PK research done today. Unlike large-scale PK, where you can actually see an object move, small-scale PK is measured by statistics. In Rhine's dice throwing PK experiments, for example, the dice tumble too fast to observe whether the mind is directing their movements as it happens; we can however measure the results (e.g. can the dice thrower consistently beat the laws of chance in terms of throwing sevens, or some other target?) Nowadays, however, researchers use high-tech target generators called random events generators (REG) in place of tossed dice and flipped coins. .

One of the first persons to propose scientific studies of PK was a founder of modern Western science, Francis Bacon (1561-1626). He suggested scientists study the throwing of dice and the influence of "imagination" on the outcome.[2]

Some of the most famous large-scale PK feats of the modern era, including reports of levitation of chairs, tables and even people, happened in conjunction with a quasi-religious movement called Spiritualism which swept England and the USA in the 19th century. Spiritualists believe that the spirits of the dead continue to survive in another plane of existence (a belief held by most religions in the world). But they also believe that spirits can communicate on a regular basis with the living through "mediums," or "sensitives"—persons with a special ability to sense their presence and communicate with them. Large-scale PK effects were often witnessed by attendees during Spiritualist séances (meetings held to communicate with the dead). These commonly included tables tilting, moving, rotating or rising into the air on their own accord; knocking and rapping noises; and ethereal lights or music. Some séances were run by frauds and charlatans seeking to capitalize on a gullible public, and their accompanying PK effects were later found to be produced by trickery, a task made easier by the darkened rooms in which most séances were held.

But at least two persons during this era, Daniel Douglas Home (1833- 1886) and Eusapia Palladino (1854- 1918), demonstrated some PK feats that were, and still are, hard to explain away. They offer some of the best scientific evidence ever collected through field research for the reality of macro-PK.[3]

Home, a Scotsman, was reported to be able to levitate his whole body; levitate tables (once with several persons sitting on it) and a heavy piano; levitate an accordion and play melodies on it ranging from "Home Sweet Home" to "Ye Banks and Braes" without touching its keys (once playing for almost 10 minutes); make plates and other small objects float and move around a room; materialize objects; and even elongate his body up to six inches.[4] Some of his demonstrations were performed under loose controls, before observers predisposed to believe him, understandably allowing skeptics to dismiss them. This was because Home was always ready to demonstrate his skills on short notice. But some of his best PK feats were tightly controlled experiments involving multiple, independent witnesses including persons skeptical of him; and demonstrations in full daylight (in contrast to the dimly-lit rooms favored by most mediums).

He also successfully submitted to laboratory testing by Sir William Crookes, the Nobel Prize-winning English physicist (among his other accomplishments, Crookes discovered the element thallium for which he won the Nobel Prize in 1911; pioneered research on electrical discharges in low-pressure gases; and served as President of England's top scientific body, the Royal Society). Crookes developed and built a variety of special devices to prevent any fraud or sleight of hand during the experiments, and carefully inspected objects touched or used by Home during the tests. Home once took a red-hot coal from the fireplace and held it in a handkerchief without the handkerchief burning up; Crookes impounded the handkerchief and took it to his laboratory to make sure it hadn't been chemically treated to make it fire-proof. He also installed equipment to measure the psychokinetic forces produced by Home (e.g. attaching a spring balance to a 32-lb. table targeted for levitation to measure the pull required to lift it off the ground).[5] When Home levitated himself in front of Crookes, Crookes didn't observe from a distance; instead, "...when he rose 18 inches off the ground, I passed my hands under his feet, round him, and over his head when he was in the air."[6] A review of the hundreds of original accounts provided by witnesses provides unusually persuasive evidence of his talents and a real challenge to skeptics.[7] Detailed attempts have been made to debunk Home,[8] but the counter-arguments of Home supporters appear convincing.[9] It is interesting to note that France's most celebrated magician/conjurer, Robert Houdin (the famous American magician Houdini named himself after his hero Houdin) personally witnessed some of these demonstrations by D.D. Home. Houdin is on record as declaring, "I am persuaded that it is perfectly impossible by chance or adroitness to produce such marvelous effects."[10]

Palladino, an Italian, demonstrated a dozen different PK feats during her career—primarily poltergeist-like phenomena involving the levitation and movement of heavy furniture and smaller household objects. On one famous occasion, in the summer of 1898, she levitated a heavy, 48 lb. table that was sitting outdoors, in broad daylight, in the driveway of the chateau owned by French scientist and Nobel Laureate (1913, for research into physiology) Charles Richet. As it hung two feet in the air, Richet and all his guests passed their hands under, over and around it to confirm that it was not being held up by some apparatus. The table itself had even been specially modified by Richet before the test to make it extremely difficult to lift by hand or feet (not that it mattered—Palladino herself stood a distance from the table, her hands also tightly held by Richet's assistants to prevent her touching or reaching the table during the experiment).[11] On another occasion, Palladino materialized a hand which Richet grasped and held to the count of 29 seconds, all the while observing both of Palladino's hands on the table. Then, "After twenty-nine seconds I said, 'I want something more, I want *uno anello* (a ring).' At once the hand made me feel a ring…It seems hard to imagine a more convincing experiment…In this case there was not only the materialization of a hand, but also of a ring."[12]

Palladino was extensively observed and tested by leading scientists, academics and even skeptical magicians in Italy, France, Russia and England. If Home had Nobel Laureate Crooks investigating him, Palladino had *three* Nobel Laureates investigating her: not only Richet but also Nobel Laureates Pierre and Marie Curie (who earned their prize in 1903 for their research into radioactivity). After experiencing Palladino's levitations and other PK effects in séance conditions he himself tightly controlled (including tightly holding Palladino's hands and legs and conducting the tests in well-lit rooms), Pierre Curie declared in an April 14, 1906 letter to his friend Georges Gouy "…these phenomena exist for real, and I can't doubt it any more. It is unbeliev-able, but it is thus, and it is impossible to negate it after the séances that we had in conditions of perfect monitoring."[13]

Among the most famous groups to investigate Palladino was a three-man "hit team" of confirmed skeptics from England's Society for Psychical Research which investigated eleven of her séances in detail in Naples, Italy in 1908 and produced a thick, detailed, 283-page report confirming her PK talents.[14] First-hand reports from magicians are obviously of considerable value as evidence: magicians make their living tricking people, and they know the tricks of the trade.[15] When they personally test someone, and can't find any trickery, their conclusions add considerable credibility to the argument for the reality of paranor-mal phenomena. The American magician Howard Thurston (1869-1936), considered by his peers as the greatest master of stage illusions, once declared. "I was forced to change my (skeptical) attitude towards spirit phenomena mainly because of the demonstrations of Eusapio Palladino…"[16] Thurston had attended a private sitting with Palladino where, in good light, Palladino had levitated a table; Thurston had crawled beneath it and passed his hands all around it to see if any devices had been used to lift it. He found none. Afterwards, he declared, "I am convinced that the table was levitated without fraudulent use of her hands, feet, knees or any part of her body, nor by any known mechanical contrivance."[17] While Palladino was caught red-handed cheating a number of times during her career, she also produced some amazing phenomena under extremely tight controls. (One theory offered to explain this occasional, verified cheating associated with some famous psychics like Palladino is that paranormal phenomena are maddeningly quirky, unpredictable and poorly understood. No psychic can produce these phenomena continuously, on demand, throughout his or her lifetime. When gifts fail, they turn to cheating to supplement their natural talents.)

As scientists developed new techniques, some were applied to psychic research. Rudi Schneider (1908-1957) was a famous Austrian medium who also was able to produce PK effects under stringent scientific controls. He cooperated patiently and whole-heartedly for years with investigators seeking to test his talents, accepting whatever conditions they chose to put on him. In 1930, he submitted to tests in Paris where, for the first time, then state-of-the-art electrical equipment was used to monitor the psychic performer and prevent cheating. Rudi did his best work in dim or low light (like many mediums), so one experimenter, Dr. Eugene Osty, devised an infra-red beam to guard the object Rudi was asked to move with his mind. If Rudi tried to cheat, and physically move the test object, a handkerchief placed on the table, the infra-red circuit would be broken, causing a camera to flash a picture or an alarm bell to ring. On numerous occasions, the flash would go off, but the photo would show Rudi unmoved, his hands and knees still held tightly by the scientists. Something was triggering the flash, but it wasn't Rudi's hands or feet. Osty ran more tests, eventually being forced to conclude that Schneider had the ability to produce with his mind an unknown, invisible (it couldn't be photographed) but clearly physical "substance" or "force"—physical because the invisible substance or force refracted or absorbed at least 30 percent of the infra-red ray (a level required to trigger the apparatus). Schneider also showed the ability to mentally control this invisible but physical substance or force, announcing beforehand to Osty when it was about to break the infra-red circuit and trigger the flash or bell. In his reports, the baffled Osty described at length the equipment he used for the tests, the experimental protocols employed, and the precautions he took to prevent fraud by Schneider. Subsequently, Theodore Besterman, an investigator from the Society for Psychical Research strongly skeptical of all PK phenomena, traveled to Paris to check Osty's equipment, and examine the possibility that Osty and Schneider had conspired together. In the end, he declared himself satisfied that no fraud or collusion was involved, and thus the invisible but measurable force or substance produced by Schneider's mind was real.[18] Despite Osty's success, the experiments were ignored by other scientists (though PK and poltergeist experimenters would eventually add videotape cameras, electromagnetic detectors and a host of other high-tech electronic metering devices to their arsenal).

By the beginning of the 20th century, the Spiritualism movement had begun to fade, and with it the popularity of mediums and séances. Psychic investigators had by now collected a mountain of anecdotal evidence for large-scale PK, but were still no closer to developing the airtight proof they sought for its existence. To get that, some concluded, psychic research would have to move into the laboratory, where controlled, repeatable small-scale PK experiments could be run; classic experiments using techniques employed by Establishment science; experiments that, if successful, would prove once and for all, without a doubt, the reality of PK.

One of the first scientists to systematically put PK to the test in the lab was Dr. J.B. Rhine who also pioneered ESP research as we learned.

Rhine began his PK tests in 1934, using volunteers throwing a pair of dice. Rhine's PK was micro-PK. You couldn't actually see the dice being directed—up or down, left or right—by the volunteer's mind because the dice moved too fast. You could only infer it from the results, measured in statistical calculations. Could someone throwing dice consistently beat the odds—in scientific terms, the "mean chance expectation"? Applying statistics and probability values to the results, he demonstrated that some people indeed appeared able to control the dice. Encouraged by this, he began to systematically reduce the possibility of design flaws in his experiment—unevenly weighted dice, etc. During the tests, he also began to catalogue the influence of the dice-thrower's mood, physical condition, expectations regarding results, and preferences and prejudices in terms of test methods on the outcome of the experiment. Rhine even tested the effect of negative, hostile or skeptical observers on the performance of the dice-thrower. (Later PK researchers would discover evidence suggesting that males do significantly better than females, and younger people do slightly better than older people, when it come to producing PK effects.)[19]

In 1943, Rhine began to publish the results of almost a decade of PK research, and received a surprisingly favorable response from the scientific community to his quantitative and statistical approach to PK. His success encouraged other scientists to try to duplicate and expand upon these experiments, and come up with various hypotheses to explain how PK worked.

But laboratory experiments on small-scale PK effects—while more credible to the scientific establishment—are simply not as dramatic or interesting as the large-scale PK effects produced by people like D.D. Home and Eusapia Palladino. And in the early 1970s, public attention in the U.S. was dramatically refocused on large-scale PK with the arrival of Israeli psychic Uri Geller. Dozens of books have been written about Geller, and you should have no difficulty finding one or more in your local library or on Amazon.com or Barnes & Noble.com. Like Eusapia

Palladino, Geller is controversial. He began his career as a stage mentalist/psychic in Israel, and has admitted to mixing in some standard magic tricks in with his PK presentation in the beginning. But before he semi-retired from public life, Geller gave many impressive demonstrations under controlled conditions in cities and in scientific laboratories around the world. In addition to his ESP feats, Geller's reported PK feats have included, among other things, the ability to bend or plasticize steel, platinum and other metals by softly stroking them; change the readout on a Geiger counter; deflect a compass needle; dematerialize objects; influence objects without direct physical contact (e.g. make objects fly through the room similar to classic poltergeist phenomenon, or make broken watches and clocks run again); influence a magnetometer; and imprint a picture on a roll of photographic film using only mental energy. Some of his feats beat chance odds of a trillion to one.

Laboratory tests conducted in the 1970s on Geller's PK abilities by various scientists in the U.S., Canada, England, France, Switzerland and Japan produced some very credible evidence for his PK abilities, despite criticism from magician and CSICOP devotee James Randi. Not all magicians share Randi's skepticism. Geller's defenders include a number of magicians who tested Geller, including parapsychologist and magician William E. Cox, who had once organized a committee within the Society of American Magicians to investigate false claims of ESP. In a thoughtful essay on the issue of Uri Geller and his claims,[20] Cox discusses some specific differences in the sleight-of-hand used by magicians and the procedures used by Geller to produce PK. The test for a skeptic magician, Cox concludes, is not to simply produce the same effects as Geller, but to produce them under the same controlled conditions imposed on Geller, e.g., frame-by-frame videotaping of the feat from multiple angles with close-up lenses. Compare every move and manipulation required by Geller versus a magician to accomplish a feat, says Cox, and the magician's techniques will be easy to distinguish from Geller's techniques.[21]

Geller wasn't the only large-scale PK performer being tested in laboratories in the 1970s. An artist from New York named Ingo Swann started out experimenting with the mind's ability to affect a plant's growth and health, and later moved on to demonstrate some psychokinesis ability under experimental controls at Prof. Gertrude Schmeidler's laboratory at the City College of New York. He eventually ended up at Stanford Research Institute in California where, under the watchful eye of physicist H.E. Puthoff, he succeeded in a task considered physically impossible—altering the magnetic field in a magnetometer (an instrument to measure magnetic fields) which was encased in an iron vault, set in concrete, and protected by four different shielding devices designed to thwart any outside influences (mu-metal shielding, an aluminum container, copper shielding, and a superconducting shield).[22] Because he also subsequently demonstrated the ability to mentally view the inside of the apparatus, producing a reasonably accurate drawing of its complex construction, Swann went on to participate in the famous U.S. government-funded Star Gate research project on "remote viewing" (Chapter 6).

Can average people produce PK effects? An American medical technician, Felicia Parise, saw a film of a Soviet Union woman doing PK and decided to try and duplicate some of her feats. In the early 1970s, she succeeded in training herself to use mental energy to move pieces of aluminum foil and a plastic container several inches across a table while being filmed and observed by a magician. She was later able, under careful laboratory controls, to expose film with her mind and deflect a compass needle 15 degrees.[23] What made Parise's feats interesting was that she never claimed to have any special powers. She had simply taught herself how to do it—much like Jack Houck teaches average people to bend spoons at his PK parties.

Parise used her mind to move inanimate, physical objects like pieces of aluminum or compass needles. Later in that same decade, other test subjects in laboratories would successfully demonstrate the ability to use their minds to physically affect the physiology and/or behavior of living organisms. Their targets ranged from cell cultures in a lab dish to plants, animals and even their fellow human beings. William Braud, at that time working with the Mind Science Foundation in San Antonio, Texas, coined the term "bio-PK" to describe this PK action directed at biological organisms, and the term DMILS (Direct Mental Influence of Living Systems) to describe these types of experiments. Braud and his colleagues designed and conducted some of the most ingenious and rigorous bio-PK experiments. Test subjects were put in one room and asked to use just their thoughts to influence shielded biological organisms in another room. They tried to affect the rate of destruction of red blood corpuscles (haemolysis) in a lab dish; or the heartbeat, blood pressure or electrodermal activity or motor movements of other human beings. Though the effect was small, the results proved significant beyond chance and were replicable by other scientists.[24] Braud's research and the work of other scientists who followed him strongly suggest that humans have the ability to affect, to some degree, the bodily functions of other people targeted by their minds (in Chapter 9 we will look at some surprising evidence for the mind's ability to affect its own body and health).

One of the most interesting and unusual demonstrations in the 1970s of the average person's ability to create PK effects came about by accident. Eight ordinary men and women in Toronto, Canada—all members of the Toronto Society of Psychical Research—originally set out to produce an apparition, or ghost, using only their minds.[25] They created an imaginary deceased person called Philip, and conducted a séance with "him." They failed to produce an apparition, but they did produce a number of PK effects, including rapping noises and table movements similar to those experienced during Spiritualist séances in the late 19th century. Their conclusion: that séance-like PK phenomena are produced not by disincarnate spirits but by the mental energy of the persons participating in a séance. They were able to levitate a table and make it rock, slide, spin, twist and flip over; make lights flicker or turn off and on; defy gravity by keeping a round object from rolling off a table tilted at a 45 degree angle; create rapping sounds as Philip "answered" their questions about his life; and produce other amazing PK effects. They later scientifically measured the intensity of the rappings, and acoustically recorded the sounds.

The Toronto PK experiments seemed to suggest a number of "rules" for producing group PK, and is an experiment testable by anyone. Their "recipe" for PK:

Recruit at least four people. PK requires a lot of mental energy and a group supplies this better than a single individual. The Toronto group had eight persons. (Jack Houck's PK parties work on the same theory— the bigger the group, the more emotional energy to create PK.)

Make sure there is good group rapport. The group needs to act in harmony, like a family. Shared feelings of friendship and affection, and the ability to be relaxed with each other, increases the chances of something being produced.

Have a common motivation. The group should share a common motivation—a curiosity and excitement about PK and a desire to test it.

Be open-minded. Everyone in the group should be at least open-mined about the possible existence of PK. Extremely strong skepticism by too many members might defeat the experiment.

Agree on the details. The group needs to create its "Philip" together, so all participants picture the same person, and agree on the details together. The closer members agree on the character's life history, motivations and physical description, the easier it is to combine mental energies.

Create a kind, good, friendly "Philip." Envision someone non-threatening, relaxing and fun to be with, someone participants genuinely like and admire. An evil "Philip" can be psychologically threatening and mentally unhealthy as a focus for group thought.

Suspend disbelief in dealing with your "Philip." People do it automatically while reading a novel or watching a movie. Participants need to make the character "come alive" to them in the same way characters become almost real in a favorite novel or movie. Many times in a darkened movie theater, or curled up with a good book, people find themselves totally engrossed in the story to the point where they forget where they are. This state of emotional involvement with a fictitious character is what participants want to achieve with their "Philip."

Avoid feelings of individual ownership. Make sure "Philip" is a group creation. In this way, if PK effects are produced, no single individual will feel like he or she caused them. The group caused them. This should reduce the individual fear and anxiety that can accompany such an adventure into the unknown.

Build in safeguards to the PK experiment. PK is poorly understood and can sometimes occur spontaneously or act erratically. Agree to limit experimentation to a single place, and only contact "Philip" as a group and with the consent of the group.

Expect a miracle. Ideally, the group should approach the task strongly expecting to produce PK effects. Believe it will happen. If PK is produced, try to accept it as a natural, normal phenomenon. Avoid outward astonishment or skepticism that might make it difficult to repeat it again.

Be patient. Retain your enthusiasm. The Toronto group met several hours each week for many months before they succeeded. It apparently takes time to build up group rapport and create the psychological conditions necessary for PK production.

Meanwhile, back in the laboratory, small scale, statistical PK experiments and equipment to test them continued to be refined and developed. In the late 1960s, physicist Helmut Schmidt developed a machine called the Random Number Generator (RNG). Schmidt's RNG was an electronic coin flipper, with the "coin" (a switch) being flipped in a completely random pattern by electrons emitted during the radioactive decay of a piece of strontium 90.

RNG machines generate truly random numbers, based on quantum mechanical processes. This ensures that the targets selected for ESP and PK experiments are guaranteed 100% random. Without truly random target generation, you never know if your results are the work of an ESP or PK effect or simply the result of a built-in bias in the experiment. In Rhine's card guessing experiments, for example, skeptics could claim that the normal card shuffling process cannot guarantee a completely random distribution of the cards in the deck. If you shuffle a deck once, many cards remain in their old positions. If you shuffle a deck a thousand times, your chances of a random order increase but, even then, it may not be perfect. The RNG eliminated this justifiable criticism from the skeptics arsenal. Schmidt's RNG also eliminated the potential of human manipulation and trickery inherent in Rhine's experiments where humans handle the target dice, coins or cards; and it eliminates skeptics' criticism that the dice used in the experiment might have been manufactured with a minute weight bias towards one number. Finally, Schmidt's RNG could be connected to a computer, allowing data collection to be automated.

Over the last two decades, some of the most interesting micro-PK research has been conducted at the Princeton Engineering Anomalies Research (PEAR) laboratory attached to the Department of Mechanical and Aerospace Engineering at Princeton University (www.princeton. edu/~pear/).

The story of the PEAR laboratory PK experiments is summed up very well in *Margins of Reality: The Role of Consciousness in the Physical World*, written by Robert Jahn and Brenda Dunne. The program was established in 1979 by Jahn, now the Dean Emeritus of the School of Engineering and Applied Science whom we met in an earlier chapter.

In 1969, Jahn had been approached by one of his students, an electrical engineer and computer scientist, who wanted to design a machine to test PK as part of an independent study project. Jahn was skeptical of PK and only reluctantly agreed to the project. And while the results of the experiment didn't fully convince Jahn of the validity of PK, it produced enough questions to make Jahn wonder about the possibility of the mind being able to affect the operation of sensitive technological systems and equipment—including delicate information processing systems found in airplane cockpits and ICBM missile silos.

Jahn proceeded as quietly and uncontroversially as possible to set up his PEAR experiments. He got private foundation funding; reported his results only in professional and technical journals; and, afraid of sensationalism, allowed no media coverage of the experiments. In contrast to most PK research and true to his bias towards engineering, Jahn decided his primary focus would be on the developing improved devices, processes and experimental protocols used to test for PK.

Jahn realized that among the biggest stumbling blocks researchers faced when trying to establish the reality of PK were 1) their use of unsophisticated laboratory equipment which could be generating biased results, 2) the limited number of successful experiments that had been conducted on the phenomenon, allowing skeptics to dismiss these few favorable results as possible statistical aberrations and 3) the inability of people to reproduce the PK effect on demand.

To solve the first problem, Jahn replaced Rhine's primitive dice-tumbling machine with several ingenious devices, including a Random Event Generator (REG)—a more elaborate and expensive form of Schmidt's Random Number Generator. Using a REG machine, Jahn could run thousands of tests efficiently and quickly. He could also feed its electronic output directly to a computer for automatic data-collection and analysis of results, greatly reducing the possibility of human error or bias from these functions. Finally, Jahn went to great lengths to shield the equipment from inadvertent or deliberate spurious disturbances—heat, vibration, sounds, electromagnetic waves, etc.—by the equipment operator or the person being tested. (Jahn also developed and used in his experiments a RMC—a Random Mechanical Cascade that dropped 9000 polystyrene balls down a pinball machine-like latticework of pegs, with the experimenter trying to make more balls fall to the left or right than would happen by chance; as well as a high-precision pendulum whose swing experimenters tried to affect with their minds.)

To solve the second problem, Jahn ran over five million PK tests. The results clearly and decisively demonstrated the existence of PK. Some people could indeed influence the REG machine to produce results that were beyond chance.[26] A battery of sophisticated statistical tests run on the database confirmed that these successful results weren't just a statistical aberration or fluke of some sort.

The huge database also addressed the third problem—the inability of single individuals to reproduce the PK effect on demand. While it was true that none of the tested individuals could produce positive results each and every time they were tested, Jahn could demonstrate that specific individuals could—over time and on average—consistently produce PK effects that exceeded chance.

Most PK experimenters sat near or next to the test devices when trying to produce PK effects. But Jahn also did experiments that indicate that PK can be produced by experimenters situated a few miles to a thousand miles away.[27] This "remote PK" effect suggests that space is no barrier to PK. As Jahn notes, remote PK also provides strong arguments against the possibility of the tested subject fraudulently manipulating the machine since he or she is miles away from the equipment. Jahn's research team also conducted some intriguing experiments in "remote perception" (clairvoyance) and precognition which provide evidence for the ability of human consciousness to operate outside the classical physics laws of time and space. The full scale and character of the PK anomaly verified in the PEAR lab was not yet known, Jahn concluded, but enough was known to justify a reexamination of science's current position on "the role of consciousness in the establishment of physical reality."[28]

In 1989, the respected academic journal *Foundations of Physics* published a blockbuster analysis of over 800 studies conducted between 1959 and 1987 testing the reality of PK—the ability of the human mind alone to control a machine (i.e. micro-electronic REG machines). Their astonishing conclusion? The odds were more than *one trillion to one* against the results being due simply to chance. The effect was small; it was not automatic or easily controlled; but it was real. PK exists.[29]

If PK, like ESP, has been proven to be a real phenomenon, scientists still don't know enough about either to produce them on demand, every time. Increasing reliability is the current goal of much current ESP and PK research.

Why can Uri Geller, or my brother John for example, produce PK effects one day, and not the other? Why do so many psychics perform well under certain test conditions, but fail under others? Two basic hypothesis have been advanced to explain this uneven track record.

The first, espoused by debunkers like James Randi, is that the paranormal powers claimed by psychics are simply the result of fraud, trickery or sloppy experimental controls. Make sure no cheating can happen, and PK won't happen. But the problem with Randi's blanket fraud hypothesis is that a number of tested psychics—including Geller—*have* in fact performed successfully under extremely demanding and rigorous experimental controls.

Some scientists studying this puzzling, uneven performance record of persons who can apparently produce PK or ESP one day and not the next, offer a different hypothesis than Randi for this failure. They theorize that since PK, ESP and other psychic phenomena are produced by human beings, not machines, the results can be affected to a degree by the relative skill, knowledge, attitude, health, emotions, belief, and level of interest the performer brings to the experiment; and even the testing environment and attitudes of onlookers and scientists running the tests.

Under this hypothesis, psychic performance can be compared in some ways to sports performance. For example, our performance in a game on any given day depends on the natural gifts we're born with; how long and how diligently we've practiced our skills; our knowledge of the mechanics of tackling correctly or swinging a bat correctly; our physical health at the time we perform; our mental mood or emotional attitude at the moment we step up to the baseball plate or basketball foul line; our belief in ourselves and our ability to do it; and even the attitude (hostile or friendly) of the crowd watching us perform. Psi performers operate on the same basis. Automatic, mechanical, repeatability of results should not be expected from psi practitioners any more than they are expected from sports players.. Even a Michael Jordan or Uri Geller can have off nights, frustrating slumps, or unpredictable failures to perform even the simplest feat; but that failure doesn't mean their earlier successes were necessarily the result of fraud or trickery.

Three well-known physicists studying Geller's performance in the laboratory under controlled experimental conditions noted in their report[30] that the traditional, completely impersonal approach to experimentation favored by the natural sciences for experimentation may not be adequate when trying to test psychic ability. Tension and hostility on the part of scientists towards the test subject, or experiments without any aesthetic or imaginative appeal to the person tested, can make it difficult for the subject to produce results. Why? Because the person producing the PK is not simply an unfeeling instrument or inanimate machine. Treating him like one can doom the experiment to failure.

Dr. J.B. Rhine pioneered many experiments on the influence of psychological, physiological, mental and emotional states of experimenter and observers on the outcome of a PK or ESP experiment. A positive, enthusiastic, attitude towards the experiment produced better results; drinking alcohol (a depressant) seemed to lower scores while drinking coffee or Coca-Cola (a stimulant) appeared to raise them; boredom with the repetitive nature of the tests slowly dropped scores; negative comments and distractions from observers lowered scores; believers in psi scored higher than unbelievers, etc.

Believing that you can produce psi helps your success rate. Even better is when you actually *expect*—indeed, you *know*—you will produce a miracle. Parapsychologist and psychologist Dr. Gertrude Schmeidler coined the term "sheep" for believers, and "goats" for skeptics. She demonstrated that "sheep" routinely score higher than "goats."[31] Again, all things being equal, if you don't believe you can hit a homer, you probably have a lesser chance than someone who does believe.

Most professional sports teams also win more home games than road games. Why? Because people perform better in front of friendly, supportive crowds. Psychics apparently do the same. It's human nature. Like a batter in an away game facing a pitcher in a hostile ballpark, far from the psychologically comfortable, friendly surroundings of his home stadium and home crowd, your performance can be affected by the attitude of people around you. If people want you to fail, let you know they want and expect you to fail, and radiate hostility, they can usually negatively affect your performance even without physically touching you. For this reason, performing psi feats before a hostile crowd of debunkers is probably harder to do than performing the same feat before a friendly audience, or even a neutral one.

Fear can also play a factor, particularly for people attempting PK for the first time. Parapsychologist and philosopher Stephen Braude once tried table-tilting as a lark and, when it actually happened, it scared the hell out of him.[32] Braude argues that this fear may lie behind the lack of large-scale PK manifestations today. D.D. Home and other large-scale PK practitioners operated in an era of the spiritualist movement, when mediums believed discarnate spirits, not themselves, produced the PK. Thus they didn't have to face the possibility that they themselves might be producing the PK. But as more and more research began to suggest that the source of the PK might be the medium himself, mediums had to deal with the possibility that they themselves might have powers they could not control or understand—a frightening thought for most people. Depending on our religious and cultural beliefs, attempting PK or any other kind of psi activity can make us extremely nervous. Though most parapsychologists believe PK is a natural, human power, anyone who has seen Hollywood films like *Poltergeist*, or *The Amityville Horror* will more likely associate table levitations or objects flying through the air with evil spirits, supernatural powers, or some rogue power from within ourselves which, if we let it out, can destroy us. Fear of the paranormal is ingrained in almost everybody.

British psychologist and PK researcher Kenneth Batcheldor has identified two blocks to PK production. The first, which he calls "ownership resistance," means that human beings are afraid to think that they themselves can cause such a phenomenon. We want to feel we are normal people, not freaks or oddballs—and people with PK powers are certainly not "normal" to most people. The second, "witness inhibition," means that when we actually see PK, we often get so frightened that we instinctively resist producing it again. For many people, witnessing a PK phenomenon could be a frightening, traumatic experience. We don't want our basic view of reality threatened by forces we don't understand. We may think we're going crazy. If Batcheldor is right, fear of the paranormal appears to be a potential major stumbling block to the ability of humans to produce psi events like PK. Consequently, Batcheldor developed a number of techniques to overcome this fear and anxiety,[33] and his work was further developed by retired British electrical engineer Colin Brookes-Smith.[34]

With some PK experiments, researchers and observers have noticed a delay effect. Positive results only become apparent after the experiment is ended. Several recorded cases of attempted PK spoon bending saw the PK experimenter try his best, then finally give up with no apparent results. A few minutes or a few hours later, the experimenter returns to the experiment only to find the spoon bent. What at first looked like a failed experiment later turned out to be a success. A number of participants in Jack Houck's PK parties have reported this phenomenon, and NDE researcher Raymond Moody, M.D. describes the same delay effect in an experiment he conducted on producing apparitions of deceased persons. [35]

What is your mental state when you try to perform PK or ESP? Apparently, how happy or sad you are, how stressed or relaxed you feel, the current state of your love life and personal relationships, how you feel about yourself and life in general can all affect performance. Some days you find that "magic groove" or "zone" and everything you do is effortless, easy; at other times, nothing you do seems to go right. Psychic performance can greatly depend on your state of mind at the moment you try to perform.

Natural gifts also appear to play a role. Some people have a natural ability to hit a fast ball, write a symphony or solve a math problem. Likewise, some people appear to be born with psychic gifts. They are often called "sensitives" because they are more attuned than the average person to "extra-sensory" perceptions. Like Michael Jordan or Mozart, either you have this gift or you don't. Parapsychologists have achieved surprisingly good results using ordinary people in some PK experiments, including Jahn at Princeton. Parapsychologists have also demonstrated in the lab that average people can often improve their performance with practice. You can train yourself to do better. But being able to produce superior results on demand may be reserved for psychic superstars.

Experiments that provide quick feedback and results often produce better overall, sustained performance. Teachers of remote viewing routinely incorporate feedback into their training methods.

Making an experiment fun can affect results. Curiosity and a love of fun are hallmarks of human beings. Most people hate the boredom of repetition, the drudgery of having to perform the same task over and over again. They like to try new things. Boredom can prevent success and kill an experiment.

Last but not least, our weak understanding of how PK and ESP actually work makes it difficult for us to know exactly how best to improve our ability to produce PK and ESP. As a result, we are much less able to guide the process, or control the outcome of a psi experiment.

Best Scientific Evidence

Princeton PEAR Laboratory Experiments (1979–Ongoing)

By 1993, the PEAR research program had conducted over 5 million PK trials. That year, Roger D. Nelson, Operations Coordinator for PEAR, presented a paper to the Society for Scientific Exploration entitled *The PEAR REG Experiments: Database Structure*. His paper analyzed data collected by the PEAR program over 12 years of research and 5.6 million trials performed by 108 individuals using a random event generator. Its conclusion: the PK phenomenon is real. Mind can affect matter. In 1997, Jahn and his colleagues at PEAR produced a paper updating their experiments.[36] That research continues today and current experiments can be viewed at the PEAR website (www.princeton.edu/~pear/) where you will find a long list of technical papers describing the experiments in detail.

What qualifies the PEAR experiments as "Best Evidence" is the sheer number of experiments conducted; the systematic approach they applied to the problem; the rigorous laboratory controls they devised to eliminate possible fraud or human or machine error; the willingness with which they have shared information on the results of their experiments and the experimental protocols they employed; and their willingness to have any skeptic examine the evidence (a number of researchers have taken up that challenge).

Jahn has invited responsible and objective skeptics to conduct an independent examination of the equipment, protocols and results of the PEAR experiments. To assist them, he has made available complete summaries of all experimental data bases, technical equipment, protocols and data-processing strategies "for whatever use any critic or colleague may choose to make of them." All he asks in return is that they focus on the evidence and "base their comments solely and logically" on that evidence.[37]

In 2000, PEAR's Roger Nelson and Dr. Dean Radin of the Boundary Institute did a massive review of over 515 different scientific PK experiments conducted between 1959-2000 (not just the PEAR experiments).[38] Scientists have conducted PK experiments asking test subjects to use just their minds to change the structure of pieces of metal; make plastic and metal balls fall in certain non-random patterns that violate the laws of chance; change temperatures in well-shielded environments; beat the laws of chance with spinning coins and thrown dice; disturb the output of sensitive magnetometers and interferometers; and influence the output of truly random number generators (REG). Their study reinforced the conclusions PEAR came to in 1993 and 1997: The effect is small, but it can't be explained away by chance or selective reporting of results. PK is real.

Perhaps the most important outcome of the PEAR experiments is their challenge to our basic concept of reality. Science says reality exists "out there," independent of us and our consciousness. The PEAR experiments suggest that human consciousness actually helps create and shape that objective physical reality. Our consciousness helps create the world; the world doesn't exist completely independently of our minds. This is obviously a radical notion of reality. Minor alterations of existing physical and psychological frameworks may not do, says Jahn. In pursuit of this mystery, the PEAR staff coordinates the work of the International Consciousness Research Laboratories (www.icrl.org), a consortium of research scholars studying the role of consciousness in the fields of anthropology, archeology, biology, engineering, physics, psychiatry, psychology and the humanities. PEAR's Internet home page includes the following quote by British astronomer and physicist Sir Arthur Eddington which perhaps best sums up the radical scientific paradigm suggested by the PEAR experiments: "Not once in the dim past, but continuously by conscious mind is the miracle of the Creation wrought."

The Palladino 1908 Naples Sittings

Eusapia Palladino, daughter of a poor Italian peasant, was born in Bari in 1854. Coarse and earthy even after becoming famous, she remained illiterate her whole life, unable to read or write anything more than her own name. As a child, after her father was killed by thieves, she ended up working as a servant in a household that practiced spiritualism. One day, during a séance, she herself produced paranormal phenomena, starting her on a lifelong career as a medium. A wealthy Naples gentleman eventually heard about her and alerted the scientific community in Italy which investigated her in 1891. Their positive reports encouraged more scientific groups to test her. In 1892, a multinational team of well-known and highly respected French, German and Italian scientists conducted 17 sittings in Milan with her, witnessing and recording furniture levitations in full light (the light was good enough that a photograph was taken of the levitated table); materializations of hands; phantom touches, and various poltergeist-type phenomena. Another 40 sittings followed in Warsaw in 1893-94. At the invitation of the French Nobel Laureate Charles Richet, Sir Oliver Lodge of England's Society for Psychical Research hastened to the Continent in 1894 to investigate Palladino. Lodge came away convinced of the supernormal character of at least some of the phenomena, but other SPR officers refused to accept the verdict, citing poor control over Palladino's movements. In 1895, the SPR invited Palladino to Cambridge, England, tested her, and concluded she was a fraud (despite being unable to show how some of the phenomena had been produced). By 1907, the bibliography of reports detailing scientific experiments conducted on

Palladino had grown to 29 pages; the scientific community was deeply divided, with English scientists dismissing Palladino and most scientists on the Continent arguing that she had demonstrated supernormal abilities to their satisfaction.[39]

In 1908, the Society for Psychical Research finally sent a "Fraud Squad" to debunk Palladino once an for all. The team consisted of three skeptics, two of whom were magicians (Carrington and Baggally). The group had a sterling track record of exposing fraudulent mediums. Mr. Baggally had spent thirty years attending séances, had investigated almost every medium in Britain, and had never found any evidence he couldn't account for by trickery. Carrington, an American, had even written a book detailing tricks used by fraudulent mediums, of which he had made a special study.

The trio of investigators set up stringent professional controls to eliminate any possible means of fraud during the sittings. They chose the hotel and rented the rooms for the test; arranged the placement of people and furniture and lighting; locked doors and windows in the specially prepared room to keep out accomplices; had Palladino strip-searched before several sessions; sat on both sides of her throughout the séances, either tightly held or tied her hands to theirs, and even tied her feet to the chair; installed a specially-designed apparatus on the séance table to prevent it from being lifted by the medium's feet; and did everything they could think of to ensure against trickery and fraud.

Despite these precautions, Palladino was able to repeatedly levitate tables in full light, some as high as two feet off the floor; make a small stool jump around, and climb up a curtain; materialize objects like hands and heads; make objects fly through the air; make a guitar inside a cabinet play notes without being touched (also a tambourine); untie four tightly-drawn reef knots (tied by Baggally to attach Palladino's ankle to the chair; the rope was specially chosen by magician Baggally because it was soft and pliable and difficult to untie because the knots, when tied, sank deeply into the cord) and ring an unreachable bell using PK; produce strong, sustained (once for up to a half-hour), phantom touches and grabs all over the bodies of the perplexed investigators (sometime on two investigators simultaneously); produce various loud sounds, bangs and raps in various places in the room ("the bangs sounded like a heavy crash with a wooden mallet"); produce blue-green and yellow lights and "a small sparkling light like the spark between the poles of a battery and emitting a similar sound"; and other baffling phenomena. The tighter the controls, the stronger the phenomena appeared. As one of the debunkers declared after the fifth of eleven sessions, the mental gymnastics involved in trying to avoid concluding such "absurd" phenomena were real produced a kind of "intellectual fatigue."[40]

In the end, the SPR fraud squad capitulated completely. Baggally summed up the opinion of the group with the following: "Taking into consideration the manner of the control, that no mechanism was found on the medium's person, that no accomplice was present, and also that the three S.P.R. investigators were men who had been accustomed for years to the investigation of so-called psychic phenomena of every variety, and who had detected fraud after fraud, I find it impossible to believe that Eusapia could have been able to practice trickery constantly during the man-hours that the séances lasted and remain undetected…Eusapia was not detected in fraud in any one of the 470 phenomena that took place at the eleven séances."[41] Their reluctant conclusion? Palladino had indeed demonstrated supernormal powers.

The detailed minute-by-minute notes taken while events happened by a professional stenographer hired by the investigators can be reviewed by any skeptic today wishing to examine the case and the evidence. The report also includes drawings of the layout of the room; where everyone was at the moment the phenomena were produced; the weight of the objects levitated; and even an invitation to skeptical magicians to try and produce the same phenomena under the same conditions Palladino produced hers.

The D.D. Home-William Crookes Accordion Experiment

Home was reportedly able to make an accordion play without touching it, or when held at the end opposite from the keys. But he also preferred to have the accordion play itself under the séance table—an obvious invitation to fraud if Home were inclined. Scientist Sir William Crookes took up the challenge testing Home while leaving the accordion where Holmes preferred it.[42] Crookes was wary of all séance phenomena and on his guard with Home. "I have myself frequently detected fraud of various kinds, and I have always made it a rule in weighing Spiritualistic evidence to assume that fraud may have been attempted, and ingeniously attempted, either by seen or unseen agents."[43] With this in mind, Crookes bought a new accordion, so Holmes couldn't use one he had tampered with beforehand. Second, he met Home at his residence and watched him change clothes so he could make sure Home wasn't secretly rigging some device in his clothing. Next, he took Home to Crookes' house where he had built a special cage for the accordion (a sketch of the ingenious cage devised by Crookes is found in Stephen Braude's book).[44] It allowed Home to reach in and hold the accordion at the end away from the keys, but not physically reach the keys on the other end of the accordion. Home's other hand remained on top of the table at all times in full view. Nine people witnessed the event. Two observers stood at each side of Home during the test, and a third went under the table with a lamp to watch the accordion. Despite these tight controls, Home was able to have the accordion expand and contract, play simple melodies and float around in the cage. But as Crookes noted, the sequel was even more striking. "...Mr. Home then removed his hand altogether from the accordion, taking it quite out of the cage, and placed it in the hand of the person next to him. The instrument then continued to play, no person touching it and no hands near it." [45]

The D.D. Home Amsterdam Tests

There are so many credible accounts of Home's powers that it is hard to choose among them. As an example, in 1858, a Dutch group of die-hard skeptics conducted three sessions with Home at a place and time of their own choosing. There were anywhere from 7-10 investigators at the sessions. Among them were a professor with a Ph.D, a medical doctor, a lawyer, and an optician, all of whom considered themselves "the most unbelieving of all believers." Home had never met any of them before. According to the skeptics' own written report drawn up shortly after the events, Home invited everyone there to observe him as closely as possible. Afraid Home might try to hypnotize them, the attendees chattered loudly with their neighbors and laughingly mocked the possibility of paranormal phenomena. But pretty soon the massive mahogany table they sat around (it could seat 14 people) started to slowly slide towards Home, despite attempts by the group to physically stop it from moving (they couldn't do so). Next, the heavy table rose up on one side so much that observers were afraid that candelabras sitting on the table would topple over. While it tilted, one of the skeptics got under the table and checked to make sure nobody or no thing was lifting the table. The baffled man found nothing. The skeptics then asked Home if he could make the table so light that they could lift it with one finger. Home did, and they could. They asked him to make it so heavy that the group couldn't lift it. "The table could hardly be lifted at all, in spite of our utmost efforts." Raps sounded in various parts of the room. "We then asked the table to rap in a certain manner, and as many times as we should indicate. This wish was carried out to the full." Thus ended session one. The next day, at noon, they switched tables and invited Home to perform his PK again. The same phenomena happened again, the new table moving around and levitating in full light. During the session, one skeptic simply formulated a request *in his mind*—asking the table to produce raps corresponding to the secret knocks second-degree

Freemasons used in rituals—and the table produced the correct knocks. Skeptics asked the table to rap out numbers at a certain rapid rate; the table did so. That night, a dramatic, third, final session was conducted with seven skeptics present. After knocks and loud raps, the ceiling over their heads and the chairs they sat on began to rock so violently that "…we felt ourselves going up and down as if on a rocking horse. We experienced the same sensation and movement as when sitting in a carriage on springs while driving along the highroad." Next, the table slowly rose into the air and descended smoothly, without any abrupt movements. Then phantom hands started touching people in the room on their arms, knees, cheeks—in one skeptic's case keeping up the touching for twenty minutes. "Another man was so violently clutched all of a sudden that he jumped from his chair." Another skeptic tossed his handkerchief on the floor and dared Home to move it into the hand of a man sitting opposite him while he closely watched the handkerchief. Moments later, the handkerchief flew up into the man's hand which was resting on his knee. The handkerchief owner got it back and wrapped it around his finger, confident it couldn't be yanked away from him. A force immediately tugged the handkerchief off his finger. All the while, participants were watching Home carefully to make sure he wasn't secretly doing something. Experiment after experiment was conducted by the skeptics; Home met each challenge. Concluded the report " All was in vain. We saw the phenomena happening but could not explain them. And nothing could be observed that could give rise to even the slightest suspicion that Mr. Home was acting in a fraudulent manner."[46]

The D.D. Home-Baron Reichenbach Challenge

One time, Home was visiting a Lady Poulett who asked him to perform for her supper guests. According to one supper guest there, "We all saw the supper table—on which there was a quantity of glass and china full of good things—rise, I should say, to an angle of 45 deg. without anything slipping in the least, and then relapse to its normal position."

This gravity-defying feat, amazing as it was, still left one guest skeptical. The tall and powerful Baron Reichenbach, the discoverer of paraffin, was present and laughed at the other guests, challenging them to move a table if he got under it and held it. "He got under the table and clasped it with both his arms, but it moved as before, dragging him all around the room."[47] The embarrassed Baron was used to mop the floor. As macro-PK research proponent Dr. Stephen Braude notes, no amount of fiddling around with random event generators can match the insights (or the effect on belief) that can be gained from mediums like Home or Palladino.[48]

Highly Recommended Reading:

Braude, S.E. *The Limits of Influence: Psychokinesis and the Philosophy of Science* (Rev. Ed.), University Press of America, 1997. This classic book is required reading for anyone serious about researching psychokinesis, particularly large-scale PK like that performed by D.D. Home and Eusapia Palladino. The book also includes a history of PK research and thought-provoking philosophical commentary on the scientific establishment's treatment of PK reports.

Jahn, Robert G. and Dunne. *Margins of Reality: The Role of Consciousness in the Physical World.* Harvest Books, 1989. This book gives you a good summary of the history of the Princeton PEAR program and its research in both PK and precognitive ESP, and Jahn's attempt to incorporate the anomalous results into an acceptable theory of how PK and ESP operate. It is sufficiently technical to satisfy a statistics freak; but it also includes some wonderful philosophical—almost mystical—speculation on the implications of PK and precognitive ESP for classical science and the way we view "reality."[49] When you're done reading it, go to the PEAR website to update the book's conclusions and view current research underway.

Margolis, Jonathan. *Uri Geller: Magician or Mystic?* New York: Welcome Rain Publishers, 1999. A very good summary of the life of Uri Geller and his psychokinesis feats over the last four decades, done by a respected British journalist (*Evening Standard* and *Guardian* newspapers, and *Time* magazine European contributor). It also includes a nice section on Jack Houck and his PK parties.

8.

Dowsing

"We must accept dowsing as a fact. It is useless to work up experiments merely to prove its existence. It exists. What is needed is its development."
Nobel Laureate Charles Richet (1850-1935)

New England holds a special place in my heart since I grew up there as a young boy. My present home, Hawaii, is filled with scenic beauty, but no place on earth matches New England—particularly Vermont—in the Fall when the maple leaves are turning gold, yellow and flaming red. Vermont is also famous for its stubborn, free-thinking individualists which is perhaps why it is also home to the American Society of Dowsers (www.dowsers.org).

Growing up in New England, I had read stories in the newspapers and on occasion heard tales of dowsers who used a forked stick to find water for farmers or homeowners drilling a well. I was always curious, but never had the opportunity to meet a dowser or see one in action.

I didn't meet my first dowser until 25 years later, and I met him by chance at the Honolulu shipyard subsidiary owned by the company I work for. I was chatting with a few friends after work about the book I was researching on paranormal phenomena when John, a welder at the yard, spoke up. "Have you ever seen anyone do dowsing before?" he asked. A native of Oregon, John had learned dowsing as a young man and had successfully used it to locate unmarked underground pipes and electrical conduits when the shipyard he worked for on the Mainland wanted to repave the yard. Shipyards have lots of buried underground pipes and cables to bring power and water to various sites on the property.

Our own shipyard was typical. Buried beneath the ground were all sorts of cables and pipes and no one knew exactly where all of them ran; only where they ended. John went to the trunk of his car and pulled out two thin copper welding rods bent in an L-shape. Grasping one in each hand, he slowly walked across the parking lot, keeping the rods level and separate, pointed straight ahead like two pistols in a showdown at the OK Corral. Suddenly, both rods swung inward together and crossed each other, making a straight line. "Here's one pipe," he said. "And it runs in a straight line in the direction of the rods." He placed a stone on the spot, walked ten feet away, then marched at a 90 degree angle to the projected line until he intersected it, his dowsing rods swinging together when he again crossed the line. He placed a stone at that spot. "If you connect these two spots with a straight line, you'll find a pipe running right below it." Since no one was going to dig up the yard to confirm his predictions, and we didn't have a map handy, I was impressed but not convinced. "Here," he said. "You try it." He handed me the rods and I slowly walked across the yard, trying to keep the rods parallel and level as he did. As I crossed John's imaginary line, I also felt the rods suddenly swing inward and cross in front of me. Perhaps I'm subconsciously willing the rods to do so, since I know the spot, I thought. So I walked to the other end of the parking lot, closed my eyes, and tried it again. When I felt the rods swing together, I opened my eyes. To my surprise, I was standing on the line John had marked. "Not bad for an amateur," John grinned.

I didn't even know dowsers looked for pipes. Most of us associate "dowsing"—if we associate it with anything—with a search for water, since dowsing is often called "water-witching" or "water-divining." But today, dowsing is used to find just about anything, according to the late dowsing historian Christopher Bird, author of *The Divining Hand* and former editor of *The American Dowser* magazine of the American Society of Dowsers. People use forked sticks, pendulums, bent coat hangers and other hand-held instruments; and they search for everything from water, oil and minerals to lost ships, planes, pets, murder victims and buried treasure.

My welder friend John used two bent welding rods instead of a forked stick or a pendulum, but what is used really seems to be a matter of personal preference. In fact, says Bird, some dowsers today don't use any instrument at all, just their hands. Further, some gifted dowsers never even leave their homes to dowse a site. Instead of physically driving out to the site and walking over a field with a dowsing rod looking for water, they simply move their rod, bob or hands over a *map* of the site and find the target.

It sounds crazy. But dowsers have apparently racked up enough successes to convince a variety of well-known companies, organizations and individuals to use their skills, according to Bird.

U.S. Marine engineers successfully used dowsing rods during the Vietnam War as a supplement to their more high-tech equipment, according to the *New York Times*.[1] The rods were also used to locate hidden ammunition and food caches, and booby traps. Evidently, it wasn't the first time the U.S. military has used dowsers. General George Patton reportedly used a dowser to locate fresh water for his thirsty troops in North Africa after the retreating Germans blew up the wells ahead of the advancing Allied forces.[2]

We don't normally associate Fortune 500 corporations with dowsing, but one of the largest global pharmaceutical companies in the world, Hoffman-La Roche, has used dowsing around the world to locate water for its new pharmaceutical plants which need the water for manufacturing and processing chemicals into drugs. Why use dowsing instead of more scientific methods? An article in the company's in-house magazine *Roche-Zeitung* quotes company dowser Dr. Peter Treadwell as saying "Roche uses methods that are profitable, whether they are scientifically explainable or not."

Since dowsing was first used to find water and minerals, it my not be so surprising to discover that companies in the energy field have a history of using dowsers to help find oil wells. The petroleum industry calls dowsers "doodlebuggers" and both big oil companies and independent wildcatters are on record as having used them. Some dowsers have flopped miserably; others have spectacular records. Since dowsing appears to be closely related to both ESP and PK, it is similarly hard to produce on demand, for probably the same reasons we discussed above. But one of the best oil dowsers was MIT graduate and electrical engineer Paul Clement Brown who used dowsing to successfully locate oil—or avoid drilling dry holes—for Signal Oil, Standard Oil, Getty Oil, Mobil Oil, and for famous independent oil producer J.K. Wadley.[3]

According to Bird, dowsing, an offshoot of divination, is an ancient art. Using a dowsing rod to find minerals goes back at least 500 years. In 1556, the German physician and mining scholar Georgius Agricola published *De Re Metallica* ("Concerning Metals") in which he describes in detail how miners should cut, hold and employ wooden dowsing rods to locate places to dig for silver and gold. The first printed reference to using a dowsing rod to find water appears a hundred years later, in the mid-1600s. That century also saw the first reference to a woman dowser, Martine de Bertereau, wife of a French baron, who together with her husband traveled all over Europe as mining consultants. By the end of the 17th century, Jean Nicholas had published the first textbook on dowsing, entitled "Jacob's Rod, the Art of Finding Treasures, Springs, Boundaries, Metals, Mines, and Other Hidden Things Through the Use of the Forked Stick." Dowsers were being portrayed on beer steins, in Meissen porcelain, and even among figurines in Christmas Nativity sets.

But the increasing popularity of dowsing also generated fear on the part of the Church, and suspicion on the part of some scientists. Since no one—including most of the dowsers themselves—really had a clue as to *why* or *how* dowsing worked, theologians suspected the Devil and science suspected fraud and trickery. Martin Luther, son of a miner himself, condemned dowsing as the work of Satan. The Catholic Church also attacked the practice and in the early 1700s started adding dowsing books to the Index of Forbidden Books. The prestigious French Academy weighed in with Science's judgment on dowsing in 1702, calling its practitioners impostors. As Bird notes, it was "official science's first debut" [4] as an opponent of dowsing, a position that has basically remained unchanged for the last 400 years.

But continued success with the technique encouraged miners to ignore the condemnation of Church and Science. They were joined by numerous Catholic and Protestant clergy, curious philosophers and scholars, and fascinated nobility who pursued the enigma unabated. In the 1700s, the study of magnetism and electricity became very popular with scientists and philosophers, some of whom hypothesized that perhaps a form of electromagnetism might provide a theoretical explanation of dowsing. But many scientists flatly refused to even theorize an explanation about something they were sure was impossible—and thus needed no explanation. They included the famous French astronomer Joseph-Jerome de Lalande who in 1782 called the idea of both flying ships and turning dowsing rods "lunacy."[5] (A year later, to his great embarrassment, the Montgolfier brothers took their first balloon ride, proving at least "flying ships" were not lunacy.)

In the early 1800s, dowsing found a champion in the German scientist Johann Wilhelm Ritter. Ritter is known today as the father of electrochemistry. Ritter was a man of many talents. He discovered ultraviolet light and invented the dry cell battery. Ritter conducted a wide range of laboratory experiments on dowsing, and tested famous dowsers like the Italian Francesco Campetti. Until this time, dowsing was primarily "field dowsing"—physically walking over a field with a dowsing stick and getting a movement from the rod. But Ritter also experimented with pendulums in place of dowsing sticks, and based on his experiments decided that the pendulum apparently could sometimes be mentally commanded or employed (like an Ouija board) to provide a "yes" or "no" movement (answer) to abstract questions, not just merely react to the physical presence of water or minerals.

This opened up the possibility of "information dowsing"—simply asking the pendulum whether water could be found on a piece of property at a specific location; or asking a yes or no answer to possible locations of lost objects (Did I leave my wallet at the restaurant? Are my keys somewhere here in the kitchen?) But if Ritter's experiments were correct, it also meant that dowsing required more than just a physical theory (i.e. a chemical, electrical or magnetic field) to explain it. It required some sort of a non-physical (mental, psychological or spiritual) hypothesis to account for the dowsing rod or pendulum's ability to answer abstract questions, or work on an abstract representation of earth (a map) instead of having to pass over the physical ground.

By the late 1800s, several British dowsers had become famous enough to attract the attention of Sir William Barrett, a physicist and one of the founders of England's Society for Psychical Research. One dowser, John Mullins, stood out as exceptionally talented. In his classic book *The Divining Rod*, Barrett and his co-author Theodore Besterman describe three notable scientific experiments in dowsing, one of which—the "John Mullins-Waterford Experiment"—they describe as "one of the strongest cases we possess." Under tight scrutiny to prevent any kind of fraud, Mullins succeeded in locating water in a rocky formation shunned by experts, while also stating before drilling began the precise depth the water would be found. And he did so after two attempts by professional engineers and an attempt by the best geologist in England had completely failed.

Barrett and Besterman personally investigated the case, interviewed witnesses and reviewed and verified a wealth of written documents, reports and correspondence related to the event. The famous event started in January 1897 when the owner of a bacon curing factory in Waterford, Ireland hired professional geologists to locate a large, steady water supply for his business. The first company, from Glasgow, Scotland, drilled down almost 300 feet with little to show for the effort. After they failed, the Diamond Rock Boring Co. of London was brought in and drilled down over 1000 feet at the spot they felt was most promising. They failed. The factory owner, increasingly desperate, called in the best expert in the field, G.H. Kinahan, Senior Geologist of the Irish Geological Survey. Kinahan used all his scientific knowledge to chose a spot to drill, and it too produced only a trickle. Having exhausted all "scientific" attempts to find water, the owner finally—with some reluctance and skepticism—turned to John Mullins. To prevent Mullins from secretly scouting the location and talking to people beforehand (Mullins had never been to Waterford or even South Ireland before), the owner deliberately had a clerk meet Mullins at the ferry dock on Mullins' arrival from England, and personally accompany him directly to the site, observing him all the time. Using his customary hazel twig dowsing stick, Mullins walked the property till the stick suddenly twisted in his hands. He announced that, if the owner drilled there, he would find at a depth of 80-90 feet an underground stream that would produce about 1,500 gallons per hour. The owner bored there and found a source at 79 feet that produced 1,672 gallons per hour when tested. Concluded the owner in a letter obtained by Barrett, "It is a most curious thing, but must be genuine without a doubt."

Barrett also received a written report from another eyewitness to the Mullins-Waterford event, an amateur geologist named Budd who answered some possible objections by skeptics. Had Mullins been tipped off by the faces of people around him during his dowsing in terms of selecting a favorable spot to drill? Impossible, said Budd.

Everyone at the site had already given up hope of finding water, and "one of their principal persons utterly scoffed at the idea of the twigs." Had Mullins been prepped beforehand on the geology of the property? Budd had cross-examined the company clerk that had met Mullins at the dock when he arrived. "He was warned to answer no questions as to wells, water or strata. Mullins did not ask him a single question."

By the early 1900s, scientists were exploring X-rays and radioactivity emissions, providing new possibilities to those who believed in a physical explanation of dowsing, while those favoring a non-physical explanation continued to argue their hypotheses.

In the 1920s and 1930s, Yale medical school Professor Dr. Harold Saxon Burr pioneered important research into organizing "life fields" or energy fields. Burr argued that all living things (humans, animals, plants, microscopic organisms) possessed an energy field, or "life field" that was physical in nature. He promoted an electrodynamic theory of life that enjoys some support today, with biomagnetics and bioelectric energy fields the focus of serious ongoing research. Some dowsers believe this is the energy field being "read" by dowsers.

Whatever the ultimate explanation to the riddle of dowsing, skeptics continue to reject dowsing and hundreds of dowsers around the world continue to have success with it.

Given the worldwide rise in population and diminishing water resources, "field dowsers" continue to be in demand around the globe. Here in America, the U.S. Geological Service and water dowsers have waged on off-and-on war with each other for decades. The USGS in a 1966 pamphlet entitled "Water Witching" called dowsing "wholly discredited" as far as scientists were concerned, prompting a counterattack by the American Society of Dowsers that eventually forced the USGS to withdraw the pamphlet, rewrite it in a more objective, neutral tone, and reissue it. Ironically, and embarrassing to the USGS, at the same time that the USGS was ridiculing dowsing, three sister agencies—the

Bureau of Land Management, the U.S. Soil Conservation Service, and the National Parks Service—were apparently using dowsers.[6]

Allied with the USGS against water dowsers is the National Water Well Association and most professional well drillers. Dowsers sometimes compete with NWWA drillers for well locating contracts. According to Bird, the NWWA considers dowsing unscientific superstition and an embarrassment to professional well drillers. Water dowsers respond by pointing to some spectacular successes by experienced dowsers in head-to-head competition with professional well drillers, geologists and hydrologists.

"Field dowsers" have also occasionally been used with some documented success to find hidden or buried archeological ruins. Among the tested archeological dowsers is Belgian Paul Margraff, who has apparently located buried foundations of castles, cloisters, houses and villages in his career.[7]

"Information dowsing" is growing in popularity but has seen fewer scientific experiments than field dowsing. It has been employed in a variety of tasks, including diagnosing medical conditions, finding lost people and objects and predicting events.

Despite its rejection by skeptics, dowsing continues to flourish. Dowsing societies exist in over 30 countries around the world. The American Society of Dowsers (ASD) has over 2,000 members in 50 states and 15 foreign countries. Each summer, the American Society of Dowsers offers a two-day Basic Dowsing School for beginners and an Expanded Dowsing School for experienced dowsers. The ASD catalogue of publications available on dowsing runs 20 pages. Stories of dowsing successes continue to be reported in national and local newspapers; in popular, mass circulation magazines like *Reader's Digest*; and on TV programs.

A small number of controlled, scientific experiments have been conducted on dowsing by scientists and academics over the last 100 years.[8] Among them are well-known tests done by skeptic and French

Academy of Sciences member Armand Vire; by English physicist and Royal Society fellow Sir William Barrett; and German physics professor Hans-Dieter Betz in the 1990s (see "Best Evidence" below). In America, U.S. physicist Zaboj Harvalik conducted a series of interesting dowsing experiments. Harvalik, born in the former Czechoslovakia, served as a physicist and scientific advisor to the U.S. Army's Advanced Material Concepts Agency. He did extensive controlled research on field dowsing (as opposed to information dowsing) and developed an electromagnetic theory that attempts to explain dowsers' ability to find underground water or buried electrical pipes. Harvalik's experiments make the case that the human body is extremely sensitive not only to man-made electromagnetic signals such as radio and TV waves but also to slight gradients or changes in the earth's natural magnetic field. Such anomalies are associated with underground running water and electrical currents running through buried pipes. Dowsing rods, sticks or pendulums might simply act as feedback or amplifying devices to help the dowser recognize these slight magnetic anomalies. Dowsers can increase their sensitivity to these anomalies by focusing their attention on the task, thus "intention" and concentration are important tools of dowsers. And what does Harvalik say about non-field dowsing (e.g. information, map, or remote dowsing)? Harvalik had some success himself with these forms of dowsing, but the physics underlying them remained a puzzle to him. [9]

But most professional dowsers, and the people who hire them, aren't interested in trying to prove the reality of dowsing in a laboratory.[10].As Bird explains, "Its *effectiveness* is the only sure proof of dowsing." Professional dowsers get hired because they deliver results; they don't want or need a seal of approval from science. Some of the best evidence for dowsing, then, comes from the documented track records of highly successful dowsers who have received thousands of dollars for their services from companies satisfied with their work Dowsing experts agree that dowsing is a skill that requires practice, and that no dowser is correct 100 percent. But some dowsers have a long, documented history of consistent successes that greatly defy the odds and exceed chance expectations. The use of dowsing by Swiss pharmaceutical company Hoffman-LaRoche is another example of good evidence for dowsing—it's not a controlled experiment in a laboratory, but the fact that a modern corporation will hire and pay a dowser hard cash is a strong vote of confidence in the reality of dowsing.

Best Scientific Evidence

Hans Dieter Betz–German Ministry of Research 1986 Experiments

In 1986, Hans Dieter Betz, a University of Munich physics professor, conducted a $250,000 study for the German Ministry of Research to examine the work and claims of dowsers like engineer Hans Schroeter (see below) who used dowsing during his German government-sponsored technical assistance program in Sri Lanka. The three-year, double-blind study included the hiring of a professional magician to inspect the test setup and help eliminate the possibility of cheating. Over 40 dowsers participated in the experiments which are described in a report called "Wunschelruten" (Dowsing Rods)[11] The report, reviewed by a special government commission before its publication, concluded that the dowsing phenomenon was indeed genuine. According to the report, "Some few dowsers, in particular tasks, showed an extraordinarily high rate of success, which can scarcely if at all be explained as due to chance...a real core of dowser-phenomena can be regarded as empirically proven." Leaving skeptics to wrestle with this study,[12] Betz later conducted additional controlled experiments in dowsing which provide further support for the possibility that at least some dowsers can to locate water better than trained hydrogeologists. In 1995, a detailed report describing these later experiments appeared in the *Journal of Scientific Exploration*.[13] A summary of some of the arguments pro and con regarding these tests are found in an article in *Science News.*[14]

Betz is perhaps Europe's leading researcher of the dowsing phenomenon. Like Professor Hans Bender whose research on poltergeists significantly changed German public opinion (see chapter on "Ghosts and Poltergeists"), Betz is credited with helping change attitudes in Germany regarding the dowsing phenomenon. The German government's involvement in dowsing research incensed professional skeptic James Randi who attacked it in a *Time* magazine essay entitled "Help Stamp Out Absurd Beliefs."[15] But the German National Service for Geological Sciences and the geological community in Germany reacted favorably and opened a dialogue with Betz and the dowsing community.

Armand Vire 1913 Tests

One of the most famous earlier scientific tests of dowsing was conducted in 1913 by biologist, skeptic and French Academy of Sciences member Armand Vire. Before conducting his tests, he felt that "anything concerning dowsing seemed to me wholly cockeyed and unjustifiable."[16] Determined to stop such a "superstitious fairy tale," he devised a test to see if dowsers could accurately locate underground caverns throughout the city of Paris, a network which he himself knew had been precisely mapped but the results never published and were held under lock and key. Vire had access to the maps because he was a specialist on organisms living in underground caverns. The results of the experiments turned him into a believer in dowsing. Some of the dowsers were able to accurately find not only the location but also the depth and width of the hidden chambers. One dowser was even able to determine whether water was flowing in a pipe buried 30 feet below the ground—and when the water in the pipe was turned off and on. As Vire later noted, "One can imagine how the precise data collected profoundly unsettled my skepticism." He admitted that dowsing skills varied, but accepted the basic reality of dowsing. "Are not many doctors insufficiently prepared to practice their art, or engineers of markedly inferior quality? Likewise, there are dowsers and there are dowsers."

Many eminent French scientists joined him in his acceptance of dowsing's reality, and the French Academy went on to establish a commission to study dowsing. Their 1921 report includes some interesting experiments which provide support for the existence of dowsing. French scientist and Nobel Laureate Charles Richet was among those who believed in the reality of dowsing. "We must accept dowsing as a fact," he declared. "It is useless to work up experiments merely to prove its existence. It exists. What is needed is its development."[17]

Barrett 1899 Carrigoona Experiment

After years of studying cases like the Mullins-Waterford event, Sir William Barrett finally decided to conduct his own personally supervised experiment in dowsing. His famous Carrigoona experiment, conducted in county Wicklow, Ireland with two different dowsers, was a scientifically well-designed and executed field experiment. To produce results that could survive skeptical scrutiny, he set several requirements: 1) the place chosen for the experiment had to be entirely unfamiliar to the dowser; 2) the person accompanying the dowser also had to be ignorant of the geology of the area; 3) the dowser had to be taken directly and immediately to the spot, without being able to talk to any local inhabitants; 4) the test site must not be immediately recognized by geologists as being either promising or unpromising in terms of its potential for producing water; 5) A professional geologist would accompany the dowser as an independent observer, and make a written record of everything that happened for subsequent verification and review by others. The successful outcome of that controlled scientific experiment, personally supervised by Barrett, is described in considerable detail (16 pages, plus photos, maps and sketches) in his book *The Divining Rod*.[18] Barrett summed up the experiment by noting that two dowsers, led independently to two fields, in a locality unknown to both, had both chosen the same unusual (from a purely geological perspective) site for drilling; and their predictions had been upheld by the test borings. "We have thus an experiment which conclusively proves the reality of dowsing."[19]

Hans Schroeter

Engineer Hans Schroeter was one of the dowsers whose work was studied by Hans–Dieter Betz. Schroeter was part of a German-government sponsored technical assistance group sent to Sri Lanka to help that underdeveloped country. When a serious drought hit the district he was helping, Schroeter used his dowsing skills to help locate over 600 wells in 350 towns and villages in just three years. His exploits are documented in a 1988 report entitled "Wasser Fur Alle" (Water For All) written by Eckhard Schleberger and issued by the GTZ, the agency Schroeter served.[20] Using a forked dowsing stick, Schroeter was also able on average to beat the results of conventional well drillers in terms of both the quantity and quality of water located.

James W. Kidd

I can't help adding this case, since it involves my old stomping grounds, New England. A former dairy farmer turned professional dowser, Kidd was working with an excavation contractor when he came to the attention of the posh, private Misquamicut Golf Club in Rhode Island in 1966. Kidd's talents were well known. His employer was so sure of Kidd's skills that he guaranteed his clients he would find water for them, and backed it up with a fixed-price drilling contract (few professional well drillers will guarantee a client they will find water for them; even fewer will offer a fixed-price drilling contract since they are not sure at what level they will hit water).

The Misquamicut Club was about to close its golf course after a four-year long drought had made it impossible for them to irrigate their course. They had broken the bank hiring geological consultants and professional well drillers to help them find water and they had failed. The consultant said no major source of fresh water existed in the district, and the test well they dug anyway turned up only salty water. Then one club director finally got up enough courage to suggest trying a dowser, and Kidd was contacted based on his reputation of success throughout New England. In one hour, using a fork cut from a black cherry tree, he identified a source of fresh water on the property, marked the site, declared the water would be found 24 feet below ground, and would produce a minimum of 34,000 gallons of water a day. When the site was drilled, the water was found at 26 feet and the flow exceeded 144,000 gallons a day. A second fresh water vein located by Kidd produced twice the volume as the first. According to Bird, ten years later both wells were still capable of producing 80 gallons a minute each (230,000 gallons a day).[21] Kidd's feat is particularly impressive given the fact that professional well drillers had failed, and professional geologists—using the scientific knowledge of their industry—had declared the site not suitable for finding water.

Paul C. Brown

Brown's dowsing work as a "doodlebugger" in the oil industry is well documented, particularly his work with famous oil wildcatter J.K. Wadley. The oil industry can normally expect to locate one producing oil or gas well for every 25 they drill. Brown repeatedly beat that average using his dowsing skills. His predictions were also normally very detailed, leaving no "wiggle room" for excuses. For example, on one well he dowsed for the Standard Oil Co., he predicted "Well will discover a new field. Oil, sand about 40 feet thick at about 7,900 feet." The results? The well tapped a new oil field, with oil produced from 7,904 to 7,943 feet depth.[22] According to Bird, ten wells dowsed by Brown for Wadley in the 1950s were later sold to Occidental Petroleum and formed the basis for that famous company's entrance into the oil business.

Interestingly enough, Brown used a pendulum instead of a forked stick to do his dowsing. It took him time to develop his skills, and he admits he made many mistakes in the beginning, but he learned from them and improved his skills that way.

Highly Recommended Reading:

Bird, Christopher. *The Divining Hand: The 500-Year Old Mystery of Dowsing.* Atglen, Pa.: Schiffer Publishing, 1993, 372 pp. The best book in the field, period. A must read if you're interested in detailed history and solid, footnoted research on the subject. The book was first published in 1979, and in the new edition Bird added a 31-page Epilogue which offers multiple, documented examples of successful dowsing. Declared *New York Times* book reviewer Doris Grumbach, "It is difficult to maintain skepticism in the face of such convincing and well-written arguments." Schiffer Publishing came out with an edition in 1997 which you can order online through Amazon or Barnes & Noble. Bird is also famous as the co-author with Peter Tompkins of the classic *The Secret Life of Plants* which described experiments suggesting that plants can sense and have emotions, like animals and man.

Barrett, Sir William and Theodore Besterman. *The Divining Rod: An Experimental and Psychological Investigation.* New Hyde Park, NY: University Books, 1968, 336 pp. This book is found in most big-city libraries. You can also usually find a copy for sale at www.abebooks.com. The book includes detailed descriptions of scientific investigations of famous French, British and American dowsers (including full details of the John Mullin-Waterford experiment described by the authors as among the best cases they uncovered in their years of research); the Carrigoona dowsing experiment described above in "Best Scientific Evidence;" and a discussion of possible hypotheses as to why it works (both Barrett and Bird concluded the dowsing phenomenon is real). In many ways, Europe is ahead of the

U.S. in scientifically examining the phenomenon of dowsing, and accepting the application of dowsing for commercial purposes. Until Bird's book, this was the best book available on scientific investigations of dowsing.

9.

The Mind-Body Connection:
Mental and Faith Healing

Note: This chapter on mental and faith healing is not meant to serve in any way as a substitute for the medical advice of a physician. The reader should regularly consult a physician in matters relating to his health, and should not attempt any form of mental or faith healing without first seeking the advice and consent of his physician.

Can the non-physical thoughts, attitudes and beliefs in our mind directly affect our physical bodies and physical health, and the health of those around us? Medical science accepts that they can. Anxiety before a math exam can give a nervous student a stomach ache. Fear of making a speech can make you break out in a sweat. A word of praise can sometimes make you blush. A sudden surprise can make your heart race.

The real debate is *how much* of an effect our non-physical thoughts, attitudes and beliefs can have on the physical body. What is the limit? Can thoughts erase a wart? Kill a cancerous tumor? Reverse heart disease? Change your blood chemistry? Allow you to undergo a major operation without anesthesia? Can happy or sad thoughts directly affect your body at the cellular level, actually increasing the number of natural killer cells in your bloodstream to boost your immune system? Can emotional support in the form of prayers, or simple, sympathetic words of comfort, actually extend your life if you have a terminal illness?

If our mind can bend a spoon, can it also bend another piece of matter—our bodies—to its will? If so, how far? What's possible? What's impossible?

In the late 1970s, I had my own small but meaningful experience with the healing power of the mind. I fell ill to a heart arrhythmia problem called premature ventricular tachycardia. When it was discovered, my doctor warned me that the condition had the potential of becoming a life-threatening condition if the heart's electrical system went haywire and into fibrillation. I was even more nervous when, after a battery of tests, they couldn't find any specific, physical cause for the racing, irregular heartbeat. They eventually gave me a pill called Quinaglute to take three times a day for the rest of my life and told me to live with it. And for a while I did. I was nervous when jogging or doing heavy physical labor for fear of setting the heart off and racing towards the nightmare of fibrillation where the heart quivers uselessly out of sync until you pass out and die.

But soon the fear was replaced by anger. I was not going to be dependent on pills all my life if I could avoid it. The doctor's didn't know the cause, but I determined I would try and read up on everything I could about heart arrhythmias and their possible causes. Then one day I came across Dr. Hans Selye's classic book on stress and its effects on the body. One of the possible effects of stress, I learned, was heart arrhythmias. I felt I had a clue, one that perhaps the doctors had missed because, on the surface, I looked like a very laid-back and relaxed person.

In reality, I was a business magazine editor with a stressful, deadline-oriented job and thus a high level of anxiety in my life. Could stress be one of the conditions causing my heart problem? I decided to see if I could reduce stress and make a difference in the frequency and duration of my missed heartbeats which had continued spasmodically even under medication. As a Peace Corps Volunteer in Thailand, I had learned a Thai form of meditation at Wat Bovorniwet Buddhist monastery where I taught English. I started to mediate 15, 30 and finally 45 minutes a day. I also bought a cheap biofeedback instrument called a Galvanic Skin Response (GSR) device that allowed me to monitor the resistance of the skin on my fingertips to the passage of a very small electrical current. As stressful thoughts entered my mind, electrical resistance changed and the GSR produced a higher pitched sound as output. When I was relaxed, the sound was a low pitch. In a few days of practice, by relaxing my body and mind through meditation, I was able to bring the sound down lower and lower and keep it there, a signal that I was no longer in stress.

A few weeks later, I began to notice that my missed heartbeats were becoming more and more infrequent. The meditation and biofeedback were producing a "relaxation response" that continued even after my meditation was done. I was also much more aware by this time of what kinds of thoughts and emotions produced stress in my body. When anxious thoughts appeared, I was aware that they were causing stress to my heart, and I worked to better control my emotions.

A year later I returned to the doctor for my annual treadmill test. He commented that my arrhythmia seemed to be well under control, and attributed it to the Quinaglute drug. I told him about my meditation and biofeedback work, and why I thought stress might be a factor in my illness. I also told him I wanted to gradually reduce, and ultimately eliminate, the drug use completely. He wisely warned me of the potentially grave risks of discontinuing the drug, but I was determined to slowly but surely try life without the drug. Over the next three years, I continued to meditate nightly and, against his advice, slowly reduced the dosage of the Quinaglute. At the end of that period, I felt confident enough to discontinue it completely. Even then, for a while longer I kept a bottle of tablets handy as backup, which reduced my anxiety about going off the drug. Twenty years later, I'm still off drugs, and I'm still meditating regularly.

Was there a direct cause-effect relationship between my meditation and my improved heart rhythm? It would be very hard to prove. A whole number of other factors may have contributed to the eventual reduction in tachycardia. Medically speaking, it was a foolish and dangerous thing to do—and *I would not recommend my actions to anyone.* But I was willing to take the consequences and did so. Today, I continue to read with interest the growing body of literature describing the intimate relationship between the mind and the body. We're all learning as we go, including the science of medicine.

Edward Jenner (1749-1823) is famous for the discovery of a vaccine against smallpox, a discovery that laid the foundations of modern immunology as a science. What is not so famous or well known is the response of the Royal Society, England's scientific establishment, to Jenner's medical discovery. They dismissed his evidence without examination and his idea with the following rebuke: "He ought not to risk his reputation by presenting to the learned body anything which appears so much at variance with established knowledge, and withal so incredible."[1]

The history of medicine is filled with such embarrassing moments. As it turned out, the only thing incredible was the failure of the best medical minds of the day to take an unbiased look at a controversial new medical treatment. Fortunately, good ideas have a way of surviving censure (Jenner's did). Medical knowledge continues to advance under the prodding of heretics and visionaries, walking a precarious tightrope between life-threatening quackery and equally life-threatening scientific hubris.

Though mind-body medicine studies are slowly changing attitudes, mental healing or faith healing largely remains a suspect idea today to a medical establishment that still operates on a philosophy of mechanistic materialism. According to this belief, a human being is a wondrously complex collection of atoms, cells and chemicals—but nothing more. Bodily illnesses have physical causes (germs, viruses, accidents, injuries, bad genes, bad diet, etc.) and require physical cures (drugs and surgery being the Big Two of modern medicine). You can't pray away a cancerous lump in your breast; you can't change your immune system with a thought. The odd, spontaneous cure that occurs without physical intervention is simply the impersonal laws of chance at work. Sometimes you win, sometimes you lose.

Reflecting this world view, modern medicine has downplayed the importance of our mental thoughts, belief, emotions, wishes, intentions and attitudes in significantly shaping our physical health. But this is a rather recent attitude.

As medical researcher Larry Dossey, M.D. notes, historically physicians commonly believed the opposite of what physicians believe today. For example, up to the 20th century, both doctors and the patients they treated accepted that the mind could help determine the course of cancer.[2] But scientific attention has since focused almost exclusively on matter, to the point where, for medicine, mind barely counts (and soul doesn't exist).

Yet the evidence for the physical effects of mental intervention are extensive. Take the humble placebo effect, for example. A "placebo effect" has been defined as the psychological or physiological outcome of a pill, injection, or surgical procedure with no known intrinsic effects.

A while back, a group of Mexican women were given what they were told was a contraceptive pill. The women took the pill and soon began reporting common reactions to contraceptive pills, including "decreased libido, increased headache, bloating of the abdomen, dizziness, stomach pain, nervousness, nausea, anorexia, acne, blurred vision and palpitations."[3] Truth was, it wasn't a contraceptive pill at all. It was a simple sugar tablet, a placebo. How can a plain sugar pill cause blurry vision? Nausea? Bloating of the stomach? Stomach pains? Acne?

Dizzy spells? Headaches? Welcome to the world of mind over matter. The sugar didn't cause those bodily physical reactions. The mind of the person that ate the pill—responding to words from a doctor—caused the physical reactions. They simply believed they were getting a contraceptive, and their physical bodies reacted as if it were true. Mental belief created physical reality.

The placebo effect in some ways is an embarrassment to modern medical theory. It doesn't play by the rules laid down by a materialistic world view. Indeed, it appears to violate scientific laws of cause and effect. How can a worthless sugar pill combined with words from a doctor ("This is a contraceptive pill") produce the same dramatic physical effects on the human body as a real chemical drug (often developed with a multi-million dollar budget in a laboratory by trained scientists in a multinational pharmaceutical company)? Yet it does. And science is getting more and more interested in how and why the placebo effect works.

Krippner notes that all sorts of factors can contribute to an effective placebo—it's reputation as treatment, the patient's expectations regarding it, the physician's belief in his own diagnosis, even the color, shape or size of a pill.[4]

In the Mexican case, the physical effect was negative. But the placebo effect can also heal. Placebo studies published in medical journals have suggested that placebos have the power to produce a variety of physical, bodily cures.

Michael Murphy is perhaps best known as the co-founder of the California-based Esalen Institute, a major influence on the popular culture of the United States and the shaping of the "New Age" movement—particularly in terms of experiments in human potential. In his fascinating book *The Future of the Body*, he presents a number of thought-provoking studies on the placebo effect.[5] For example, a famous 1955 Harvard University study reviewed 15 double blind experiments done with placebos on 1,082 subjects. It found that the simple placebo alone produced a cure rate of 35 percent on a wide variety of medical problems, including postoperative pain, headaches, colds, angina pectoris discomfort, seasickness and nausea, among others. Noted researcher Henry Beecher, "Many 'effective' drugs have power only a little greater."[6] In other words, the mind alone was nearly as effective as modern drugs in producing physical cures for these tested (though not life-threatening) conditions.

In another double-blind clinical study [7] cited by Murphy, doctors used real medicine (sulpharsphenamine) to treat the warts of a group of 105 patients, with a resulting 53 percent cure rate. The same doctors also tried curing the warts of another 120 patients using nothing but colored, distilled water given as a placebo. Some 48 percent of these patients saw a complete remission of their warts. In short, the mind, tricked by a placebo, was just about as effective as a modern drug in eliminating warts.

Documented clinical studies have shown the placebo effect has successfully relieved or cured hay fever, coughing, insomnia and sleep disorders, colds, headaches, diabetes, peptic ulcers, seasickness, and various kinds of pain including angina pectoris; reduced obesity and urinary incontinence; matched the effectiveness of anti-arthritic pills in treating the symptoms of arthritis and the effectiveness of chemical anti-depressants in treating depression; and treated anxiety. Placebos can speed up or slow down a heartbeat rate; alter moods and perceptions, produce observable calm or its opposite, nervousness; and even produce feelings of euphoria.

In 1956, psychiatrist Arthur Shapiro reviewed 100 years worth of medical journals to see what patterns of treatment emerged. He found that medical fads came and went, producing good results for a while before disappearing. *Something* seemed to work, but what was it? The evidence suggested that the constant "something" might be the placebo effect, and that the history of medicine was basically the history of placebo effects—the power of the mind to believe. [8]

There is some fascinating evidence to support Shapiro's argument that the effectiveness of many medical treatments is not due to the treatments themselves, but to the placebo effect—if the medical community enthusiastically believes in a treatment, it often works; but if they stop believing, the therapy often stops working. For example, a study conducted by Dr. Herbert Benson and David McCallie, and published in the *New England Journal of Medicine* in 1979, reviewed the history of over a dozen medical treatments used for angina pectoris. The list included heart muscle extract, pancreatic extract, various hormones, x-irradiation, anticoagulants, monoamine oxidase inhibitors, thyroidectomies, radioactive iodine, sympathectomies, various vitamins, choline, meprobate, ligation of the internal mammary artery, epicardial abrasions, and even cobra venom! The authors noted that most of the therapies tried started off very effective but later were abandoned as ineffective. Indeed, most of these once-successful therapies were later found to have *no specific physiological effect on angina*. Then what made these scientifically worthless therapies effective in the first place? The placebo effect, concluded Benson and McCallie. Their suggestion to doctors? Don't ridicule or disregard placebos—they're cheap, safe, and have withstood the test of time. Use them. If Benson and McCallie are correct, the minds of doctors and patients—their beliefs and mental attitudes—can apparently transform a scientifically worthless therapy into an effective medical treatment. The mind is an active healer.

Indeed, various mental healing procedures are now being used by millions of people in an attempt to utilize the potential of the mind to heal the physical body. They include hypnosis and suggestion, biofeedback, meditation, visualization, emotions management, and old-fashioned prayer, a form of mental healing humans have used for millenia which is attracting fresh attention from scientists.

A placebo relies on a physical intervention to trick the patient into healing himself. Having something physical which the patient can see or touch (a sugar pill, a saline solution injection, or in earlier times perhaps a sacred stone, feather or drink) gives the patient something to focus his mind on. In reality, however, you apparently don't even need a physical placebo to help the mind produce a dramatic physical change in the body. You can produce many of the same effects using nothing but words—in the form of a suggestion which the patient is willing to accept and believe in.

British medical research, for example, has confirmed that if a doctor suggests that a patient will get well quickly, such patients improve faster than patients who weren't given such optimistic forecasts.[9] What caused the accelerated healing? The patient's belief in the doctor's words. Belief can sometimes even change bad medicine into good. Krippner cites a study where a group of people with upset stomachs were given a medicine actually designed to worsen their nausea, but were told it would help their stomachs.[10] Belief triumphed. A verbal suggestion was more powerful than physical matter (a medicine) in determining how the body would react.

Receiving suggestions while in a hypnotic trance has often proven even more powerful.[11] The power of the mind while in a hypnotic trance has been used to successfully treat a number of physical and mental conditions and manage pain. Hypnosis is now generally considered part of mainstream medical practice (though in 2001 you can still find a breathless article in *Scientific American* written by skeptical editors declaring their surprise over their findings).[12] Its acceptance by Science can make us forget that hypnosis used for medical intervention is really a form of mental healing.

Indeed, hypnotism started out as a healing therapy. The Austrian medical doctor Franz Mesmer is credited with drawing the Western world's attention to the powers of hypnotism in the late 1700s. His theory of "animal magnetism," which incorrectly combined various insights into magnetism and healing, eventually fell by the wayside, but not before one of his disciples, the Marquis de Puysegur, accidentally produced a hypnotic trance in one of his patients. Puysegur explored the hypnotic trance phenomenon in a variety of experiments and is credited with discovering most of the features now associated with hypnotism. Due to Mesmer's fame, the new trance phenomenon became known as "mesmerism."

What mental healing feats can the mind do under hypnotic suggestion? Studies cited by Murphy suggest that it can speed healing from burns; relieve or eliminate herpes, psoriasis, dermatitis and fish-skin disease, help treat asthma; relieve allergies; and control gastric acid secretions.[13] The human skin is especially amenable to suggestion. Using hypnosis, researchers are able to produce *real, physical blisters,* bruises and skin inflammations on test subjects *simply with words—a suggestion.* Hundreds of tests have been conducted in this area confirming the power of thought alone to produce such dramatic physical changes to the skin. In one experiment cited by Murphy, a hypnotist suggested to a woman that she was sitting on a sunny beach. The skin on her face, arms and shoulders turned beet red. Her body responded as if the suggestion were reality.

One of the most dramatic features of the hypnotic trance is the ability of many entranced subjects to ignore pain using just the mind. By the mid-1800s, notes Murphy, some European doctors were using hypnotism (the new term for mesmerism) to serve as an anesthesia during surgery. Using hypnotism alone, they were apparently able to perform an astounding array of surgical operations including amputations of arms, legs, fingers, breasts, penises and a wide variety of tumors; and do teeth extractions and cataract operations. Thanks simply to the power of the mind, the patient could allow the doctor to hack, saw and cut off various limbs without feeling significant pain during the procedure.[14]

Despite these successes, hypnotism in the West never became commonplace in surgery, and eventually lost out to ether and chloroform as the surgical anesthesia of choice. Not everyone could be hypnotized to the depth necessary to block out pain, whereas ether and chloroform worked with or without your help. The physical treatment (ether or chloroform) was easier to use, less risky and more predictable and reliable than using the mind. But the ability of the mind in a hypnotic trance to control pain continued to attract investigators. In the late 1800s, France's greatest neurologist, Jean-Martin Charcot, brought new respect to hypnotism while greatly advancing understanding of the hypnotic trance and how it operated. Other French medical doctors and scientists experimented with the power of suggestion and developed hypnotic therapies for various physical and mental illnesses. U.S. researchers made valuable contributions to hypnotism starting in the 1930s, and in the early 1960s developed the Stanford Hypnotic Susceptibility Scales that helped define the types of personalities most susceptible to suggestion and hypnotic procedures.

As an anesthesia, hypnotism continues to see limited use, but the power of the mind to control pain is still astonishing. In 1979, researchers Josephine and Ernest Hilgard published a list of operations conducted between 1955-1974 that employed hypnotism rather than drugs or other anesthetics to control pain. They included appendectomies, Cesarean section birth deliveries, mammoplasties, breast tumor excisions, vaginal hysterectomies, skin grafts and even cardiac surgery.[15] In terms of chronic pain, a technology assessment panel at the National Institutes of Health is now on record as judging hypnosis to be effective intervention for alleviating pain from cancer and other chronic conditions. In fact, the degree of pain relief can match or exceed that provided by morphine.[16] Under hypnosis, the mind can also apparently control the flow of blood from a cut or incision, increasing, reducing or stopping it altogether during dental and medical surgery or after an injury.[17]

In addition to controlling pain and blood flow, the mind under hypnosis has also demonstrated its ability to eliminate physical growths on the body. As we saw above, the mind can make warts disappear almost a well as medicine. In fact, a 1959 review of the medical literature by psychiatrist Montague Ullman concluded that suggestion was more effective than drugs or surgery in eliminating warts (not to mention much cheaper!).[18] Based on his research, Krippner has concluded that "There are few medical conditions today that cannot be improved if you know how to trigger the body's tremendous power to heal itself."[19]

Visualization researcher Jeanne Achterberg agrees with Krippner that the mind's ability to make a wart disappear holds tremendous implications for medicine since a wart is caused by a virus. The same process used to remove a wart is the same process for getting rid of cancer.[20] Achterberg, a professor of psychology and the author of *Imagery in Healing: Shamanism and Modern Medicine*, and *Rituals of Healing: Using Imagery for Health and Wellness*,[21] has done pioneering scientific research into how we mentally visualize the outcome of our disease and its effect on the ultimate outcome.

Besides hypnotic trance, another way to increase the mind's ability to affect the physical body is by means of biofeedback training. In combating my heart arrhythmia, I used an inexpensive biofeedback instrument to alert me to my level of stress. Once I could measure it, I could see the direct effect a calm thought had on reducing stress—calm thoughts made the tone produced by the GSR device fall. I could clearly hear the effect my mind was having on my physical body.

The invention of sensitive electrical and electronic machines like this has given us the ability to gain instant feedback about physical processes which Science long believed to be outside our voluntary control and manipulate them with the mind. Everyone knew we could voluntarily control our big muscles and skeletal actions. For instance, we could tell the muscles in our arm to reach into the refrigerator and our hand to grasp a milk carton, or tell our foot to raise itself to step up a stair, or tell our falling body to right itself before our ice skates slipped out from under us. But for many years, scientists believed humans could not voluntarily control or modify at will such activities as our heart rhythm, blood pressure, brain activity, skin temperature and other processes. For example, no one expected that humans could simply tell their hand to get warm and subsequently raise their hand temperature 3-4 degrees on demand. But scientists now say such things are indeed possible—and biofeedback training can help us apply our mind to the task of controlling and modifying these bodily functions once considered beyond the mind's control.

One of the earliest biofeedback instruments, developed before World War II, was an alarm system triggered by urine to help train children to stop bed-wetting. The availability of the electromyograph to measure muscle tension, the electrocardiograph to measure the electrical activity of the heart, the electroencephalograph to measure the electrical activity of the brain, and galvanic skin response (GSR) devices like I used for my arrhythmia problem open new ways to provide the mind with instantaneous feedback regarding these physical, bodily processes. Doing so can allow doctors and patients to try a mental process and see how it affects the body.

I later found studies of great interest to me that showed the mind, using biofeedback equipment under clinical test conditions, had the ability to regulate heartbeat in order to control, and sometimes even eliminate, such heart malfunctions as sinus tachycardias, fixed atrial fibrillation, and even my premature ventricular contractions.[22]

What other physical, body functions can the mind control? Using biofeedback, the mind has demonstrated its ability to voluntarily lower the body's blood pressure, helping reduce or eliminate hypertension.[23] One biofeedback experiment involved seven patients who had been using prescription medicines for hypertension for periods up to 20 years. After training in biofeedback, 6 of the 7 were able to control their blood pressure so well with just their minds (aided by feedback) that they completed eliminated the need for any medicine at all. And eight years later, they were still off medication, using biofeedback alone.[24]

Using feedback, the mind can actually isolate, pinpoint target and consciously control specific, single individual muscles or groups of muscles, allowing us to cure or relieve problems like facial tics, eyelid spasms, and the symptoms of cerebral palsy.[25] Using biofeedback, the mind can control the frontalis muscle to relieve tension headaches; and alleviate migraine headaches by redistributing blood flow through hands and feet [26]—an example of mind directly affecting matter: the flow of blood in the body. The mind, with the assistance of biofeedback instruments, can help epileptics control seizures by altering the brain's circuitry. In one medical study, it succeeded in reducing seizures in some 60 percent of the patients treated with biofeedback. And NASA has used biofeedback to teach astronauts to control motion sickness as well as 20 other physiological responses. Some 65 percent of astronauts using the technique were able to completely suppress their motion sickness symptoms. The first biofeedback-trained astronauts flew aboard the shuttle in 1985. Again, it's important to remind ourselves here that a machine (the biofeedback instrument) isn't causing the changes in the physical body—the mind is causing the changes in the physical body.

Besides hypnosis and biofeedback, there's a third proven method of improving mental control over our physical body—meditation. Scientific research on the use of meditation practices in healing stretches back to field research by Western scientists and academics in the 1930s on the mental powers of Indian yogis and Japanese Zen monks. Researchers were interested in testing claims that during meditation these adepts could, at will and on demand, control autonomic bodily functions like heartbeat, skin temperature, blood pressure, brain wave activity and breathing. Enough good research was produced to suggest that at least some humans, through years of intensive training, could indeed perform amazing feats of bodily control using only the mind.

In the late 1950s, psychologists Basu Bagchi of the U. of Michigan Medical Center and M.A. Wegner of UCLA spent five months traveling through India with a carload of scientific instruments that could register brain waves, skin temperature and skin conductance, respiration and finger blood-volume changes. Their studies appeared in serious American scientific journals and their conclusions, while cautious, suggested the image of the Indian fakir as faker was not always accurate. Others were encouraged to continue the research.

Researchers at the famed Menninger Foundation in Kansas tested one Indian yogi who could, at will, produce with his mind an 11 degree Fahrenheit difference between the left and right sides of the *same* palm, with one side turning pink from heat and the other turning gray from cold. Demonstrating his control over his heartbeat, the yogi also voluntarily produced, on demand, a heart fibrillation that raced at 306 beats a minutes and lasted 16 seconds.[27] Even more impressive was an experiment with a man with no yogic training who demonstrated the ability to voluntarily stop his heart—to produce cardiac arrest—on demand. EKG tests showed his heartbeat did indeed disappear completely. (As he began to faint from lack of blood, the subject would take a deep breath and revive himself.)[28]

In the early 1970s, landmark research on meditation conducted by Dr. Herbert Benson and Keith Wallace appeared in *Scientific American* and *Science* magazine at a time when thousands of young Americans were embracing Transcendental Meditation. Benson, a cardiologist and Harvard Medical School professor, pioneered research into the "relaxation response," a stress-reduced condition often generated during meditation. He spent his career researching the physiological effects of stress management and is the author of five books and more than 100 scientific papers on the subject. Ironically, for years he resisted publicly practicing what he preached—the relaxation response. Why? Apparently because he didn't want to be criticized for being an unscientific "believer" in squishy, New Age nonsense. (Which makes you wonder—if a Harvard professor is that afraid of what his peers think of such a relatively mild unorthodox idea, how much more pressure would an iconoclastic thinker from a smaller university feel about advancing evidence for mind-body healing? Today, Benson is President of Harvard's Mind/Body Medical Institute.)

In 1981, Benson and a group of researchers from the Harvard Medical School instrumented three Tibetan monks in India practicing a form of meditation called Tum-mo. The monks could take a blanket soaked in cold water, wrap it around themselves, and sit in the snow on a mountain top in a meditative trance. In the Harvard tests, the monks meditated for 55 minutes in an unheated, cold room, using their minds to raise their internal body temperature. The researchers attached sensors to measure temperature at their fingers, toes, lumbar region, navels, rectum, and nipples. All three monks produced dramatic body temperature changes. One 50-year old monk was able to raise the temperature of his toes by 15 degrees Fahrenheit; another 59-year old monk raised his finger and toe temperatures 11 and 12 degrees Fahrenheit respectively, and raised the overall temperature of the room he was meditating in by 2.7 degrees Fahrenheit. [29]

As Murphy notes, meditation research has come a long way since Bagchi and Wegner. Scientists have explored "cardiovascular, cortical, hormonal, and metabolic changes, several behavioral effects, and alterations of consciousness resulting from meditation," and experimental techniques and equipment used in meditation experiments have also improved tremendously. The results are uneven, the effects are not always consistent, but there is little doubt that the meditative mind can be used to significantly manipulate physical, bodily processes.

Hypnosis, biofeedback and meditation can all help the mind control the physical body and produce mental healing effects. Can visualization techniques do the same? Does our future health depend in part at least on what outcome we visualize in our minds? Researchers say a doctor's diagnosis usually sets a patient's mind visualizing the outcome predicted by the doctor. As a result, doctors have a dangerous power. A credible doctor giving a patient a fearful diagnosis can have the same effect as a Haitian witch giving a victim a hex, says Dr. Jeanne Achterberg, a psychology professor and leading visualization researcher.

What would run through your imagination if you were told you had cancer? Achterberg cites the case of a woman who had been given the diagnosis of breast cancer in its early stages. She died within hours of the diagnosis, leaving doctors amazed. The patient's early stage cancer couldn't have caused her death, notes Achterberg. More than likely, she feels, it was the patient's own imagination. The patient had seen her mother suffer and die from the same painful illness, and had declared she would not let herself suffer the same way. Faced with the same bleak diagnosis as her mother, her mind may have simply shut down her body's vital functions.[30] She visualized her death from cancer—although breast cancer is not automatically a death sentence—and her body enacted the visualized outcome.

Visualization of a diagnosis can also work the opposite way. Achterberg cites the case of a critically ill man whose heart was failing.[31] The patient overheard the doctor on his rounds say that the patient had a "wholesome gallop" to his heart—implying that the heart was actually failing. Despite this grim prognosis, the patient made a complete recovery. The next time he met the doctor, several months later during a follow-up check, he told the doctor he knew exactly what had gotten him better—when he overheard the doctor's observation that he had a wholesome gallop to this heart. The man mistakenly had assumed that the diagnosis meant he had a lot of kick and spirit to his heart. Therefore he knew he would get better. "The medical profession is omnipotent in creating imagery," argues Achterberg, and these powerful mental images "can determine life or death independently of any medical intervention."[32]

Using the imagination to create healing images was standard medical practice for centuries and is still widely used throughout the world. Traditional healers understood that mental images can create real, physiological changes in the body and acted accordingly. But modern medicine embraced Descartes philosophical world view that saw the mind and body as completely separate from each other. Mentally visualizing a healing situation and expecting a physical change in the body was useless, unscientific nonsense—a laughable form of superstitious quackery.

Today, clinical studies in visualization like Achterberg's (see "Best Evidence" below) conducted over the last two or three decades suggest that Descartes was wrong. The mind-body separation is a myth. The mind can indeed produce physical effects on the body.

In the emerging mental healing practice of visualization. the patient is encouraged to create personally-meaningful images, usually involving specific bodily changes they want to turn into reality; experience them on an emotional level during the exercise; and repeat the exercise a specified length of time and number of times.

A good example is a visualization exercise developed for a glaucoma patient by psychiatrist Dr. Gerald Epstein.[33] For almost eight years, the patient had been suffering from glaucoma, an illness involving insufficient drainage of fluid in the area surrounding the lens of the eye. This results in build-up of pressure and can eventually lead to blindness. The patient was taking three different medications at the time he started his visualization program. Working with the patient and the patient's physician, Epstein developed a three-week visualization program during which the patient discontinued the medication. Before the imagery program started, the patient looked at a picture of the eye area he was going to visualize in order to reinforce his visualizing powers. Then for 1-3 minutes three times a day, for three weeks, he conducted his visualization exercise. The exercise involved imagining a flow of air coming into the pupil every time the patient breathed in, sensing the air creating a ripple in the built-up aqueous fluid, and pushing the fluid away into the canal of Schlemm, a venous sinus which drains the fluid away from the eye. As the patient did so, he told himself that the ocular pressure had returned to normal. After the three weeks were finished, the patient's doctor confirmed that the glaucoma was gone and it was remaining normal without medication. Five years later, Epstein checked up on the patient. The patient was still maintaining normal ocular pressure using the visualization technique and the help of one medicine.

Achterberg has collected a number of dramatic cases of visualization's power to alter the physical body. In one instance, a physician was diagnosed with cancer of the pancreas, which normally leads to death within 3-5 months of diagnosis for 90 percent of those stricken with the disease. At the time Achterberg first met him, he had already lived for over a year and was taking a mild form of chemotherapy. He was also conducting visualization techniques each day in a Japanese garden. After putting himself into a state of near sleep, characterized by theta brain waves, he would imagine knights in shining armor spearing cancer cells in his blood stream. The patient managed to live 17 years past his diagnosis.[34]

Physicians, psychiatrists, psychologists and medical researchers have found visualization exercises helpful in varying degrees for a variety of other medical conditions. They include circulatory, digestive, skin, musculoskeletal, respiratory, immune and genitourinary disorders.[35] Controlled clinical studies have shown that in some cases—migraine headaches, for example—regularly practicing visualization techniques can be more effective than taking conventional medicine.[36] Visualized mental images, then, can directly affect critical physiological processes in our body.

If visualization can create mental scenes that directly heal our physical bodies, how about just looking at an actual pleasant scene? Believe it or not, the emotional lift gained from looking out a hospital window has been clinically proven to be a powerful medicine. Studies suggest that a patient who can look out of a window during recovery from certain types of surgery will have a shorter hospital stay than a patient denied that simple pleasure. Environmental conditions affect recovery rates.[37] Given that most hospitals today are huge, sterile, high-tech, impersonal factories, a view of trees, flowers, sunshine and perhaps the busy activity of healthy people outside a window may produce healing emotions of hope and joy.

Can the words spoken to us by other people—spouses, friends, neighbors, acquaintances and even strangers—help heal or kill us; wreck or restore our immune system; or increase or decrease our survival rate when suffering from a major illness? There's growing scientific evidence that the words spoken to us by those around us can indeed can do just that (the same goes for words we ourselves speak to others).

Imagine your boss comes in today and says "You're fired!" His words alone can produce mental emotions (anger, fear, anxiety) that produce tremendous physical effects to your body. The anger, fear and anxiety can cause intense stress, which, depending on how you emotionally react to the stress, can contribute to a variety of illnesses ranging from headaches and ulcers to cancer, heart attacks and cardiovascular disease. David Felten, M.D., is Adjunct Professor of Neurobiology and Anatomy at the University of Rochester School of Medicine, and Editor of the journal *Brain, Behavior and Immunity*. Felten points out that people are always warning each other not to get so stressed out that they become sick, not realizing that "there is an actual biological basis for that."[38]

Conversely, can kind words of love and encouragement from your spouse, friends or family reduce stress and help you to actually live longer if you have a serious illness like cancer? One intriguing clinical study suggests it can. Dr. David Spiegel, M.D., professor of psychiatry at Stanford University School of Medicine, conducted a landmark study in 1989 on the effects of psychosocial treatment on patients with metastatic breast cancer.[39] He found that standard cancer treatment combined with group emotional therapy not only improved the quality of life of these cancer patients, but also resulted in them living twice as long as persons who only received standard cancer therapies. Spiegel heads up Stanford University's Psychosocial Treatment Laboratory (www.med.stanford.edu/school/Psychiatry/PSTreatLab/) and is co-author of the 1999 book *Group Therapy for Cancer Patients* which presents the rationale, methods and results of intensive supportive care given to cancer sufferers.

Mind/body researcher and heart specialist Dr. Dean Ornish echoes Spiegel's belief that social isolation leads to stress, which in turn can lead to heart disease and other illnesses. Unfortunately, personal isolation is increasing in modern society as people disconnect from their families, churches, neighborhoods and community. Folk wisdom has always held that love and understanding is powerful medicine, and its presence helps keep us healthy. Feeling wanted and understood, accepted and loved by somebody; having someone you can talk to honestly and without pretense or concealment; someone with whom you can share your deepest fears and worries; someone who can give you a shoulder to cry on—these forms of emotional support are increasingly being clinically examined by scientists to try and measure more precisely what effect they have on physical health, illness and disease.

Several hard-nosed statistical studies suggest some real relationship between communicated emotional support—in the form of non-physical thoughts and words—and overall physical health and longevity. For example, statistics show married people with cancer live longer than unmarried cancer patients.[40] The same is true for isolation's effect on heart disease, says Ornish. In fact, he argues, isolation hurts the health of just about everyone. Studies exist demonstrating that isolated individuals suffer three to five times higher mortality rates from all causes compared to people who remain connected to others. And the rate has been shown to be independent of such factors as the person's cholesterol. rate, blood pressure, or whether they smoke or not.[41] Other studies have shown that loneliness can lower a person's immune response and ability to fight off infectious diseases and viruses.[42] Still other studies at Duke University show that people who attend church at least once a week have healthier immune systems than those who don't.[43] We're all potential healers, says Felten. Heath care workers and family members probably don't think of themselves as being able to affect the chemistry and pharmacology of an ill person, but they probably do just that. [44] (Although physical touch is not relevant to our review of scientific evidence for mental healing, it's still fascinating to note that simple touch can help break isolation and actually create specific, physical changes in the brain.[45] At a meeting of the Society for Neuroscience in New Orleans in 1997, researchers further confirmed that a mother's hugs, touches and caresses of her baby can profoundly affect the biochemistry of the brain, with lifelong effects on the child's physical growth and mental abilities. A lack of physical touch caused unusually high levels of stress hormones; and a lack of attention from a mother or caregiver towards a child can actually cause brain cells in an infant to commit suicide. "What we found shocked us," said psychologist Mark Smith of the DuPont Merck research laboratory in Wilmington, Delaware.) [46]

Can we create health by learning to control our own emotions? When you get angry, your heart rate goes up, your blood pressure goes up, the arteries in your heart may begin to constrict and the blood may clot. Learning to control your anger by mental healing procedures such as meditation can prevent or help cure physical illness. Changing you mental attitude can change your physical health.

Laughter, the opposite of anger, may also have a measurable healing effect on physical illness. Perhaps the most famous case of laughter being used to help cure illness is that of the late *Saturday Review* magazine editor Norman Cousins and his recovery from a serious collagen illness called ankylosing spondylitis—which meant the connective tissue of his joints was literally disintegrating. He had difficult moving his neck, arms, hands, fingers and legs, and his jaws were almost locked. Doctors told him his chances of full recovery were 1 in 500. A well-read man, Cousins had read ten years earlier Yale doctor Hans Selye's book *The Stress of Life* which described the negative effects of negative emotions on body chemistry. It set him thinking: if negative emotions produced negative chemical changes in the body, could positive emotions produce the opposite—a healing effect? Instead of falling into despair over his diagnosis, Cousins tried three things to which he later credited his eventual recovery—large doses of vitamin C, a well-developed will to live, and laughter. Cousins believed that affirmative emotions were a factor in enhancing body chemistry and aggressively pursued laughter. He spent hours looking at Allen Funt's "Candid Camera," a TV program that set up unsuspecting people in hilarious situations and filmed them using hidden cameras. He also watched all the Marx Bros. comedy films he could find, and had the nurse read humor books to him as he lay in bed. After he had recovered from the disease, Cousins wrote the bestseller *Anatomy of an Illness*. It describes how doctors measured his body chemistry just before and several hours after his laughter sessions, and found that such activities did produce a small but cumulative positive effect on his body chemistry. Laughter was indeed good medicine. Cousins also did another unusual thing to lift his spirits and make him feel happier—he moved from the hospital to a hotel room after concluding that a hospital was no place for a sick person to be. The hotel room, he noted, cost only one-third as much as a hospital room, and provided more privacy and serenity, factors that helped him get better faster.

Medical researchers in both Japan and the U.S. have since conducted scientific studies confirming Cousins' insights into the healing power of laughter. Pediatricians at the ULCA Medical Center pain lab, hoping to teach children ill with cancer how to better manage their pain through laughter, devised an experiment where healthy kids submerged their hands in ice water (a painful experience). Those watching funny videos were able to endure the ice bath 40 percent longer than kids not watching the videos. Was the explanation simply that the videos helped distract their minds—or is something happening at a physical level? Researchers in the field of psychoneuroimmunology suspect it's more than simple distraction—they've measured actual physical changes in the body caused by humor—changes in hormone levels and a strengthening of the immune system. Emotions can have a direct physical effect on the body. A Japanese team of scientists in 2001 reported in the *Journal of the American Medical Association* that they were able to actually reduce skin welts in allergy patients by showing them Charlie Chaplin's comedy classic *Modern Times.*[47]

Why do some people get sick easier than others? Dr. Candace Pert argues that our mental state (non-physical thoughts, emotions, beliefs) may affect whether we get sick from the same loading dose of a virus—whether that virus be a simple, common cold, or a life-threatening virus like AIDS. Pert is a neurobiologist, research professor and former Chief of the Section on Brain Biochemistry of the Clinical Neuroscience Branch at the National Institute of Mental Health. She pioneered medical understanding of the chemicals that travel between the mind and the body and was featured in Bill Moyer's PBS TV series "Healing and the Mind." Emotions can weaken or strengthen our immune system's ability to respond to threats. Loneliness, as we mentioned above, has been linked to lower immune responses in studies done of persons in nursing homes.[48] Also, the more severe the mental depression, the more likely you'll find a diminished immune response in the physical body.[49] Pert notes data showing people have more heart attacks on Monday mornings (the start of an unpleasant work week) than other days; and that deaths for Christians peak the day after Christmas while for Chinese people they peak the day after Chinese New Year (when most people suffer a post-holiday emotional letdown).

Can you die of a broken heart, like folk wisdom says? Data exists showing that people who lose their spouses are at increased risk for dying themselves during the 6-12 months following the loss of their spouse. One hypothesis: resulting mental depression from losing someone you love may lead to physical, biological changes increasing your vulnerability to heart attacks and other diseases.[50]

People who can put their mental feelings into words may end up healthier than those who hold them in. According to Pert, controversial research done in Europe suggests that the suppression of grief, and suppression of anger, in particular, is associated with an increased incidence of breast cancer in women.[51] Traditional healing ceremonies involving catharsis, letting all your feelings pour out, may turn out to be scientifically valid. Researcher Lydia Temoshek studied patients who had a serious form of cancer called malignant melanoma. Those who expressed their feelings had more beneficial immune activity at the site of their lesions than those who didn't express their feelings. They also had thinner lesions.[52]

Whatever the ultimate limits of the mind in terms of healing—or hurting—the body, they are apparently not what Science believed even a decade ago.

Unfortunately, mental healing is usually not as therapeutically reliable and predictable in its effects as a pill or surgery. To advance further, mind/body medicine researchers are working hard to develop a better understanding of exactly *how* mental healing works. How do non-physical thoughts, beliefs and feelings actually affect the physical body and perform its healing or hurting? How can something purely mental—a thought, memory or idea—have a physical effect on the body powerful enough to kill a tumor, erase a wart, or lower blood pressure sometimes as effectively as physical interventions like surgery or drugs?

The answer offered by some researchers is that there is a "psychosomatic communications network"[53] linking the mind and the body together. Under this hypothesis, our mental thoughts, beliefs, wishes and intentions create emotions. These emotions, in turn, trigger chemical messenger molecules (neuropeptides) which diffuse through every cell in our body, affecting autonomous nervous system functions like blood pressure and heart rate; weakening or strengthening the immune system; and changing hormonal levels in the endocrine system thus causing physical changes to the body.[54] Emotions produced by non-physical thought are thus the bridge between the mental and the physical worlds. Dr. Candace Pert helped pioneer the theory and popularized it in her book *Molecules of Emotion.*[55]

Researchers have also identified some key differences between simple wishful thinking and effective mental healing techniques using hypnosis, biofeedback, visualization, expressions of love and concern, and prayer. All of the latter typically involve deliberate, purposeful, focusing attention; they are real mental "work." Wishful thinking is typically an idea with no focus to it. It is undisciplined and fleeting. The two are different mental states, different states of consciousness.

Professor William Braud of the Institute of Transpersonal Psychology (www.itp.edu) in Palo Alto, California, has directed laboratory investigations into the effects of psychological exercises such as relaxation, attention, intention and visualization on the immune system. In one paper, he identified five major mental techniques that he believes have important effects on self-healing processes. They include 1) the need for relaxation and quietude; 2) learning to focus your attention on one thing (e.g. your breathing) which allows you to develop mental self-control and avoid distractions; 3) learning visualization or imagery techniques since pictures are the preferred language of mind-body interactions; 4) incorporating intentionality into the process, a wish that some goal be reached, and an expectation that it will; and 5) the evocation of strong, positive emotions during the healing process.[56]

Psychologist/parapsychologist Krippner also sees multiple personality disorder research as another window to understanding exceptional human abilities and the mind's power to influence or modify the physical human body. Persons suffering from multiple personality disorder (MPD) provide us with bizarre evidence that the mind can indeed control the body in exceptional ways. Different personalities (a function of the mind) can cause astonishingly different physical reactions in the same shared body (matter). One personality might need glasses for nearsightedness, the other for farsightedness; one personality might have an allergic reaction to cats while another have no problem with felines. In one case, says Krippner, a former heroin addict developed MPD. One of his other personalities was a heroin addict. When that addicted personality emerged, so did actual physical needle tracks on his skin. Mind over matter. Change your personality and change your glasses prescription. Why does this happen? MPD studies may help us identify the factors that make these mind-body feats possible, and develop testable hypotheses.

A growing number of physicians and medical researchers—like some quantum physicists—suspect that the mind and the brain are not the same. They include Candace Pert who argues that the mind is not just three pounds of meat inside a skull on top of your neck. Rather it's an enlivening form of *energy* operating throughout every cell in the body.[57] For this reason, she feels physicists may figure it out first.

Last but not least, is there any scientific evidence supporting the reality of that special type of mental healing called spiritual healing? Mental healing doesn't require a belief in God; an atheist can use visualization, meditation, biofeedback or hypnosis to unleash the power of the mind to heal. Spiritual healing, in contrast, employs a special type of mental thought called prayer, specifically directed to a Higher Power than man; and attributes ultimate responsibility for any resulting healing not to the human mind but to that Higher Power, often called God.

It's impossible to scientifically prove the *ultimate* responsibility for any healing (it's essentially a philosophical or theological question as to whether our own mind, some collective super-mind or energy, or a supernatural, divine being is ultimately responsible for the results). But it is possible to scientifically determine if the specific form of mental healing defined as prayer can produce healing results.

When Dr. Larry Dossey. M.D. decided to check the scientific literature for any proof of prayer's efficacy in healing people, he found over 100 well-design scientific experiments, half of which showed prayer was effective in bringing about significant changes in living beings. Dossey was initially surprised that this body of apparent scientific proof for the efficacy of prayer was not more widely known among the scientifically trained medical community But he eventually concluded, like many historians of science, that knowledge which doesn't fit prevailing ideas can be basically ignored no matter how scientifically valid it is.[58] Dossey reviewed some of this scientific research in his *New York Times* bestseller, *Healing Words: The Power of Prayer and the Practice of Medicine.*

Researchers have produced some intriguing, controlled experiments on the power of people who believe in a God or a Higher Power, and use prayer to call upon that God for help, to affect the health of sick people. These include a successful 1998 research experiment on distant healing with AIDS patients, and a 1999 experiment on prayer's effect on hospitalized heart attack victims (see "Best Scientific Evidence" below).

Another example is a study done by a Columbia University team of medical doctors who found in a randomized, blind study conducted in 1998-99 that the pregnancy rate for women receiving in-vitro fertilization doubled when they were prayed for. "We set out with the expectation that we would show no benefit of prayer," noted the surprised study team leader, Dr. Rogerio Lobo of the Columbia Presbyterian Medical Center, New York. "We could have ignored the findings, but that would not help to advance the field." None of the researchers were employed by religious organizations or were asked by religious groups to perform the study. The study appears in the *Journal of Reproductive Medicine.*[59]

Outside the laboratory, meanwhile, a number of well-documented "miraculous" cures offer strong evidence for the power of faith and prayer to heal the body. In his book *The Future of the Body,* Murphy focuses attention on healing cases collected by the Medical Bureau at Lourdes, where three children reportedly saw a vision of the Virgin Mary in 1858 and which today is a major pilgrimage stop for the crippled and the ill. [60] Since 1954, the Medical Bureau has sent scientifically inexplicable cases to an international panel of physicians for review and comment. These reports usually include the medical records, X-rays, photographs, records of biopsies and summaries of other lab tests done on the person before and after they were healed, and are filed in the archives at Lourdes.

Murphy describes the rigorous scrutiny each miraculous healing claim undergoes, and summarizes a half-dozen, well-documented cases in his book. As Murphy notes, a wide range of illnesses have been cured at Lourdes. They include ulcers with extensive gangrene, amyotrophic lateral sclerosis (ALS), tuberculosis, peritonitis, leg and abdominal tumors, blindness of cerebral origin, sarcoma of the pelvis, and other diseases.

Francis Pascal, for instance, suffered meningitis when he was three. It left him blind and partly paralyzed. In 1938, when he was four, he visited Lourdes. He was instantly cured of both his blindness and lameness after two immersions in the Lourdes waters. The Medical Bureau confirmed that both his blindness and paralysis were organic, not just functional (i.e. the illnesses were not simply psychosomatic, caused by the mind). Gerard Bailie, for his part, was stricken with an incurable eye disease at age two and a half, and lost his sight after an operation. In 1947, at age six, he visited Lourdes and his blindness was cured. Vittorio Micheli experienced complete remission from a highly malignant, fast developing tumor that had attacked his bones. The Medical Bureau report on the 1963 cure shows that Micheli's iliac bone was eventually restored after suffering massive disintegration. At Lourdes he experienced relief from pain and a sense that he was cured; several months following his visit, his pelvis was reconstituted.

Since most persons coming to Lourdes believe in God and specifically pray to God for a cure for themselves or their children, these documented cures can reasonably be attributed to the power of that specific form of thought defined as a prayer.

Best Scientific Evidence

The scientific evidence for the power of the mind—using hypnosis, biofeedback, meditation and visualization—to affect the workings of the physical body is extensive and relatively accepted by open-minded physicians and medical researchers. The debate is now switching to *what degree* the mind can affect the physical body. What exactly are the outer limits of the human mind's power to heal, change, transform the physical, material body and thus the course of a physical disease or illness?

Clinically Demonstrated Powers of the Mind

Scientists now have preliminary clinical evidence that, at a minimum, the non-physical thoughts, emotions, beliefs and intentions directed by some human minds can, under certain circumstances, modify or influence the following physical bodily functions to the following degree:

- using a placebo, produce a cure rate of 35 percent on a wide variety of medical problems, including postoperative pain, headaches, colds, seasickness, nausea, and angina pectoris discomfort.[61]
- using hypnosis as the only anesthetic, undergo successful appendectomies, Cesarean section birth deliveries, mammoplasties, breast tumor excisions, vaginal hysterectomies, skin grafts and even cardiac surgery.[62]
- using biofeedback, control and sometimes eliminate heart malfunctions such as sinus tachycardias, fixed atrial fibrillation and premature ventricular contractions[63]; cure or relieve facial tics and the symptoms of cerebral palsy[64]; affect the flow of blood through the body to alleviate migraine headaches.[65]
- increase the number and effectiveness of natural killer cells in the immune system which are used to fight viruses, infectious diseases and tumor cells. [66]
- using visualization techniques, reduce or eliminate glaucoma[67]

- reduce or stop completely the flow of blood from an injury or cut.[68]
- reduce gastric acid secretions by up to 40 percent.[69]
- control systolic or diastolic blood pressure[70] thus reducing or eliminating hypertension

1998 Study on Distant Healing of AIDS Patients

Can mental/spiritual healing happen at a distance—even when the person doing the thinking or praying lives hundreds of miles away from the sick person targeted for healing? A group of 40 experienced healers living all over the U.S. and professing different faiths (Christian, Jewish, Native American, Buddhist, shaman and even secular "bio-energetic" practitioners) were invited to try and do just that under rigorous scientific controls. Their goal was to influence from a distance, using only their minds, the medical outcomes of a population of San Francisco men with advanced AIDS whom they had never met. The first pilot study was a rigorous, random, double-blind, research study carried out at California Pacific Medical Center. The remarkable results? Four out of ten control subjects died, but all of the subjects in the distant healing group survived. A similar follow-up study corrected a potential age bias identified in the first study. The results were the same: those men treated with healing from a distance experienced significantly better medical outcomes and quality-of-life outcomes—fewer outpatient doctor visits, fewer hospitalizations, less severe illnesses and less emotional stress. The editor of the *Western Journal of Medicine,* which published the study, noted that the paper had been carefully reviewed by nationally-known experts in statistics and medicine (i.e. it was solid, scientific research) and hoped the provocative paper would stimulate similar studies. It was time, he declared, for "more light, less dark, less heat." [71]

1999 Study on Prayer Effect on Heart Disease

Researchers in this experiment were intrigued by an earlier 1983, double-blind experiment in distant healing involving a Catholic prayer circle's influence on the health of 393 heart disease patients at San Francisco General Hospital. That famous study, known as the Byrd study after the name of its chief researcher, had produced positive results.[72] Determined to conduct an even more rigorous scientific experiment which would either validate or throw into question Byrd's study, William Harris and a research team from the Mid-America Heart Institute at St. Luke's Hospital in Kansas City, Missouri launched their own test.[73] They recruited a group of Christians (including Roman Catholics and Protestants) to pray for 990 hospitalized coronary care unit (CCU) patients. All the prayers had to agree to the following statement: "I believe in God. I believe He is personal and is concerned with individual lives. I further believe that he is responsive to prayers for healing made on behalf of the sick." The result? Patients prayed for stayed in the hospital the same average length of time as patients who weren't prayed for, but their overall hospital experience was measurably better. Only 51 (10.9%) of the prayed-for patients required major surgery, whereas 76 (14.5%) of the control group (non-prayed for patients) did. In another measurement, only 12 (2.6%) of the prayed-for patients required intra-aortic balloon pumps while 20 (3.8%) of the control group did. Designing prayer experiments to control all variables is extremely difficult at best, but the results do suggest prayer can have some real, measurable effect on health.

Futterman Study on the Effect of Mind on the Human Immune System

Dr. Ann Futterman trained actors to improvise a monologue that would elicit happy or sad emotions. When they voluntarily got in that mental state, she measured changes in their immune systems caused by these short-term emotional states. She found that manufactured thoughts of both intense happiness and intense sadness caused an increase in the number of natural killer cells in the actor's bloodstream, and that the cells were working more efficiently than when the actor was in a neutral state. The effect also happened very quickly—within 20 minutes. The potential implications of the study? We can voluntarily use the mind to produce emotions that can affect our immune systems, and can enhance our chances of surviving a disease.[74] When we increase the number of natural killer cells, we're improving our body's first line of defense. These cells have the ability to kill virus-infected cells and "potentially they're also able to kill tumor cells."[75]

The Achterberg Cancer Visualization Study

Can you look at drawings made by cancer patients and end up with predictions of the disease's progression that are more accurate that trained doctors can make in the same situation? Achterberg found a fascinating and close correlation between how a patient visualizes his disease when asked to draw it, and what course the disease ultimately takes. Her Imagery of Disease test was able to predict the status of cancer with 93% accuracy for patients who had total remission, and 100% for those who eventually died or whose condition rapidly worsened. The findings were so unbelievable that medical journals at first refused to publish them. It sounded more psychic than scientific. So Achterberg gave them to the *Journal of Multivariate Statistics*. They confirmed the validity of the statistics.[76]

The 1903 Carrel-Lourdes Prayer Healing Case

Michael Murphy, in his book *The Future of the Body*, offers several spectacular cases of spiritual or faith healing that took place at the religious shrine of Lourdes in France. One of the best involves Alexis Carrel, a skeptic, Nobel Laureate in medicine and a medical director at the Rockefeller Institute who witnessed an amazing cure on his first visit to Lourdes in 1903.[77] On the train trip down, Carrel decided to observe a young woman named Marie Bailly (he gives her the pseudonym Marie Ferrand in his book) who was suffering from the last stages of tubercular peritonitis and on the verge of death. In his book,

The Voyage to Lourdes, he notes that her condition was considered absolutely hopeless by two doctors—the woman's personal physician as well as a famous Bordeaux surgeon. There was nothing medicine could do for her. She was doomed. He agreed with their conclusion after also personally examining her on the train trip down to Lourdes, for he himself had seen many similar cases in his practice. He believed that the power of Lourdes, if any, was simply the power of suggestion, and thus could have absolutely no effect on an organic disease like hers. He was not even sure she would survive the trip to Lourdes before dying. Her heartbeat was irregular and racing, her breathing rapid and shallow. She finally arrived at Lourdes at 2:30 PM that afternoon and was eventually wheeled down to the Grotto, a rock cave where the shepherd Bernadette had seen her vision of the Virgin Mary. Its entrance was hung with rosaries and discarded crutches; inside stood a statue of the Virgin, illuminated by hundreds of votive candles. Carrel stood and watched the dying girl carefully; she was motionless, her breathing still rapid and shallow, her heart racing, her face turning blue. He looked around the room, then eventually back at the girl. She was slowly changing right before his eyes, beginning to rally. Carrel thought he was "hallucinating" but felt the hallucination itself was scientifically interesting, so he started taking notes. It was 2:40 PM. He fixed his eyes on her as her face continued to change, the pain disappearing from her eyes, the blanket covering her distended abdomen slowly flattening out and her stomach returning to normal. Carrel felt he was going mad. A few minutes after the basilica bell rang out three o'clock, the distension in her abdomen had completely disappeared. By four o'clock, her condition had improved to the point that she was talking, looking around, moving her limbs without pain, drinking a cup of milk. At seven PM that evening, when Carrel visited her in the hospital to inspect her, she was sitting up in bed, the gleam back in her eye, the color back in her cheeks. Her abdomen was normal, the hard tumor masses Carrel had personally seen and touched only a few hours earlier completely gone. Carrel came away convinced that some Lourdes miracles were indeed authentic. He wasn't happy about it. As Carrel notes, all he had ever believed had been turned upside down. It was "distressingly unpleasant to be personally involved in a miracle." But he reported the case honestly to colleagues and friends, and publicly supported the position that science should investigate fairly and fully claims of faith healing like the one he had personally witnessed and examined. "To say something is not true without having first investigated the facts is to commit a grave scientific error," he declared. Certainly science should be on guard against charlatanism and credulousness, "but it is also the duty of science not to reject things simply because they appear extraordinary or because science is powerless to explain them." For Carrel, "The only thing that matters is to look at the facts."[78] What makes this case so impressive is the medical training and reputation of the observer. It's not often you get a skeptic and Nobel Laureate in medicine as a witness to a spiritual healing.

Highly Recommended Reading:

Murphy, Michael. *The Future of the Body: Explorations into the Further Evolution of Human Nature.* Los Angeles: Jeremy Tarcher, 1993. This book is a must read for anyone interested in the potential of the mind to influence the physical body. Murphy gathered data and anecdotal evidence from medical science, anthropology, sports, the arts, comparative religious studies and psychical research to see exactly how grand the human potential might be. It is grand indeed.

Moyers, Bill. *Healing and the Mind.* Main Street Books, 1995. Like Michael Murphy's book *The Future of the Body*, this now classic book is also an absolute must-have for anyone seriously interested in the mystery of mind-body healing. Sometimes it reads like a medical textbook, but it contains provocative scientific data on the mind/body connection, presented by top authorities in the medical field.

Achterberg, Jeanne, et al. *Rituals of Healing: Using Imagery for Health and Wellness.* New York: Bantam Doubleday Dell, 1994. Offers a good look at how the medical community has taken clinical research findings in visualization and applied it to healing programs for patients. If you're a skeptic looking for a more scientific report on visualization, try Achterberg's earlier book, *Imagery in Healing: Shamanism and Modern Medicine* (Boston: Shambala Publications, 1985). This scientifically-oriented book (very well documented and footnoted) shows how the systematic use of mental imagery has helped patients affect the outcome of disease states. You can usually find a copy at www.abebooks.com.

Targ, Russell and Katra, Jane. *The Heart of the Mind.* Novato (CA): New World Library, 1999. Targ, a retired senior staff scientist for Lockheed Missile and Space and one of the giants in parapsychology research, was co-leader (with Hal Puthoff) of the original remote viewing project run out of Stanford Research Institute in the 1970s and 1980s which evolved into the famous STAR GATE program. Katra is a veteran spiritual healer with a Ph.D who works part-time as an "immune-system coach." This thought-provoking book contains a layman's summary of the scientific experiment conducted in 1998 on distant healing with AIDS patients described above in "Best Scientific Evidence." It also offers readers an excellent overview of modern scientific exploration of parapsychological phenomena (ESP, PK, life after death, mental/faith healing) and their implications regarding the nature of mind and man himself.

10.

Death Bed Visions

*"Death-bed visions, combined with other afterlife research, make possible
a fact-based, rational and therefore reasonable belief in life after death."*
Osis and Haraldsson

I'm getting older, I admit it. My hair is thinning, my elapsed time for the
mile is steadily rising, and I can no longer party all night. I'm in Middle
Age. So is everyone around me (except my son Christopher, 14, who
points out my bald spot to anyone who visits us). When I bought more
life insurance recently, I couldn't help but notice the mortality tables
and my place in the ranks of advancing years.

Who isn't interested in whether they will survive death? America is
probably in for an explosion of interest in the subject as millions of
Baby Boomers begin to feel the aches and pains of their advancing mortality. I certainly am. This is one mystery where you and I and every
human alive have a personal stake in the outcome of the investigation.
As a result, scientific evidence for life after death probably ranks at the
top of the list of paranormal subjects of interest to Boomers (Trust me,
when you hit 50 you'll feel the same).

Death is the ultimate mystery, and man has been grappling with it
for hundreds of thousands of years. Up until relatively recently, most
peoples and cultures in the world accepted some form of life after death

as a given. The primary basis for this belief in life after death wasn't modern scientific evidence or laboratory experiments; it was faith. People believed in life after death because most people believed in religion, and most religions of the world hold this belief. And this belief was constantly being reinforced by the experiences of human beings throughout history who have repeatedly reported encountering ghosts and spirits of the deceased people. In addition, most cultures and societies right up to today have mediums or channelers (shamans, priests, mystics and psychics) who claim the ability to communicate with the dead, often while in a trance.

Faith was supported by other human experiences as well. In many cultures, children sometimes told their bewildered parents of previous lives. Throughout human history, people on their deathbeds have seen a world on the Other Side—a world where often their departed relatives friends or family awaited them. By the 20th century, medical science was literally bringing back people from the dead—people whose hearts had stopped and whose brains had ceased functioning. Some of these patients who had near death experiences (NDE) visited another reality while clinically dead during which their minds continued to function and they encountered and communicated with previously deceased family members.

But the rise of rationalism and skepticism during the 18th century, Darwin's discovery of evolution in the 19th century, and knowledge about the body and brain uncovered in the 20th century have combined to cast doubt on these millions and millions of anecdotal experiences. Science demanded more than anecdotal evidence to "prove" life after death, particularly since Science embraced a philosophy of materialism. The materialist argues that consciousness cannot exist or function without the body because human consciousness is simply an electro-chemical function of a piece of matter called the brain. When the brain dies, consciousness is extinguished forever. Man is an ingenious wonder, but ultimately he is nothing more than a collection of atoms, a sophisticated piece of matter.

But life outside the clinical laboratory—where most humans live, play and exist—suggests the opposite: that consciousness is more than the brain; that it can continue to function even when the brain and the body are clinically dead; that the deceased communicate with the living and the living with the deceased; that human beings may have a non-material "spirit" or "soul" as described by many religions.[1]

Among phenomena suggesting life after death which can be scientifically examined are death bed visions; near death experiences (NDE); ghosts and poltergeists; communications through mediums (human or electronic) purporting to be in touch with the deceased; and reincarnation memories.

Death bed visions are particularly interesting, and I was surprised to find that someone had actually studied them scientifically. At or near the moment of death, a number of dying people share with bystanders around their bed visions they see of an afterlife world, and hold conversations with invisible people, reported to be relatives, friends or family members who have died before them.

Dr. Karlis Osis, a pioneer in scientific research on deathbed visions, notes that most of us apparently pass away without awareness of the moment of death. But some persons remain clearly conscious right to the end and describe what they "see" approaching before they die—apparitions of dead relatives and friends, religious and mythological figures, heavenly environments filled with light, beauty and intense color. The experiences can transform the dying person, bringing serenity, peace and even elation.[2]

These deathbed visions exhibit some common characteristics across cultures, and a small handful of researchers have systematically collected and analyzed them. They want to see how frequently they occur, what is seen in the typical deathbed vision, and whether the visions can be explained away by normal means. The majority view of modern medical science is that they are a hallucination, evidence of a psychological or physical disorder. But a growing minority view argues that they may be evidence of another reality—life after death.

Anecdotal reports of deathbed visions can be found in the literature of many cultures. But it wasn't until the mid-1920s that the first systematic collection of deathbed observations in the modern era was published. *Death-Bed Visions*,[3] appearing in 1926, was written by Sir William Barrett, a physics professor at the Royal College of Science in Dublin (and a member of Britain's Society for Psychical Research). Some of the cases collected by Barrett were very impressive.

The catalyst leading Sir William Barrett to compile his pioneering collection of deathbed visions was an experience[4] described to him by his wife, a physician and obstetrician. On the night of January 12, 1924, Lady Barrett rushed home from the hospital to tell her husband about a remarkable deathbed vision seen by one of her patients, Dora, who delivered a child safely but died after the delivery. As Dora lay dying, she suddenly looked across the room and broke into a radiant smile. When Lady Barrett asked what she saw, Dora replied, "Lovely brightness—wonderful beings." Dora was fully and intensely absorbed in the vision. Then she announced to Barrett that she saw her father who was indicating to her how glad he was that she was coming to join him. When the nurses brought Dora her newborn baby for her to see, Dora wondered aloud whether she should stay for the child's sake, but then announced that she couldn't turn her back on the beautiful world she was seeing in her vision. She wanted to go there.

It must have been an extremely real and attractive vision for a mother to willingly give up her own baby, and her life as well, to embrace it. But such complete and total belief in the reality of their deathbed visions by the dying is not uncommon. What makes the case so strong is what happened next. Dora turned to Lady Barrett with a puzzled expression. "He has Vida with him," she said.

The Paul Harvey, "rest-of-the-story" twist ending? Vida was Dora's sister, who had died three weeks before. Because her family was afraid it would upset Dora's fragile health, Dora had not been told that Vida had died. Thus Dora's surprise at seeing her sister with her deceased father.

Unfortunately, Barrett's work was conducted towards the end of the "golden age" of serious postmortem survival research which started in the 1880s with the founding of the Society for Psychical Research. During that period, research on ghosts, mediums and the survival hypothesis held center stage as the Spiritualist movement swept the U.S. and Europe.

By the 1930s, however, overall interest in ghosts, mediums and evidence of life after death—including deathbed observations—had begun to wane along with the whole Spiritualist movement. Hard-nosed science was making exceptional discoveries using controlled experiments in the laboratory. Death-bed observations, in contrast, were anecdotal evidence, and anecdotal evidence was viewed as second-class evidence compared to repeatable laboratory experiments. In addition, to medical doctors weaned on the prevailing philosophy of materialism embraced by establishment Science, post-mortem survival was tainted with religious overtones. Parapsychologists seeking peer approval and respect from their university colleagues were thus more attracted towards Dr. Rhine's new and exciting laboratory experiments in ESP and psychokinesis.

From the 1930s to the late 1950s, limited research of note was conducted on deathbed visions. In 1948, an Italian researcher collected peripherally-related reports of strange, unexplained events happening at the moment of death (the ringing of bells, watches and clocks stopping, photos and painting falling off the wall).[5] But the consensus of the medical community was that death-bed visions were simply hallucinations produced by a dying brain, perhaps aided by drug reactions. Doctors pointed out that certain drugs and pain killers given during terminal illnesses can cause hallucinations. Anesthesia also sometimes produces hallucinations as a side effect. Did the dying person receive any of these medications? If so, the visions could have been caused by a drug reaction. Also, certain medical conditions can cause hallucinations at times. These include high fevers, brain diseases, extreme pain, and nephritis. Were any of these factors present?

Modern psychiatry, also steeped in the philosophy of materialism, offered another possible hypothesis. According to their theories, when fearful human beings face imminent death and permanent extinction, the brain reacts by producing comforting hallucinations or fantasies that help them avoid facing the truth. The brain might also produce hallucinations of deceased relatives as a form of intense wish fulfillment. Perhaps severe stress caused depersonalization or a schizoid experience. Or the person may have had a previous history of psychological problems making him prone to fantasize or hallucinate.

For the scientific establishment, at least, deathbed visions had been laid to rest, explained away by consensus theories.

But Barrett's seminal book had earlier caught the eye of the late Karlis Osis who was impressed because the book had been written not by some starry-eyed Spiritualist but by a noted physics professor. He decided in 1959 to take a second look at the whole question.

Osis had done his Ph.D. research on ESP (Munich, 1950) and did most of his early work on that subject, particularly long-distance ESP experiments. Osis first got interested in ESP and other paranormal phenomena as a child. At age 14, he was ill in bed with tuberculosis in a house his family shared with an old, paralyzed aunt who was on the verge of death. He was alone in his room one day when "suddenly all the room looked like it was being filled with light...and a big wave of joy came over me." At that moment, someone came into the room and told Osis his aunt had just died. For Osis, the coincidence was unmistakable. "I couldn't get it out of my mind, it was so shaking." It launched him on a life of investigation in an attempt to get to the bottom of the mystery. "Something attracted me, and something also said, 'This can't really be.' That was what shaped my life."[6]

Osis subsequently worked with the famous Dr. J.B. Rhine at the Parapsychology Laboratory at Duke University from 1951 to 1957. In 1957, he became director of research at the Parapsychology Foundation in New York, and investigated mediums, ghosts and poltergeists. As director of research, Osis was in a perfect position to do something. He had the qualified workers, the funding and the blessing of the Foundation's backers to pursue a mass survey of doctors and nurses regarding the deathbed visions of their patients. He received enthusiastic backing from the president of the Foundation, Eileen Garrett, one of the most famous and gifted psychics of her day. Other well-known friends of the Foundation, including the eminent writer Aldous Huxley, also offered their encouragement.

In 1959, Osis mailed out questionnaires to 5,000 physicians and 5,000 nurses nationwide as part of his first pilot study. Some 640 medical observers filled out and returned the questionnaires, providing information on over 35,000 observations of dying patients. The results indicated that over 1,300 dying patients saw apparitions and almost 900 reported visions of an afterlife. Osis selected 190 of the most interesting cases, did telephone interviews with the observers, and sent out follow-up questionnaires. In the end, some 150 apparition cases and 25 deathbed vision cases were examined in depth as part of the pilot study.

The major objective was to determine which hypothesis the data supported best: a) the "sick brain" hypothesis—the visions of apparitions and afterlife worlds were hallucinations caused by delirium, schizoid reactions when faced with death, or disturbed brain processes caused by high temperature, sedation, medication, etc. or b) the afterlife hypothesis—what the dying sees is an afterlife.

When the data was analyzed, the pilot study supported the afterlife hypothesis. Among its conclusions:

The typical deathbed vision experience was of a shorter duration, more coherent and more related to the situation of dying and an afterlife than the rambling experiences of a sick brain. One report provided Osis dealt with a rather matter-of-fact, unemotional woman, a buyer for a department store in her 50s who was dying of cancer. According to the medical specialist who observed her vision, the woman saw gates opening into a beautiful garden and an invitation to enter. The patient got angry when the medical specialist for disturbing her during the vision, but also clearly understood she was in the hospital room during and after the vision.

Most of the visions did not exemplify the normal characteristics of ordinary hallucinations. The patient was rational, logical and well oriented in all respects except his insistence that he was seeing something real. Osis received a report of a 69 year old woman dying of cancer, holding a conversation with the apparition of her deceased husband: They talked for some time in soft, loving conversation about how much they loved and missed each other and would soon be together again. The patient even reached out her hand as if reaching for his, declaring that he looked well cared for. The nurse who submitted the case was no true believer in apparitions. In fact, as she told Osis, she found it startling, frightening and unnerving because she didn't believe in such things. Yet she was positive drugs hadn't produced the vision. In the end, she wished she had had a camera to catch the expression on the woman's face, wrinkles gone and lit with a pleasant smile. [7]

Delirium was not the basis for the deathbed apparitions; the apparitions seemed to have an external source and were not mere projections of wishful thoughts or unfulfilled desires. Another case involved an intelligent, 76-year-old woman who had suffered a heart attack. The nurse confirmed to Osis that the patient at the time of the vision was not under sedation, had no history of hallucinations, and her mind was very clear and sharp. She was also convinced she would make a full recovery and return home to a daughter who needed her. But then suddenly she called her nurse over and asked her if she didn't also see what she (the patient) saw—her dead husband Charlie, standing with open arms waiting for her. She continued on, describing the beautiful place she saw, with its flowers and music, and Charlie patiently waiting for her. The nurse concluded she had seen her husband.[8]

Two-thirds of the apparitions seen by the dying were of deceased people; only one-third were of living persons. The opposite is typical of hallucinations by persons in normal health.

Of the apparitions seen, 83 percent were of relatives: mothers, fathers, spouses, siblings and offspring. This contrasted sharply with hallucinations of the mentally ill who most often conjure up strangers or bizarre characters.

The majority of patients who saw apparitions described the mission of the apparition(s) as aiding them in making the transition to the Other World. An 11-year old girl with a congenital heart malady saw her mother in a pretty white dress just like the one the girl was wearing, and told the nurses her mother had come to take her on a trip. The vision lasted for half an hour. The girl died peacefully four hours later.[9]

The predominant reaction of patients who see apparitions coming to take them away is that of serenity and peace. One 65-year-old American male cancer patient exhibited no confusion in his thinking but "saw the other world." He looked over at the wall and brightened up as he saw friends and relatives. He said hello to them, gestured to them and, after it was over, seemed very peaceful and serene. Before the vision, he had been sick and nauseous.[10]

Based on the promising results of this pilot study, Osis went on to conduct a second American study in the early 1960s, sending out questionnaires to 2,500 doctors and 2,500 nurses in the Eastern U.S., and receiving over 1,000 responses. The questionnaires sought information on deathbed visions experienced by both terminally ill patients and patients who later recovered from a near-death experience.

A decade later, in the early 1970s, Osis and his colleague Erlendur Haraldsson conducted a third major study, this time collecting over 700 cases in Northern India. Haraldsson was a native of Iceland, and a journalist and writer before getting his masters degree in psychology and doing his internship in clinical psychology at the Dept. of Psychiatry at the University of Virginia in Charlottesville (home of reincarnation researcher Dr. Ian Stevenson). He earned his doctorate in psychology in 1972 from the U. of Freiberg (Germany) with a thesis on ESP. He worked as a research associate at the American Society for Psychical Research from 1972-73 when Osis was there.

This third study allowed the two researchers to compare the American data with results gathered from a non-Western, non-Christian country to better gauge the effect of culture on death-bed visions. Out of 1,708 cases from these two later studies, they selected 807 for detailed follow up interviews. Then they sat down and analyzed the results.

The follow up studies reconfirmed the conclusions of the original pilot study.

Medical factors:

- There was no acceptable evidence that drugs were generating the afterlife visions. Those patients who received drugs (e.g. morphine and Demerol) did not have a greater frequency of afterlife visions than other patients.
- There was no acceptable evidence that brain disturbances were generating the afterlife visions. Brain disturbances caused by disease, injury or uremic poisoning decreased the afterlife vision phenomenon or did not affect it at all.
- The presence of a medical history suggestive of hallucinogenic factors did not increase the frequency of afterlife visions.
- Osis and Haraldsson had a separate search of medical literature done for them to find any evidence that lack of oxygen (anoxia) caused hallucinations in dying patients. No support was found for this thesis.

Psychological factors:
- Such factors as stress, patient expectations of dying or recovering, or a desire to see someone they loved did not affect how often people had death-bed visions. No evidence was found from the data to suggest that psychological factors encouraging hallucinations also encouraged afterlife visions. Patients didn't automatically see in their visions people they specifically wanted to see; and people who didn't expect to die also saw death bed visions. These results, noted Osis lent support to the hypothesis that the people seen in the visions were not just wishful projections of the patient.

Cultural factors
- Patients often saw something that was "unexpected, untaught and a complete surprise to them."
- Afterlife visions often did not conform with religious beliefs about the afterlife. Among Christian American patients, there were many reports of visions of heaven; visions of hell and devils were almost totally absent. Christian ideas of "judgment," "salvation" and "redemption" were not mirrored in their visions. In India, basic Hindu afterlife beliefs like reincarnation and dissolution in Brahma were never mentioned in the visions.
- Eleven core phenomena suggestive of an afterlife were found to be common to both Indian and American death-bed visions. Similarities outweighed the differences by a large margin, indicating a universal human experience rather than a culturally-produced experience.

These three studies taken together are among the best evidence death-bed observations have to offer in terms of supporting the post-mortem survival thesis. Although they offer anecdotal evidence, the questionnaires were professionally designed; the information was systematically collected; the data was scientifically evaluated in a way designed to minimize the possibility of bias; and the methodologies and research processes are described in enough detail to allow critics to raise questions. Osis and Haraldsson concluded that the evidence gathered through deathbed observations favors the postmortem survival hypothesis. Noted Osis, "It cannot clinch it, but it can give it support."[11] And they invited other scientists to pick up the challenge, concluding their book *At the Hour of Death* with the words, "Above all, we need more research."

Today, the Division of Personality Studies, University of Virginia Heath System (www.med.virginia.edu/personality-studies/) continues to pursue the phenomenon of death-bed visions studied by Osis and Haraldsson. The Division's mission is "studying how mind and brain relate and the question of postmortem survival." Researchers there note that death-bed visions may be more common than people recognize, and they use their website to invite people who have experienced death bed visions to send in their reports.

Seattle pediatrician Dr. Melvin Morse, who pioneered the modern investigation of near death experiences in children (see Chapter 11), has conducted a detailed study of death-bed visions and come away surprised and upset at the way the medical establishment routinely denies the reality and importance of this relatively common (based on surveys he found) paranormal phenomenon.[12]

Best Scientific Evidence

The Osis and Haraldsson Surveys

The three major survey projects conducted by Osis and Haraldsson over two decades were scientifically designed; covered over 5,000 death bed vision experiences; and included pioneering cross-cultural comparisons (the U.S. and India). They thus provides a strong, scientific body of evidence suggesting that death-bed visions are not simply caused by medical or psychological problems. As the authors note, their evidence best fits a life after death hypothesis best, and thus "makes possible a fact-based, rational, and therefore realistic belief in life after death."[13]

The Horace Traubel-Walt Whitman Case

This case[14] offers unusually strong evidence suggesting the objective reality of death bed visions. The reason? Not only did the dying person see a vision of a visitor from beyond—a healthy friend visiting the dying person at the same time witnessed the same death bed apparition. In addition, a record of the testimony of both witnesses was written down the same day. On Sept. 6, 1919, Horace Traubel, a close friend, poet and biographer of the famous American poet Walt Whitman, lay dying in Bon Echo, Ontario. Sitting in the room with the dying Traubel was Lt. Col. L. Moore Cosgrave. At 3 AM in the morning, Cosgrave noticed that Traubel had fixed his eyes on a spot in the shadow of the room, some three feet above the bed. Fixing his own gaze on the spot Traubel was looking at, Cosgrave watched in amazement as a light haze appeared which eventually resolved itself into the form of Walt Whitman. Cosgrave noticed that the apparition, now standing next to the bed, wore an old tweed jacket, an old felt hat, and had his right hand in his pocket. Cosgrave saw the apparition smile at Traubel and nod twice. Traubel saw the apparition and said, "There is Walt." Cosgrave watched the apparition pass through the bed towards him, then felt a kind of low, electric shock as Whitman's ghost brushed against Cosgrave. With a final smile towards Traubel, the apparition faded away. Later that day, both Cosgrave and Traubel recounted the experience to a Mrs. Flora MacDonald Denison who made a written record of their description of the experience in her diary. Nine months later, Cosgrave wrote two letters describing the experience to Dr. Walter F. Prince, head of the Boston Society for Psychical Research.

The Lady Barrett Case

The Lady Barrett case described at the beginning of this chapter remains one of the best. There is some evidence to rule out hallucination (the most common objection made to a death bed vision). If Dora's dying vision had only included her deceased father, it would be easier to dismiss the vision as dying person's wish fulfillment. But Dora's mind saw something she had not expected to see, her sister Vida. She didn't know Vida was dead, and was truly puzzled to see her on the "Other Side." The case also has other strengths. The patient who had the deathbed vision was observed to be alert, clear and rational throughout the vision experience. The deathbed observation was made by a trained physician (Lady Barrett). The details were reported to another person shortly afterwards, when the event was still fresh in the mind. And the person who wrote up the case (Sir William Barrett) was himself a trained scientist, a physicist.

Highly Recommended Reading:

Osis, Dr. Karl and Haraldsson, Dr. Erlendur. *What They Saw At the Hour of Death: A New Look at Evidence for Life After Death (3ʳᵈ Ed.)*, Mamaroneck, N.Y. Hastings House, 1997. If you're going to read one book, this is it. It's the latest edition of the popular classic originally published by two veteran researchers of the life after death question. It provides perhaps the best scientific research ever conducted specifically on the subject of death-bed visions. It also includes a preface by Dr. Elizabeth Kubler-Ross.

Barrett, William. *Death Bed Visions: The Psychical Experiences of the Dying.* Aquarian Press, 1986 (Reprint). You can usually find a copy of this classic for sale at www.abebooks.com. It is the source of the Lady Barrett case cited in "Best Scientific Evidence" above.

11.

Near Death Experiences (NDE) and Out of Body Experiences (OBE)

"Anomalies need to be investigated. Maybe only 2% are validated, but they can be the driving force for paradigmatic shifts."
Marcello Truzzi

My sister Rosie went to school in Italy to study art, met a cute Italian guy named Giuliano, got married and a few years later had a beautiful daughter, Olivia. It was a very difficult birth, with lots of bleeding, and at one point the doctors almost lost her. She felt herself dying and then found herself out of her body, floating above the room and looking down on the doctors frantically trying to save her. They ultimately did. She had no explanation for the experience at the time. Few people wrote about or studied near death experiences in the early 1970s. Out of body experiences like her's were simply considered hallucinations. She strongly believed what had happened to her was no hallucination; that it was real. Still, she told very few people, reluctant to be considered odd or crazy. I only heard about it when I began researching this book. My sister Jody told me the story, and Rosie confirmed it. Like the ESP experiences of my relative Father Weibel, her story is especially interesting to me because it comes from someone I know and trust completely. Perhaps a similar story is waiting to be uncovered in your family.

Near death experiences have happened throughout human history and have sometimes been the subject of famous tales. Some 2,400 years ago, Plato featured the NDE-like experience of the soldier of Er in his book the *Republic*. The soldier went through several of the NDE stages (see below) typically experienced by modern NDE experiencers, including an out-of-body (OBE) experience, a life review and a return to life with a message for others.[1] Accounts with some similarity to the modern NDE can be found in various religious treatises such as the Egyptian and Tibetan books of the dead, and in the life stories of spiritual leaders like the prophet Mohammed, the Old Testament prophet Ezekial, Joseph Smith of the Mormons, George Fox of the Quakers, Jonathan Edwards of the Congregationalists and Native American spiritual leader Black Elk. An NDE experienced by British soldier Capt. David Perry (1741-1826) in the autumn of 1762 during a bout with typhus could easily pass, in its essentials, for an NDE experienced today—including Perry's poignant comment "I never dared say anything about it for a great many years afterwards for fear of being ridiculed."[2] In more modern times, Sigmund Freud's best-known disciple, C.G. Jung, had a classic out-of-body experience as part of an NDE during a heart attack which he reported in his autobiography *Memories, Dreams, Reflections*. As he noted, "It was not a product of my imagination. The visions and experiences were utterly real. There was nothing subjective about them; they all had a quality of absolute objectivity."[3]

But it is only recently that NDEs have become a serious focus of scientific research. Part of the reason is because modern medicine can resuscitate clinically dead people who can describe what they see and experience after they die. Today, thanks to advances in emergency medicine and improved equipment and techniques, many more people are surviving near-fatal heart attacks, electrocutions, drownings and terrible car accidents and recounting their NDE experiences shortly afterwards to trained medical professionals who personally observed the patient's clinical death. And while many medical doctors, trained in the prevailing philosophy of materialism, have trouble accepting the stories told by near death survivors, more and more physicians are taking a closer look at what NDE survivors are reporting.

Dr. Raymond Moody was one of the first physicians to systematically collect anecdotal evidence of the near death experience and gather stories of survivors. Moody was uniquely equipped to pursue the NDE phenomenon. He was a philosophy student at the University of Virginia when he first heard someone recount an NDE experience. The person telling the story was a local psychiatrist, Dr. George Ritchie. As a young Army private in 1943, Ritchie had been pronounced dead of pneumonia in a Camp Barkeley, Texas military hospital. He had no observable vital signs (heart beat, respiration, etc.) for over nine minutes and doctors had given up on him. During his NDE experience, he found himself out of his body and his spirit able to travel around the country. At one point, he traveled to a city on a river and alighted in front of an all-night cafe with a neon Pabst Blue Ribbon beer sign in the window. When his spirit finally returned to the hospital late at night, he almost couldn't find his body in the dark. In the end, he recognized it by the Phi Gamma Delta fraternity ring he wore on his finger. After being clinically dead for almost ten minutes (before an orderly convinced the doctors to try one last direct heart injection that revived him), he was unconscious for another four days before recovering. Ten months after his experience, he was driving through Vicksburg, Mississippi when he recognized the all night cafe he had seen during his out-of-body experience.[4] Impressed with the account, Moody never forgot it. Later, as a philosophy teacher, he heard additional similar cases from students who learned of his interest in the subject. Moody eventually entered medical school which offered him the opportunity to systematically collect NDE experiences, professionally evaluate them, and talk at length with some of the patients who reported them.

What is a NDE? Moody, who coined the term, originally identified fifteen commonly reported elements. Other researchers since then have reworked the list,[5] but the typical NDE includes one or more of the following elements:

A Feeling of Being Dead

A person dying from a heart attack, car accident, drowning, etc. loses consciousness and realizes that he has died, but he typically feels no pain—just a sense of peace.

An *Out-of-Body (OBE) Experience*

He then finds himself conscious and floating above his lifeless physical body which he can see below him. Occasionally he can also see (and later report to others for independent verification) details of what is happening below him—doctors or nurses working on his body, people crying, etc. Sometimes the NDE experiencer travels out of the room and down a hospital hall, into a waiting room, or to other nearby places and observes actions there as well. These observations of remote places, if proven accurate, are obviously impossible under our current understanding of the laws of physics and science.

Passing Through a Tunnel to Another World

He experiences himself rushing through a dark tunnel until he emerges into a realm of light, another world. It often looks like a brighter, more colorful form of earth, with flowers, gardens, forests, music and scenes typical of this life, much like the heaven most Americans believe in. But NDE experiencers can sometimes find difficulty describing the scene in words. Time and space don't operate the same way as in our physical world, explain some NDE experiencers.[6]

Meeting Friends, Relatives and Beings of Light

Emerging from the tunnel, he may be welcomed there by a deceased parent, relative, or friend; and/or angelic or spiritual beings radiating a wonderful light. He may or may not see Jesus or Mohammed or other religious figures he expects to meet, but commonly sees some kind of Being of Light. And this Being is the central point of the encounter.[7] Communication with this Being, or other beings, is by mental telepathy.

A Life Review

The NDE experiencer see his whole life pass in review, all his good and bad deeds, and has an opportunity to see himself as he really was. He gets a chance to evaluate for himself his own behavior. He judges himself. This life review element is apparently not that common, happening in anywhere from 4 percent to 29 percent of all NDEs. It is apparently more common with incidents involving violent, unexpected death.

A Wish to Stay There

Many NDE experiencers want to stay in this other world and not return to their former lives. They must be told or encouraged to return by the Being of Light who helped them conduct their life review. Others are given the choice of staying or returning and decide to return because their children or spouses need them.

Return and Transformation

The NDE experiencer suddenly finds himself back in his physical body, often arriving with a jolt, alive once again. Doctors and nurses tell him that they thought they had lost him. After recovery, the person may end up changing his attitudes and actions and beliefs for the better. He enjoys the moment more fully, often has a heightened sense of purpose to his life, loses the normal fear of death, and becomes more loving and tolerant towards others. He may have an increase in psychic abilities. And if he had an NDE during a suicide attempt, the risk of him attempting suicide again are greatly reduced. [8] Sometimes, though not always, he may come back more spiritual but less religious in terms of sectarian belief in an exclusive, specific, religious dogma. If this happens, it can sometimes be upsetting to the NDE experiencer's priest, minister or rabbi.

For the atheist, the NDE can obviously be a surprise. Most modern Jews do not believe in an afterlife, so Jewish NDE experiencers provide some very interesting accounts.[9] One woman who realized she had died and was in an out-of-body state also noticed that the nightgown she was wearing didn't match her robe. She found herself furious about two things—first, she would spend eternity walking around with an outfit that didn't match; and second, she had been wrong about an afterlife, something she hadn't believed in, and didn't like to be wrong!

Experiencers may interpret certain details of the experience in terms of their cultural or religious background. For instance, the Being of Light may appear to be Jesus for a Christian, Mohammed for a Muslim, Krishna for a Hindu, or a being of pure energy for an atheist. Likewise, the other world which they enter may look like a Christian paradise, a Muslim paradise, an abstract world of extremely vivid colors and music, or simply a beautiful forest, landscape or city. But an encounter with a superior entity in a world of pervasive all-encompassing love is common to the majority of NDE experiencers. In a minority of cases NDE experiencers have also encountered terrifying or fearful events or worlds.[10] These hellish experiences appear to be primarily encountered by people who have deep or repressed guilt, fear or anger; or who expect some kind of judgment or punishment after death.[11]

By the mid-1970s, Moody had over 150 cases in his files. In 1975, he published *Life After Life*, presenting many of the cases and his commentary on them. He freely admitted his anecdotal data was not a scientific study or a proof of life after death. The book went on to become a national bestseller.

The book helped spark the founding in 1978 of an International Association for Near-Death Studies (IANDS), a worldwide organization of scientists, scholars, near death experiencers and the general public, dedicated to the exploration of NDEs and their implications. The Connecticut-based IANDS (www.iands.org) has since developed a library and archives of near-death related materials which members can use to research the phenomenon. The association also puts out a quarterly newsletter *Vital Signs*, and a quarterly scholarly journal entitled *The Journal of Near Death Studies*. It has chapters in many states and in foreign countries as well.

In 1982, national pollster George Gallup, Jr. wrote a book based on survey data he collected on the topic of life after death.[12] One focus of the surveys was Americans' involvement in near death experiences. The poll results were based on a standard national sampling of 1,500 adult Americans as well as two smaller-scale surveys focused on national leaders in science and medicine. Both were done in late 1981. They produced some fascinating data. About one in seven Americans reported having been close to death at least once; and about 35 percent of these reported an NDE. These NDE experiencers had a higher belief in reincarnation than the general public—31 percent for NDE survivors vs. 23 percent of the general public. His data suggested the possibility of under-reporting of NDE experiences by physicians: while 67 percent of the general public believed in life after death, only 32 percent of physicians did. Gallup's book and his methodologically rigorous survey lent serious credibility to the NDE experience in the early 1980s when the NDE phenomenon was still struggling for scientific credibility. In many ways, it legitimized the phenomenon like no amount of anecdotal stories could do.

Moody's bestseller had also caught the attention of the medical community as well as the layman. While Moody concentrated on anecdotal evidence, two other physicians decided after reading *Life After Life* to conduct some more systematic, formal scientific surveys to take Moody's stories a step further. Both men had helped Moody found IANDS (along with Bruce Greyson who we met in Chapter 3). Kenneth Ring, M.D. was sympathetic after reading Moody's book; Atlanta cardiologist Michael Sabom, M.D. was skeptical.

Working independently, Sabom and Ring first confirmed Moody's assumption that the NDE was not uncommon for near-death survivors, and relatively consistent in terms of the stages of the experience. Next, they confirmed Moody's assumption that while religious background, belief and personal variables (sex, age, education, social class, marital status, etc.) did influence the specific content of the NDE experience, the overall content was relatively consistent regardless of religious background and demographic factors.

Turning to the question of whether the NDE was a hallucination (the most common skeptical argument), they both noted that a hallucination is accompanied by heightened brain activity. But their studies produced data showing that NDEs happened more often when neurophysiological activity was reduced, not increased. Sabom also found that NDEs were more likely when the person was unconscious for longer than 30 minutes; Ring found that the closer people were to physical death, the more extensive the NDE.[13]

Before conducting his research, Sabom was especially skeptical of Moody's reports that patients could observe their own resuscitation effort while out of the body. Expecting negative results, Sabom decided to put their claims to the test. He was convinced the patients' out-of-body observations were simply educated guesses.[14]

Sabom took 32 patients who reported an OBE experience during cardiac arrest and asked them to describe in detail what had gone on during the resuscitation effort while they were clinically unconscious and unable to observe the event by normal senses. To make sure the NDE patients weren't just providing lucky guesses, he recruited a control group of 25 veteran cardiac patients to attempt a description of their resuscitations. The result? Twenty out of 23 who attempted the task in the control group made at least one major error in their descriptions; the accounts of the 32 NDE experiencers "did correspond in at least a general way to the known facts" of the NDE. Sabom concluded that the NDE accounts of these patients were "not subtle fabrications based on prior general knowledge."[15]

More importantly, six of the 32 NDE experiencers could recall specific details of their near-death event—despite the fact that they were unconscious during the event—providing Sabom with specific facts to check against the records. The recollected details in each case were quite accurate and not interchangeable with details from other near-death crisis descriptions.[16] These specific details included things like which family members were waiting where in the hospital and their emotional reactions, the type of gurneys the patients themselves were riding, the type and description of equipment used to treat them, etc. In one thought-provoking instance, an NDE survivor made an apparent error in describing the work of a defibrillation meter—until Sabom found out that the older model the patient described was exactly the kind used back in 1973 when the patient had his cardiac arrest. Based on his research, Sabom ruled out a common explanation skeptics give for dismissing the reality of these details seen during an OBE: that the accurate portrayal of the near death crisis event is due to prior general knowledge the patient has of how a resuscitation works, and thus his description is merely an educated guess.

Sabom also went on to eliminate two other common explanations: The first was the possibility that the accurate portrayal of the near-death crisis event was based on information supplied to the patient by medical personnel after the event. Sabom found this unlikely for two reasons: doctors and nurses don't normally furnish resuscitation victims with descriptions of their resuscitation as detailed as those recounted by NDE survivors; and in several cases, NDE patients recounted the details to medical personnel shortly after being revived and before their own doctors could have told them anything.

The second common explanation offered by skeptics was that the accurate portrayal of the near-death crisis event might have been based on visual or verbal perceptions made by the patient while in a semiconscious state. Since hearing is the last to go, a skeptic could argue that patients might have picked up a description of their resuscitation from remarks made during the effort. But in the six best cases Sabom examined, several of the autoscopically perceived events were visual, not auditory. Also, many of the details described in these cases were of objects and events outside their visual field, in other rooms or places. Thus none of these possibilities were found to be plausible explanations by Sabom.

Last but not least, Ring and Sabom provided scientific research supporting the belief of NDE experiencers that their experience was real, not a hallucination or dream. The NDE experiencers could tell the difference between the two. One NDE experiencer explained to Sabom that he had previously been in a coma for a week, and had suffered convulsions and hallucinations, but they were different. In the hallucinations, he was like a spectator; in the NDE OBE experience, he knew "it was *me.*"[17] Ring and Sabom further confirmed that NDE experiencers also showed a dramatic decline in their fear of death compared to patients who were near death but had no classic NDE experience.[18] The NDE literally changed their view of life and death.

By 1983, Seattle pediatrician Dr. Melvin Morse had published the first known description of a NDE in a child. That year, in an article in the *American Journal of Diseases of Children,* he told the story of his first encounter with a NDE patient, a young girl called Katie. Morse was the doctor who resuscitated her in the emergency room after she had drowned in a swimming pool accident. The story she told Morse after she miraculously came back to life started him on a medical literature search to see if anyone else had ever come across such a case. There he found the research of Dr. Moody and other pioneers, and decided to conduct research himself, focusing on children's NDEs. He was especially eager to see whether children's NDEs differed from adults (whose NDE reports are more likely to be "polluted by culture" than the stories of children with little life experience).

Morse's Seattle Study answered these and many other questions, and appeared in his book *Closer to the Light.* The federally-funded study team included eight highly-qualified researchers, including medical doctors specializing in anesthetics and the brain, and in child neurology and psychiatry. Hundreds of hours of research and questioning of over 120 seriously ill children led Morse to conclude that the NDE could not be explained as a result of drugs or anesthesia, or hallucinations, or brain-produced chemicals, or oxygen deprivation.

The NDE experience, if real, suggests that the mind can continue to function normally even when a person is considered "dead" by the materialist's definition of death, i.e. the heart has stopped beating as measured by the recording of an electrocardiograph (EKG); and brain activity is non-existent, a flat line as measured on the recording of an electroencephalograph (EEG). It also suggests that humans can "see" and "hear" things happening around them even when there is no active brain to process sensory information (impossible under the materialist philosophical model of reality). Further, the clinically dead person in this NDE state remains a separate, specific individual, retaining his or her personality and memory throughout the NDE. If such activities are possible for the relatively short time people are clinically dead, it is theoretically possible that consciousness could survive for weeks, months, or even for eternity after bodily death.

Moody (www.lifeafterlife.com), Morse (www.melvinmorse.com), Ring and Sabom remain NDE researchers and have collectively authored many books and given hundreds of speeches (Moody himself has six books to his credit). In the last decade, they have been joined by dozens of ordinary laypersons who have written books and articles about their own personal NDE experiences.[19] In terms of scientific research, both Ring and Sabom have produced notable data in recent years. In 1998, Sabom, still a practicing Atlanta cardiologist, wrote *Light and Death: One Doctor's Fascinating Account of Near-Death Experiences*.[20] The book includes findings from his 1994 Atlanta Study as well as a NDE case that is included in our "Best Scientific Evidence" section below. In 1999, Ring, now professor emeritus of psychology at the University of Connecticut, co-authored *Mindsight: Near-Death and Out-of-Body Experiences in the Blind* [21] describing a study of 31 blind and sight-impaired people—including some blind from birth—who reported being able to "see" during their NDE experiences, even though they had no physical sight.

Another co-founder of IANDS, Bruce Greyson, who has served as Director of Research for IANDS since 1983, continues to research the phenomenon in his capacity as a professor in the Department of Psychiatric Medicine, University of Virginia. Some 30+ scientific papers on NDEs and OBEs that Greyson has authored over the last three decades are listed and available through the university website at (www.med.virginia.edu/personality-studies/). They include a study he co-authored and published in the *Journal of Scientific Exploration* entitled "Do Any Near-Death Experiences Provide Evidence for the Survival of Human Personality After Death? Relevant Features and Illustrative Case Reports."[22] Single features of an experience near death do not necessarily suggest survival after death; they may have other explanations. The authors suggest, however, that when three features occur together, the experience does suggest survival. The three features are: enhanced mental processes, seeing the physical body from another position in space, and paranormal perceptions (awareness of events elsewhere that are not accessible to the person's five ordinary senses). The paper describes 14 cases which offer some or all of these features.

In one case investigated by Greyson, a patient named Al Sullivan underwent an emergency quadruple bypass operation and had a typical NDE, including an out-of-body experience. While out of the body, he watched the surgeons operate on his body. One of the surgeons seemed to be "flapping his wings as if trying to fly," and Sullivan told the surgeon what he saw shortly after the operation ended and he regained consciousness. When Greyson investigated the case, the surgeon confirmed that Sullivan had made the comment after he awoke, and that the description of the highly unusual behavior was accurate.

To avoid touching anything with his hands after scrubbing in for the surgery, the surgeon was in the habit of holding his hands against his chest and pointing to things with his elbows to give instructions to other people in the operating room. It's hard to imagine Sullivan coming up with such a highly specific, highly unusual and highly accurate description of events by simply guessing or speculating on what happened during his operation; or for a doctor or nurse involved in the operation telling Sullivan after the operation about the surgeon's odd habit before starting surgery.

Greyson is quick to admit that NDEs can only provide indirect evidence for the survival of consciousness after death because in the end NDE experiencers don't actually die. But he concludes that the Sullivan case and similar ones he has investigated "provide convergent evidence that warrant our taking seriously the idea that consciousness may survive death."

The evidence is indeed beginning to mount. In the Feb. 2001 issue of the *Journal of Resuscitation*, doctors working at Southampton General Hospital in England describe a fascinating, year-long study they conducted involving 63 heart attack patients who were deemed clinically dead but were subsequently resuscitated. Each was interviewed within a week of his/her experience, while memories were fresh. Four of this group remembered NDEs involving thinking, reasoning and moving about (i.e. conscious activity) even after doctors determined their physical brains were not functioning. According to Sam Parnia, one of the physicians who conducted the research, "The studies are very significant in that we have a group of people with no brain function...who have well-structured, lucid thought processes with reasoning and memory formation at a time when their brains are shown not to function."[23] Encouraged by the findings, the Southampton team has since gone on to collect over 3,500 cases of people apparently demonstrating consciousness at a time when they were considered clinically dead by doctors.

Another study at the end of 2001—this time published in the prestigious English medical journal *The Lancet*—added more scientific support for the possibility that consciousness continues even when people are clinically dead and show a flat EEG.[24] A team of doctors in the Netherlands studied 344 patients who were resuscitated after cardiac arrest, including 62 patients (18% of those revived) who reported NDEs. They found that the NDE experiences weren't explainable as reactions to medication; by a fear of death on the part of the patient (a hypothesis offered by some psychologists to explain NDEs); or by physiological changes in the brain caused by a lack of oxygen which can cause sensory distortions and hallucinations. Concluded the researchers, "The NDE pushes at the limits of medical ideas about the range of human consciousness and the mind-brain relation." They call for more research, and a willingness by scientists to include as an explanation for NDEs the possibility that the mind is more than just the physical brain, i.e. "that the NDE might be a changing state of consciousness (transcendence) in which identity, cognition and emotion function independently from the unconscious body…"

Near death studies focus on *involuntary* out of body experiences. But do you have to wait for an accident or heart attack to have an out of body experience? Can you *voluntarily* have one? What if you were able to travel anywhere in the world without spending a cent on airline tickets. Check up on your elderly mom living 500 miles away in another state, or see what's going on behind closed doors in another room. Better yet, how about possibly being able to travel anywhere in the universe, to different dimensions of reality, including the afterlife state. Both scientists and ordinary people are currently experimenting with voluntary out-of-body experiences (as opposed to the involuntary OBE experience that accompanies an NDE experience).

Belief in the ability to voluntarily separate your consciousness from your body is common in many cultures around the world. D. Shiels, in his 1978 study of nearly 70 non-Western cultures around the world found that, despite cultural differences, OBE beliefs are strikingly similar, indicating consensus on the basic elements of the phenomenon.[25]

What about in the rational, scientific West? Belief in the OBE experience is also surprisingly common in modern, post-World War II America. A number of surveys done in the United States, dating back to at least 1954, indicate substantial acceptance of the reality of the OBE experience in America too. Anywhere from 14 to 34 percent of those polled in five different cited surveys responded that they had experienced an OBE. For example, a 1975 a survey of a randomly selected group of 1,000 students and townspeople in a small town in Virginia reported that 25 percent of the students and 14 percent of the townspeople reported having an OBE.[26] But we can probably thank near death studies for making the scientific community more open to the possibility that some persons can *voluntarily* do the same thing that near death experiencers do involuntarily.

The founders of England's famous Society for Psychical Research (see next chapter) conducted a number of thorough investigations of reports of "apparitions of the living," some of them produced voluntarily by curious experimenters determined to project themselves into another place to be seen there by friends or lovers. Some of the best cases of successful, voluntary OBE experiments were collected and written up by Hornell and Ella Hart.[27] The exploits of a young gentleman named S.H. Beard, described below in "Best Evidence," is one of these carefully investigated and verified OBE experiments.

In more modern times, one of the most famous OBE experimenters in the U.S. was the late Robert A. Monroe. The son of a college professor father and a medical doctor mother, he was a graduate of Ohio State University where he studied engineering and journalism. His 50-year career in broadcasting and advertising included the creation or production of over 400 radio and TV network programs. He later became owner and operator of a string of radio stations in North Carolina and Virginia.

Monroe had his initial out-of-body experiences in early 1958. They scared him badly. He thought he was dying, or had epilepsy, or a brain disorder, or was suffering from hallucinations and going insane. But despite batteries of tests and physical examinations, neither his family doctor, Dr. Gordon, nor his psychologist friend, Dr. Bradshaw, could find anything wrong with him. A rational man with an above-average grounding in both medicine and science, Monroe began to read everything he could find about the history of the concept, and began to experiment, using himself as the guinea pig. The story of his initial experiments is found in his first book, the 1971 classic *Journeys Out of the Body*.

One early OBE Monroe experienced, which took place Sept. 10, 1958, gave Monroe what he felt for the first time was proof that his OBEs were real and not simply vivid dreams or hallucinations. He took an OBE with the idea of visiting Dr. Bradshaw, who at the time was supposed to be sick in bed. As he approached the Bradshaw house, however, he was surprised to see Bradshaw and his wife walking along outside. When he returned to his body, he called Bradshaw. Bradshaw informed him that he had decided some fresh air would help him and was indeed taking a walk outside at the time Monroe had seen him. For Monroe, this was proof that he was not hallucinating, that his mind was not producing what it expected to see (Bradshaw in bed) but rather something real. For Monroe, it was a "simple incident, but unforgettable." [28]

Monroe was also a certified sane OBE experimenter. To demonstrate to skeptics that he was a normal, average human being and not a kook, Monroe voluntarily presented himself to the Topeka V.A. Hospital in 1977 so they could do in-depth psychiatric and psychological investigations on him. The personality tests were conducted by Stuart Twemlow, M.D., a psychiatrist and chief of research on the faculty of the Menninger School of Psychiatry there. The results of these tests can be found in *Journeys Out of the Body.* The tests found no evidence of a psychologically disturbed or troubled individual; instead, Monroe was judged to be sane, normal and rational.

Several of Monroe's OBE trips themselves were also studied as they happened by scientists in various controlled laboratory experiments.[29] The earliest were conducted in 1965-1966 at the Electroencephalographic Laboratory of the University of Virginia Medical School by psychologist Charles Tart (the results of these tests are described in the preface Tart wrote to Monroe's *Journeys Out of the Body*). While Tart tentatively concluded that Monroe's OBE might have been something more than just a dream,[30] he also demonstrated that researchers could investigate the OBE scientifically in a laboratory. Tart is responsible for popularizing Monroe's term "out-of-body experience." He went on to conduct a number of fascinating scientific OBE experiments, including one where a woman in an OBE state was able to accurately "see" a random, 5-digit target number placed on a high shelf above the bed where she lay wired up to electrodes. The odds against her simply guessing the target number 25132 by chance alone were 100,000 to 1. Tart eventually concluded that in some—though not all—OBEs, "the mind may, at least partially, really be located elsewhere than the physical body." In other cases, the mind may still be in the physical body, but getting its accurate information by ESP.[31]

In May 1980, Twemlow presented to attendees at the annual meeting of the American Psychiatric Association in San Francisco a study detailing the OBE experiences of 339 individuals. The paper, entitled *The Out-Of-Body Experience: Phenomenology,* can be found at the back of Monroe's second major book, *Far Journeys.* Among the study findings: the OBE experience does not appear to be simply a vivid dream or hallucination, but rather the experience of a true sense of separation of the person's mind from his or her body; the OBE experiencers as a group reflect a broad range of age, educational and geographic characteristics, and demonstrate good psychological and physical adjustment; and most of those tested had experienced more than one OBE experience.

In 1984, respected paranormal researcher D. Scott Rogo presented an interesting paper entitled, "Researching the Out-of-Body Experience: The State of the Art."[32] Rogo reviewed the existing research literature seeking answers to several fundamental questions crucial to understanding the OBE phenomenon. Citing data from over 60 studies and reports (which are listed in the references section of the paper), Rogo concluded that:

- The OBE experience was a common human experience, with roughly 10-20 percent of the adult population undergoing an OBE sometime in their lives.
- OBE experiencers weren't special types of persons (e.g. persons with pathological states of mind, or over-anxious about death, prone to fantasy, etc.).
- At least some OBE experiencers can be "detected" at distant locations during their OBE travels by the use of animal, human and sometimes physical detectors.
- At least some gifted OBE experiencers can sometimes make surprisingly correct observations at distant locations while traveling out of the body.
- At least some OBEs are certainly not dreams or hallucinations.

Like NDEs, in the last decade OBEs have become the subject of dozens of popular books written by persons who report they have experienced an OBE. Some of these books include instructions for attempting an OBE yourself. Monroe himself died in 1995 at age 79. He left behind in Faber, Virginia an OBE research and educational facility called the Monroe Institute of Applied Science where interested persons may try Monroe's method for experiencing first-hand an OBE themselves. Visitors to the institute's online website (www.monroeinstitute.com) are greeted with a quote from Monroe: "The greatest illusion is that man has limitations."

Best Scientific Evidence

1991 "Pam Reynolds" Case

The "Pam Reynolds" (a pseudonym used by Sabom) case found in Sabom's 1998 book *Light & Death*, offers a well-documented case of someone "seeing" and "hearing" things during an OBE that were physically impossible to see or hear but were later verified as accurate and true. Sabom himself has called it "the most incredible case I have come across in the 20 or so years of NDE research."[33] While her body was unconscious on the operating table, Pam left her body and floated up to the ceiling where she could look down and "see" the surgeon as he cut open her skull with a pneumatically-powered bone saw, and "hear" nurses talking about how small her veins and arteries were. Her visual observations in this OBE state were not vague or general, but rather extremely detailed and specific. For instance, she described the Midas Rex bone saw as resembling an electric toothbrush with a grove or dent on top where it went into the handle; and interchangeable blades stored in a neurosurgery instrument case which to her looked like a socket wrench case. Sabom provides in his book photos of both the saw and instrument case to illustrate how accurate Pam's OBE "sight" was.

But the real value of Pam's case lies in the fact that her NDE experience continued on during the 1991 operation while she was in a state of stone-cold death. In fact, you probably can't get any deader than Pam was during her NDE. For her amazing "standstill" brain operation, doctors had put her in full, hypothermic cardiac arrest. They dropped her core body temperature to 60 degrees, then completely drained all the blood from her head, and left her with no measurable breathing, heartbeat or brain waves. Verifying this absence of life, or vital signs, were just about every medical measuring device available, including instruments which monitored her blood pressure, blood flow, oxygen level in her blood, core body temperature, urinary temperature, and cortical brain activity. Her NDE (near death experience) was actually by all known standards a "DE" (death experience). Yet while in this verified (by full instrumentation) state of extreme clinical death, Pam progressed through a typical NDE, through a tunnel, into the light, were she met her cousin, grandmother, grandfather, great-great aunt, and other people. When it was time to return, her uncle took Pam back through the tunnel to her physical body. This NDE case perhaps comes closest to providing solid, scientific evidence suggestive of post-mortem survival of consciousness.

Case of Mr. "S", Retired Air Force Pilot

In his book *Recollections of Death*, Sabom provides us with six other well-researched and documented NDE cases where very specific details seen by unconscious NDE patients during their OBEs are independently corroborated by medical records or witnesses. My personal favorite is the case of Mr. "S," a retired Air Force pilot who had a massive heart attack when he was 39.[34] Sabom interviewed him in May 1978, five years after he had experienced his heart attack.

In the interview, Mr. "S" describes how he observed the frantic resuscitation efforts as a disinterested observer, standing on the sidelines. As Sabom notes, among the wealth of very specific details the patient observed while unconscious and out of body included: doctors and nurses rushing in to save him; an injection into his IV line; the cardiac board being placed behind his back; movement of the dials on the face of the defibrillation machine while it was being charged up; the pressing of "buttons" on top of the defibrillator paddles to discharge the defibrillator; the jolt of his body from three successive defibrillation attempts; external cardiac massage between defibrillation attempts; and the holding of a light-green oxygen mask, hissing under pressure, over his face during the procedure. Sabom was able to confirm the basic details of the near-death crisis event with medical records obtained from the hospital and noted that the man's description accurately matched what you would expect to happen in an ICU unit during CPR. But Sabom was particularly fascinated by his accurate description of the unusual movement of two needles on the face of the defibrillation machine. The description also matched the operations of the type of machine in common use in 1973, but which were not found on newer machines.

Sabom asked Mr. "S" if he had been exposed to CPR resuscitation techniques in the Air Force because Mr. "S" used some sophisticated medical terms in his account of the events that implied he had a knowledge of medical jargon and procedures. The patient explained to Sabom that during his OBE he had paid attention to the medical staff as they worked and overheard them using the terms. Mr. "S" accepted his amazing NDE as simply a fact of life, something hard to explain, but that's the way it was.

Ring and Lawrence Trio of Cases
Three fascinating reports of independently verified perception during an NDE have been described by Dr. Kenneth Ring and Madelaine Lawrence, R.N. Ph.D., Director of Nursing Research at Hartford Hospital in Connecticut.[35] Nurse Kathy Milne was working as a nurse at Hartford (CT) Hospital in 1985 when she got to talking with a woman who had been resuscitated. The patient described floating out of her body, watching the frantic resuscitation effort, then finding herself above the hospital roof, looking at the Hartford skyline. After marveling at the interesting view for a bit, she looked over and spied a red object, a shoe. But while she was thinking about it, she was sucked back into her body where she subsequently related the story to Milne. Milne told a skeptical doctor who mocked the story but got a janitor to help him get up on the roof. He found the red shoe, and became a believer too.

1881-1884 S.H. Beard OBE Experiments
Mr. Beard was a member of the London Stock Exchange and a gentleman of some means and reputation. His character and honesty were

personally known to Mr. Edmund Gurney, a founder of the Society for Psychical Research (SPR). Beard also was seen by multiple witnesses, and twice witnesses experienced his physical touch; in one instance he announced in advance the date, time and target of his attempted OBE projection; and written reports and signed affidavits from witnesses were routinely collected by the SPR in their follow-up investigation of Beard's claims.

The series of experiments[36] began one Sunday evening in London in Nov. 1881 when Beard, after reading a book describing the amazing power of the human will, on the spur of the moment decided to try and project his spirit into the second-floor front bedroom of a house three miles away where two lady friends of his slept. His targets were Miss L.S. Verity and her younger sister, E.C. Verity. The following Thursday, he was visiting the ladies when, without prompting (later confirmed under cross-examination by the SPR), the older sister, L.S. Verity, blurted out that she had been terrified by seeing him standing in her room the previous Sunday. She had been awake at the time (around one AM., the time Beard was trying to project his spirit) and a gas lamp was burning in the room. When Beard's apparition started to approach her, she screamed and awoke her sister E.C. who also saw Beard's apparition. Beard was very startled by his success, and wrote down a detailed account of the events in his dairy within the same week, preserving a record of the independently verified (two witnesses) OBE. The Verity sisters later supplied the SPR with written testimony to the accuracy of Beard's account. Intrigued by his success, Beard eventually tried it again in Dec. 1882—same target, the long-suffering Verity sisters. This time, he wanted to not only make them see him but also feel his touch. The next night, out on the town, he accidentally encountered Mrs. L, the married sister of L.C. and E.C. Verity. She told Beard without prompting that she had seen him twice the previous night. She had been staying with her sister in the Verity house and around 9:30 PM saw him in the hallway. Later, while still awake about 12 midnight, Mrs. L saw the door open, Beard enter the bedroom, walk over, and touch her hair. Afterwards, Mrs. L woke he sister up to tell her what she saw (the sister later confirmed Mrs. L's story in writing to the SPR investigators).

At Gurney's suggestion, Beard ultimately agreed to conduct an experiment involving letting Gurney know in advance of a date, a time and a target. On March 22, 1884, Beard wrote Gurney: "I am going to try the experiment tonight of making my presence perceptible at 44, Norland Square, at 12 PM." Who lived there? As might be guessed, it was the poor Verity sisters. A week later, Gurney received a written and signed statement from L.S. Verity attesting to Beard's unexpected presence in her room at the date and time Beard had targeted. She had seen him while she was wide awake, and with such vividness, that she almost had a nervous collapse and a doctor had been called. She had also felt his touch on her hair, something Beard had promised Gurney in advance he would do during the experiment to make the success "complete in every detail."

Highly Recommended Reading:

Sabom, Michael, M.D. *Light and Death: One Doctor's Fascinating Account of Near-Death Experiences.* Zondevan Publishing, 1998. A Christian, Sabom does a good job in this book of separating his religious beliefs from his scientific research. This book carries the details of the "Pam Reynolds" case cited in "Best Scientific Evidence"; the complete, detailed statistics from his 1994 Atlanta Study; and an excellent chapter on why hypotheses raised by skeptics (endorphins, hypoxia, temporal lobe seizures, reconstructed hallucinations, imagination) to explain away veridical OBEs like Pam experienced simply don't work.

Ring, Kenneth and Cooper, Sharon. *Mindsight: Near-Death and Out-of-Body Experiences in the Blind,* William James Center for Consciousness Studies, 1999. This book was chosen best NDE book of the year for 1999. Ring is also author of *Heading Toward Omega: In Search of the*

Meaning of the Near-Death Experience (1985) and co-author of *Lessons From the Light: What We Can Learn from Near-Death Experiences* (1998). Two earlier NDE books of Ring are out of print.

Morse, Melvin, M.D. *Closer to the Light: Learning from Children's Near-Death Experiences,* New York: Villard Books, 1990. The medical profession is starting to take NDEs seriously. Morse cited 70 scientific studies which are included in the medical bibliography that appears in the back of the book. Pages 183-193 are especially interesting since many skeptics variously explain away NDEs as a product of hallucinations, anesthesia, hypoxia, transient depersonalization, birth memories, endorphins, drug reactions. In these ten pages, Morse gives his reasons why these explanations have problems. Morse went on to write *Transformed by the Light* (1992) and *Parting Visions: Uses and Meanings of Pre-Death, Psychic and Spiritual Experiences* (1994). Morse argues for the reality of the near death experience and near death visions. Even if people's experiences can't be readily duplicated in the laboratory, " We arrive at truths by listening to patients," he says.[37]

Sabom, Michael, M.D. *Recollections of Death: A Medical Investigation.* New York: Harper and Row, 1982. Sabom's research was the first systematic study to provide strong scientific evidence for the ability of some NDE experiencers to accurately see things while out of the body which can later be independently verified. Such evidence is critical for any "proof" of the ability of the human consciousness to operate independently of the brain (and the physical body) in some sort of life-after-death existence. The "Mr. S." case described in "Best Scientific Evidence" comes from this book.

Moody, Raymond, M.D. *Life After Life.* New York: Bantam Books, 1975. This is the classic which introduced millions of average Americans to the concept of the Near Death Experience. It presented over 100 NDE cases for the reader to ponder. Moody dedicated the book to Dr. George Ritchie whose NDE experience spurred Moody to pursue his original investigations. Over 14 million copies of the book have been sold. Moody went on to write five more books, including *Reflections on Life After Life* (1977); *The Light Beyond* (1988); *Coming Back* (1992); *Reunions* (1993); and *The Last Laugh: A New Philosophy of Near-Death Experiences, Apparitions and the Paranormal* (1999). Moody was the first to recognize how common and consistently uniform the NDE experience was. In his book *Life After Life*, Moody concludes that the mind separates from the body at death, and passes on to other realms. [38]

Monroe, Robert A. *Journeys Out of the Body.* New York: Main Street Books, 1973. A classic, first-person account of unexpected out of body experiences. Monroe's story is perhaps one of the most well-known in the field. Monroe coined the term "out-of-body" as a replacement for "astral travel," an older term he felt was too identified with the occult, and fringe science. Monroe also wrote two other books: *Far Journeys* (1985), and *Ultimate Journey* (1996).

12.

Ghosts and Poltergeists

"There are things that we do not understand, and Science, to its eternal shame, is making little attempt to understand them."
Legendary English ghost hunter Harry Price

I and my five brothers and sisters grew up in Connecticut in a large, old colonial house built in 1760 that had served as a tavern in the Revolutionary War. As kids, we never encountered a ghost in the dark cellar or creaky-floored attic of Farnam House, but we were always on our guard. New England is famous for its ghosts, and its history, landscape, weather, and plentiful supply of ancient, brooding houses conspired to create an atmosphere conducive to belief in ghosts. On late winter evenings, I always hurried past the town cemetery on South Street without looking back as I delivered newspapers on my paper route, and I loved Halloween every year. Halloween is a major celebration in New England, where orange pumpkins shine from windows and deserted country roads wind through dark woods populated with shadowy branches and scurrying sounds. Not far from our town lies the famous Sleepy Hollow, home of the headless horseman immortalized in Washington Irving's wonderful ghost tale of the same name. Although I later left New England, I retained a curiosity about ghosts that persists to this day. I've never personally seen a ghost, but I'm ready if one should come knocking on my door some night.

Ghosts are a universal phenomenon, seen again and again and again without end by people of every culture, every religion and every country on earth. They have been reported for thousands of years by people from every economic strata; every educational strata; and every social strata. They have been seen by kings and peasants, hamburger-flippers and nuclear scientists, aborigines and bank presidents, doctors and laborers, by famous people and by average citizens, by men and women and children of every age and sex. The famous 18th century philosopher Immanuel Kant (1724-1804), speaking of ghost stories, said, "...although I doubt each one taken by itself, when they are considered as a group I have some belief in them."

Ghost sightings continue to this day, to this minute (somewhere in the world, at this very moment, someone is probably encountering a ghost). You'll find ghosts haunting the literature of every language, from Shakespeare's *Hamlet* to the Japanese folk tale of the wronged maidservant Okiku whose ghost would not leave samurai Aoyama Tessan in peace. As Charles Dickens said of ghost Jacob Marley's death in the opening page of his delightful little ghost story *A Christmas Carol*, "There can be no doubt about this." Likewise, there can be no doubt about whether the phenomena called "ghosts" *exist*; the only debate is exactly what "ghosts" are.

The first-known written collection of ghost cases in the West was published in Latin in 1573 under the title *Ghostes and Spirites Walking by Nyght*.[1] But modern, systematic, scientific ghost and poltergeist research began in 1882 with the establishment in England of the Society for Psychical Research (SPR) by a small group of prominent British academics and scientists. They approached the ghost phenomenon with an open mind and a commitment to quiet, scholarly investigation: "The very last thing we expect to produce is a collection of narratives of a startling or blood-chilling character; our pages are far more likely to provoke sleep in the course of perusal than to banish it afterwards."[2] When they put out their call to friends and colleagues for any experiences or encounters they or their associates might have had with ghosts, they were deluged with reports.

The sheer number of reports they received led them to believe they were not wasting their time studying the phenomenon. As they noted, "The point in the evidence that impresses us is not its exciting or terrific quality, but its overwhelming quantity—overwhelming, we mean, to any further doubting of the reality of the class of phenomenon."[3]

In 1886, the SPR published a thick, two-volume, 1400-page summary of their ghost research to that point entitled *Phantasms of the Living*. It included extensive details on over 700 apparition cases collected and personally investigated (including careful follow-up verification of details and witness statements) by society researchers, and remains a classic in the ghost-hunting field. The SPR went on to collect hundreds of additional reports, and develop most of the different scientific hypotheses offered today to try and explain the various ghost phenomenon (ESP and telepathy were among the prime possibilities considered by SPR researchers).

The SPR's credible work and sober reputation encouraged the formation in America in 1885 of a similar organization, the American Society for Psychical Research (ASPR). The ASPR vigorously collected, analyzed and investigated ghost encounters in the U.S. and published additional, solid reports on the puzzling phenomenon.

One of the most important contributions made by SPR to the scientific understanding of ghosts was the classification system they developed, grouping different types of apparitions according to common, shared characteristics. Ghosts come in many different forms. Researchers have identified up to 20 different kinds, but ghosts are typically classified into several major categories according to a system devised by former SPR president G.N.M Tyrrell.

Crisis Apparitions

A mother suddenly awakes in the middle of the night to see the specter of her soldier son standing by her bed. He has a bullet wound in his chest. He smiles and waves goodbye to her. The next day, she gets a telegram from the Army that her son has been killed in battle. This is a typical crisis apparition, occurring within a short period (12 hours, by SPR definition) of a major crisis such as actual death, impending death, falling into a coma, or another life-threatening situation. The person in peril appears to someone he knows, to inform them of the dramatic change or imminent change in his situation. Based on reports collected by the SPR and ASPR, crisis apparitions are statistically the most frequently reported type of ghost. A classic crisis apparition is the case of Lt. David McConnel in World War I, cited in Best Scientific Evidence" below.

Post-Mortem Apparitions

This is the classic ghost—the apparently disincarnate spirit of some specific individual who has been dead for more than 12 hours: it might be a day, a week, a year or even several centuries. These apparitions are often able to communicate with the living, react to the actions and thoughts of living persons, or pass on information. Among the apparent reasons cited for the return of these ghosts: a desire to fulfill a promise made before death or remind someone living of a promise they had made; an attempt to atone for a wrong or seek forgiveness; a wish to reassure or console someone living; a need to deliver important advice or a warning; or an attempt to secure justice or exoneration. The James Chaffin apparition case, described below in the "Best Scientific Evidence" section of this chapter, is an excellent example—the ghost coming back four years after his death to pass on to his son important information about a secretly revised last will and testament. A disembodied spirit hypothesis most closely fits the evidence provided by post-mortem apparitions. Surveys have shown that widows and widowers quite frequently have a visionary encounter with their deceased spouse.[4]

Haunting Apparitions

Also called "continuing" or "recurring apparitions," these ghosts are like projected holograms, or psychic movies that run and rerun again and again. They usually appear in the exact same place all the time; they perform the same repetitive action for any viewer (walking down the stairs then turning left through a wall, sitting in a rocking chair knitting, etc.); and unlike post-mortem or crisis apparitions, they don't communicate interactively in any way with the viewer. They take no notice of them. An often-cited example of this type of haunting apparition is the Cheltenham house haunting of 1882. It's interesting to note that the ghosts of dogs, cats and other animals have also been encountered along with human beings. Some researchers hypothesize that haunting apparitions are best explained as an unknown form of invisible, residual energy from an exceedingly powerful, emotionally explosive event—a horrible murder or rape, a bloody battle, an overwhelming experience of grief or pain, etc. These super-intense emotions somehow leave a psychic residue or 'force field" in a place which can be "received" by sensitive persons. This energy would be analogous to radio waves, another form of real but invisible energy that exists all around us but can only manifest itself to something tuned to its frequency.

Apparitions of the Living

A number of cases have been reported of people seeing apparitions of persons still alive. Some crisis apparitions take place before the person dies, and thus technically speaking are apparitions of the living. In addition, living persons have reportedly had their spirits seen by witnesses in other places during voluntary or involuntary out-of-body experiences, or during telepathic projection experiments. The German language even has a term for a person's double, or second self—a *doppelganger*. Norwegians use the term *vardogar* to refer to their double, and a number of cases have been reported in that country of a person's *vardogar* arriving at home before the person himself did. Most people today would not include these apparitions under the concept of a "ghost," but rather under the category of out-of-body experiences. The SPR, however, included such cases in its 1886 *Phantasms of the Living* study.

Poltergeists

The unseen "noisy ghost," or poltergeist, certainly lives up to its German name. Parapsychologist Alan Gauld poetically catalogues some of the clatter and uproar they cause in his book *Poltergeists*. They include "raps, taps, thumps, thuds, crashes, bangs and bombinations." They also throw, tilt, move and lift objects as small as a pin or as large as a dining room table; communicate by raps and noises; play musical instruments, cause fires and deluges of water; annoy and upset animals; interfere with radios, TVs, light bulbs and other electrical and electronic equipment; tear clothes and even sometimes beat or bite people.

Interestingly enough, despite popular belief, ghosts and apparitions aren't seen only at night. Psychologist Dr. Walter Franklin Prince found that over 40 percent of apparitions appear in daylight and another 10-20 percent are seen under good artificial light conditions.[5]

Ghost and apparition cases involving multiple, independent witnesses are obviously more believable than those involving a single witness. In the early 1930s, two SPR members, Hornell Hart and his wife Ella, collected into one report[6] some 80 authenticated, investigated, multiple witness apparition cases, taken primarily from the files of the SPR. Their best or "primary evidence" cases involved two or more witnesses who separately and personally experienced the same event at the same time who had filed written records of their experience within one year of the date it occurred. They also presented some high-quality "secondary" and "tertiary" cases. One of the best primary cases from their files happened in 1931. A chimney sweep named Samuel Bull died of cancer in June of that year, leaving behind in his house his widow, grandson James and later a married daughter and her five children and husband. In Feb. 1932, the married daughter and the grandson saw Sam Bull's ghost for the first time, walking up the stairs and passing through a door into the room where he had died. Between February and April, everyone in the house saw the ghost, including a 5-year old girl who recognized the ghost as "grandpa Bull." On one occasion, the ghost was visible to them for a half-hour. He was seen in great detail by all of them, both in daylight and by artificial light. He twice laid his had on the brow of his widow and once called her name. When word got out of the strange occurrences at the family home, the local Vicar investigated the case and interviewed them, coming away with the opinion that they were telling the truth. Subsequently, a number of notables visited them and interviewed them, including Lord Balfour. Signed and written statements were also collected from members of the family, documenting their observations and claims.

The objective reality of the ghosts described in their report, concluded the Harts, could be measured in number of ways, including: a) the extent to which they affected more than one sense (in three reported cases the ghost was not only seen but also heard and felt); b) how consistently multiple witnesses described the same apparition from wherever they were at the time (what the ghost was wearing, what specific actions it took, what facial expressions it showed); and c) to what extent the apparition affected the physical, "real" world in which we live (in various cases, the ghost cast a shadow, appeared as a reflection in a mirror, opened a door, extinguished a light and, in one case dragged the observer along when the observed grabbed it). The best apparitions, they noted, presented themselves to the observers as an ordinary sense experience.

Unfortunately for ghost research, as the 20th century progressed, the controlled, repeatable laboratory experiment emerged as the only acceptable standard of scientific truth. Anecdotal evidence—stories told by fallible human beings of strange, often fleeting phenomena whose existence rested primarily on the authority of the reporter (no matter how honest and credible that person's reputation)—was no longer acceptable to a science whose underlying philosophy of materialism deemed ghosts impossible anyway.

Ghost investigations slowly began to fall out of favor, even with paranormal researchers. Dr. J.B. Rhine's success with his controlled laboratory experiments on ESP in the 1930s further encouraged ambitious, young psychic investigators to adopt the experimental approach. By mid-20th century, ghost research had declined in both quality and quantity, both in England and America, and the number of serious ghost-hunters dwindled to a handful of stubborn parapsychologists, including Dr. Gertrude Schmeidler and the late Dr. Karlis Osis.

Schmeidler, who taught psychology at City College New York and has conducted significant ESP and PK research, pioneered a number of scientific, qualitative techniques for investigating hauntings. In the 1960s, she started investigating ghosts at the request of a friend bothered by one. She tested ghost and poltergeist witnesses to determine their credibility and susceptibility to fantasy (among those she tested was Julio Vasquez, focus of the famous 1967 Miami poltergeist case). She employed psychics and "sensitives" to tour a haunted house, and matched their reports of "cold spots" and their mental impressions of the "ghost" against ghost witness reports, using statistics to identify any significant correlation. She also used confirmed skeptics as control groups in her research.

But those hardy parapsychologists who remained interested at all in ghosts and poltergeists could be forgiven for perhaps seeing poltergeists as a less career-threatening target of research among the two. Poltergeist phenomena could at least be hypothesized as a form of psychokinesis produced unconsciously by the human mind. Post-mortem apparitions, in contrast, almost force investigators to honestly consider such hypotheses as the existence of disembodied spirits and life after death. But such hypotheses automatically entangled you in questions of religion, the supernatural and post-mortem survival which establishment science rejected as superstition. Offering a paranormal phenomenon like psychokinesis as an explanation for poltergeist phenomena was bad enough; offering spirits of the dead as an explanation could end your career.

Today, poltergeists remain less controversial within the broader scientific community. Professor William G. Roll is among the most well-known and respected living scientific investigators of poltergeist phenomena (he also investigates ghosts). Roll studied at UC-Berkeley and Oxford University in England and later became director of the Psychical Research Foundation in Durham, North Carolina. He subsequently worked as Professor of Psychology and Psychical Research at the State University of West Georgia where he still teaches parapsychology courses. His faculty appointment was the first professorship in the U.S. devoted to teaching and research in parapsychology. Most of his poltergeist research is presented at conventions of the Parapsychological Association and appears regularly in the *Journal of Parapsychology* (www.parapsych.org). In 1995, Roll co-authored the book *Psychic Connections: A Journey into the Mysterious World of Psi.*[7]

Roll, who investigated the famous 1966-67 Miami poltergeist case offered below in "Best Scientific Evidence," is among those who prefer to exclude poltergeists from the ranks of disembodied spirits and put them instead in the category of "recurrent spontaneous psychokinesis" (RSPK). He has noticed that many poltergeist outbreaks are often associated with the presence at the scene of some living person in or near the age of puberty; for example, an emotional teenager unhappy at home. Roll doesn't rule out the possibility of discarnate spirits, but believes it more likely that a living person is producing the poltergeist effects through a form of psychokinesis.

In both the Miami, Florida and Rosenheim, Germany poltergeist cases described in "Best Scientific Evidence" below, Roll's hypothesis works as well as the disembodied spirit hypothesis. In each case, the poltergeist phenomena were closely linked to the physical presence of a specific, living person—Anne Marie Schneider in Germany and Julio Vasquez in Miami. Their unconscious minds could have been causing the poltergeist phenomena through psychokinesis. Of course, not everyone buys the RSPK theory for poltergeist activity. Disembodied spirits, working through Anne Marie and Julio Vasquez and using them as agents, could also explain the Miami and Rosenheim cases.

Meanwhile, serious scientific investigation of reports of ghostly apparitions and hauntings (as opposed to poltergeist phenomena) remains rare today. The Division of Personality Studies, University of Virginia Health System, which we saw studies death bed visions and NDE/OBE phenomena, invites the public to send them anecdotal ghost reports, especially reports of crisis apparitions. Researchers there believe that ghost apparitions may still be happening as often as they were a century ago, but are simply not being reported like they used to be. Gallup poll numbers continue to show a high number of ghostly encounters by the public. In 1990, one in seven Americans polled by Gallup reported they had been in a haunted house, and one in ten reported encountering a ghost. If the ten percent of Americans who reported encountering a ghost ever did report their experiences, researchers would indeed be swamped with millions of reports.

Dr. Ian Stevenson, who works at the Division of Personality Studies, is best known for his reincarnation research. But he has also done research on apparitions in an attempt to remind his colleagues in the scientific community that, whether they study them or not, apparitions haven't disappeared. Ignoring them is not making them go away. One investigation[8] published in 1995 involved six apparition cases occurring between 1955 and 1989 in the U.S. and England. It included a "collective apparition case"—a ghost seen by more than one person at the same time. When two or more people see the same thing, it obviously makes the case stronger by reducing the chances of the sighting being a hallucination. Stevenson notes that between one-third to one-half of all ghost sightings involve multiple witnesses. He also believes it is a "folk myth" to say all people embellish or confuse their facts over time when recounting experiences with apparitions. Highly emotional and unusual experiences like seeing a ghost, he argues, are likely to be remembered more accurately.

Could ghosts make a comeback as a target for research? Recent increased scientific investigation of phenomena suggesting the possibility of life after death (especially NDEs) may be slowly changing attitudes of younger scientists towards ghost research. Once you accept the possibility of human consciousness functioning even when the body is clinically dead—in effect, a human mind operating freely of a material body—you are almost forced to accept the possibility of disembodied spirits.

An example of this synergy between NDE and ghost research is the work of Dr. Raymond Moody, M.D. who pioneered NDE research with his groundbreaking book *Life After Life.* Perhaps due to his training in both philosophy and medicine, he is one of the most intellectually daring among his parapsychology peers. He is uncomfortable with the abstract, intellectualized approach favored by modern parapsychology which "seems almost to have renounced its connection to the soul."[9] Moody himself has personally undergone past-life regression, and his Theater of the Mind, described in his book *Reunions: Visionary Encounters With Departed Loved Ones,* is an exceptionally bold and unusual controlled experiment in ghost research—specifically post-mortem apparitions. Moody uses a modern version of an ancient Greek mirror-gazing technique to allow people the possibility of contacting post-mortem apparitions in the form of their deceased loved ones. In his book, Moody tells stories of real people who tried mirror-gazing and concluded that they actually did contact their dead relatives. Incidentally, Moody checked with ghost/poltergeist expert Roll before he started his experiment. Roll assured Moody that apparitions—if they appeared to those trying mirror-gazing—were not something that would harm the contactee. Reflecting on his mirror-gazing method of inducing visionary encounters with the dead, he says new techniques like his are needed to supplement and invigorate paranormal research. The interesting thing about Moody's idea is that it is a testable laboratory experiment. You can try it and see if it works. Moody continues to operate his Theater of the Mind laboratory as a research facility, conducting professional workshops for educators and clinicians.

Best Scientific Evidence

There have undoubtedly been millions of ghost sightings throughout history. They are among the most common paranormal phenomena experienced around the world. Relatively few however have been investigated scientifically. Some of the most thorough and credible investigations were conducted almost a century ago by the Society for Psychical Research, and put modern ghost investigations to shame.

1925: James L. Chaffin Apparition

This is one of the best investigated and verified "post-mortem" apparition case from the files of the SPR.[10] When North Carolina farmer James L. Chaffin died from a fall on Sept. 7, 1921, his wife and four sons knew that the farm would go to Chaffin's third son Marshall. In a signed and witnessed document the whole family knew about, James Chaffin had given Marshall the farm in his will of Nov. 16, 1905. Consequently, no one contested the will. What no one knew was that in January 1919, two years before he died, James Chaffin had actually changed his mind and written a new will, giving all four sons a share in the property. This amended will he stuck in the pages of an old family bible. For four years, Marshall enjoyed the farm his father had apparently willed to him alone. But in June 1925, one of Marshall's brothers, named J.P., began to have very vivid dreams in which his father James appeared at his bedside, wearing his old black overcoat. In the dream, he told his son, "You will find my will in my overcoat pocket." The son awoke convinced that his father had come back from the dead to explain some mistake dealing with his last will. He found out that his mother had given his father's coat away to his brother John who lived 20 miles away. When he went there and examined the coat, he found sewn in the lining a piece of paper in his father's handwriting that said "Read the 27th Chapter of Genesis in my daddie's old Bible." Now convinced more than ever that something important was about to be revealed, J.P. asked a neighbor to be a witness when they actually opened the bible. After searching the house, they finally found the bible and the updated will. The second will was then submitted to the court and the State of North Carolina ruled it to be valid. Thus a ghost successfully communicated with a living person the existence of a document apparently unknown to anyone but the ghost. The SPR carefully investigated the case, sending a lawyer down to North Carolina to review the written court documents, sworn testimony of witnesses, and interview family members and inspect the second will. Had someone faked the handwriting of James Chaffin? Ten witnesses were on court record as recognizing the handwriting as Mr. Chaffin's. Did J.P. know about the will all along? Then why did he wait four years to claim his inheritance, instead of submitting it when his father died? And why would he have let the valuable overcoat be sent away, perhaps to be lost or discarded before he could recover it? Concluded the SPR's investigator: "It is hard to suggest a satisfactory explanation of the facts on normal lines."

1918: Lieutenant David McConnel Apparition

Among the best-known and documented "crisis apparitions" is the case of British Lt. David McConnel, a pilot trainee who took off on a flight to another air base and died in a plane crash on Dec. 7, 1918. The exact moment of his death, 3:25 PM, was known because the watch on his wrist stopped when the plane hit the ground. About the same time that he crashed, his roommate, Lt. J.J. Larkin, saw him walk into the pilot lounge. Larkin asked him if he had a good flight, and McConnel answered "Yes. Got there all right. Had a good trip." Then he left. Fifteen minutes later, another friend of Larkin and McConnell came in the room and said he hoped McConnel would be back by evening so the trio of friends could go to dinner. Larkin told him that McConnel was already back. Later that night, they both finally learned of McConnel's death earlier that afternoon. Larkin, stunned by the apparition, reported it to his commanding officer the next day, with his friend confirming the sequence of events. On Dec. 22, 1918, Larkin set down the events in detail in a letter to McConnel's family, which had heard the story when they came to claim the body of their son. The Society for Psychical Research investigated the case and it remains among the best stories of its kind in their files. It had a reliable, no-nonsense witness whose claim was confirmed by another independent witness, and the details themselves were written down in detail very shortly after they happened, when memories were very fresh. McConnel's story can be found in the *Journal of the Society for Psychical Research*, Vol. XIX, 1919-1920, available from the England's Society for Psychical Research. The SPR's Eleanor Sidgwick, who in 1923 produced an updated edition of the 1886 classic *Phantasms of the Living*, called the McConnel case "perhaps the best evidenced death coincidence" report in her collection.[11]

1863-1938: Borley Rectory, Essex England

It's been called "the most haunted house in England." Built in 1863 and destroyed by fire in 1938, this minister's house experienced three types of ghostly activities—poltergeists, hauntings and post-mortem apparitions—that continued for over 75 years. Almost everyone who lived at Borley during that period apparently reported experiencing strange sights and sounds, and over 100 persons are on record as having encounters with paranormal phenomena. These included encounters with seven different ghosts; a phantom coach; disappearing and reappearing objects; messages that suddenly appeared on walls and scraps of paper; and unexplained footsteps, voices, and music, among other things. The Borley hauntings have been the subject of four full-length books, as well as numerous magazine and newspaper articles and radio and TV shows.

More importantly from an evidential point of view, Borley rectory was the target of a serious, scientific field investigation—a sustained, year-long stakeout conducted in 1937-38 by a team of investigators led by the famous but controversial English ghost-hunter Harry Price. He describes his investigation in his book *The Most Haunted House in England: 10 Years' Investigation of Borley Rectory*. It includes photographs and floor plans of the rectory and its various rooms; reproductions of writings that mysteriously appeared on walls; excerpts from detailed dairies and original statements gathered from witnesses who experienced the extraordinary and often unpleasant phenomena; transcripts of séances and communications with mediums; and accounts of the many and varied scientific experiments conducted by the ghost hunting team during the year they lived in the rectory (June 1937-May 1938). Famous British ghost hunter Peter Underwood believes Borley Rectory "stands alone in the annals of psychic research as a continuing problem for the materialist and an exciting challenge for the psychical researcher."[12]

1967-1968: the Rosenheim Poltergeist

This extensively investigated and documented case, together with the publicity surrounding it, had a significant impact on the German public's belief in poltergeists. Before Rosenheim, 18 percent of those polled believed in poltergeists; after Rosenheim, 28 percent of the German public believed in poltergeists. It was the subject of television documentaries in both Germany and England. The Rosenheim poltergeist activity started in November 1967 at a law office in Rosenheim, Bavaria and centered around a 19-year old female employee, Anne Marie Schneider. Sometimes when she walked through the office, light bulbs unscrewed themselves or exploded and ceiling lamps mysteriously began to sway. Pictures hanging on the wall spun around in circles on their hooks, desk drawers opened by themselves, phones dialed themselves, and a 400-pound storage shelf moved itself away from the wall. Because some of the effects were electrical, the investigating team led by Dr. Hans Bender brought in electricians, telephone company specialists, and even physicists from the famed Max Planck Institute to conduct electrical, mechanical and magnetic field tests. No one was able to produce a normal explanation for the events, or even to control them. The Rosenheim case is neatly summarized in William Roll's book *The Poltergeist*.[13] Bender's personal discussion of the case can be found in English in the *Proceedings of the Parapsychological Association*.[14] The original German report—if you read German—is found in the *Zeitschrift fur Parapsychologie und Grenzegebeite der Psychologie*, Vol. 11, 1968. A photo of a swaying lamp taken by Bender's team during the investigation is found in Alan Gauld and A.D. Cornell's book *Poltergeists*.[15]

Germany invented the word "poltergeist" and German scientists have done some of the best research on them. The late Hans Bender, a professor of psychology at Freiburg University was among the most well-known. He also served as Director of the Freiberg Institut which is devoted to parapsychology research using tools such as PK and ESP tests, psychological testing and on-site field investigations. Bender himself personally investigated dozens of cases besides the Rosenheim case. Bender was particularly interested in the physics of objects materializing and dematerializing in space or passing through solid walls—occasionally reported poltergeist phenomena. Bender was perhaps the first parapsychologist to produce a poltergeist movement on demand, during a 1966 investigation of a poltergeist case involving a 15-year old electrical apprentice.[16] He was also among the first to use videotape extensively to document poltergeist phenomena, including swinging lamps and pictures rotating on a wall during the famous Rosenheim case.[17]

1966-1967: the Miami Poltergeist

In January 1967, police were called in to the Tropication Arts warehouse in Miami to investigate the mysterious, spontaneous breaking of numerous glass and ceramic souvenir objects stored on shelves. When the police couldn't find a culprit or a rational explanation for the events which continued to take place even while they were there, the owner called in the ghostbusters. As parapsychologist Alan Gauld wryly observed of the Tropication Arts warehouse with its thousands of breakable glass and ceramic knick-knacks, "It is impossible to imagine a more congenial stamping ground for a destructive poltergeist." [18]

This is truly a classic poltergeist case: numerous reputable witnesses, including four police officers, company managers and supervisors, stock clerks, and professional parapsychologists; over 224 separate incidents recorded over several months; two weeks of intensive, on-site investigations by two well-known parapsychologists (Dr. William Roll and Dr. J.G. Pratt); over 120 incidents which happened while the investigators were there, including 44 seen as they happened by one or both of the investigators themselves; the use of "target" objects kept under visual scrutiny at all times; and incidents logged as to time, date, place, observers and their positions at the moment events happened; distance and direction traveled by objects (in one case, a large, two-quart glass jar on the back of a shelf traveled 22 feet). The amount of professionally collected data from the poltergeist case "marked a new high point in the recording of poltergeist phenomena."[19]

Like the Rosenheim poltergeist case, the phenomena were closely associated with the presence of a specific individual, in this case a 19-year old Cuban shipping clerk named Julio Vasquez. Only one incident happened when he wasn't there. Julio was never caught faking the phenomena; indeed, some incidents happened with Julio under close observation and distant from the incident. The Miami poltergeist case remains a mystery, and one of the best documented cases on record.[20]

Highly Recommended Reading:

Banks, Ivan. *The Enigma of Borley Rectory*. London: Foulsham, 1996. Getting a handle on the complex, 81-year history of paranormal events and scientific investigations that took place at Borley Rectory takes patience and a lot of reading. Tom Perrott, President of England's venerable Ghost Club (founded in 1862), calls Banks' book "probably the most comprehensive of its kind so far produced." This 225-page book, latest in a long line of tomes dealing with the Borley mystery, includes a detailed history of Borley Rectory from its construction in 1863 to its tearing down in 1944; a description of almost every recorded paranormal event that took place there (ghosts, apparitions, poltergeist effects), based on diaries, interviews and published records of witnesses; a summary of every important investigation conducted on Borley Rectory by believers and skeptic alike for the last 50 years; photos and layouts of the rectory and grounds; and a selected bibliography of 27 books dealing with the controversy. If you want to credibly argue a case for or against Borley Rectory and its paranormal claims, you need to know your facts. This is a good place to start.

Sidgwick, Eleanor. *Phantasms of the Living*. New York: Arno Press, 1975. The original classic book *Phantasms of the Living*, written by Edmund Gurney, F.W.H. Myers and Frank Podmore for the Society for Psychical Research and published in London in 1894 by Trubner, is not available anymore. But you'll find references to it, and cases from it, sprinkled throughout serious literature on the ghost phenomenon. Fortunately, Eleanor Sidgwick subsequently produced an edited, updated version of the book. If you're serious about looking at the best scientific evidence for ghosts, you should consider buying it. You can usually find a copy at www.abebooks.com. The Lt. David McConnel case cited above in "Best Scientific Evidence" can be found in this book.

Roll, William G. *The Poltergeist* New American Library, 1983. This book, by one of America's leading poltergeist researchers, focuses on well-documented case histories (some of which Roll himself researched as a principal investigator). Among them are the Miami and Rosenheim poltergeist cases mentioned in "Best Scientific Evidence." Roll also gives a history of the poltergeist phenomenon worldwide, and devotes several convincing chapters to his preferred explanation for the phenomenon—a form of psychokinesis. A new edition is due out soon.

Fitzhugh, Pat. *The Bell Witch: The Full Account.* Armand Press, 2000. This case is the only documented case in U.S. history of a spirit/poltergeist actually causing a man's death. The Bell "witch" terrorized John Bell's family and community in rural Tennessee for four years (1817 and 1821). During that period, hundreds of people witnessed the events and personally interacted with the spirit/poltergeist, including then U.S. President Andrew Jackson. Though not scientifically investigated like the Miami and Rosenheim poltergeists, the Bell "witch" remains one of the most intriguing and believable spirit/poltergeist cases in American history.

Gauld, Alan and Cornell, A.D. *Poltergeists.* Boston: Routledge & Kegan Paul, 1979. This book by two English parapsychologists can often be found in larger libraries, or bought online at www.abebooks.com. It provides an in-depth history of the poltergeist phenomenon. It also features an appendix with citations on 500 poltergeist cases. For each case, the authors provide the country it happened, the location of the first manifestation of the phenomenon, dates, duration of the event, and a reading list of materials printed about the case. A separate chapter is devoted to an in-depth statistical analysis of the 500 cases. Gauld is a past president of the London-based Society for Psychical Research.

Moody, Raymond, M.D. *Reunions: Visionary Encounters With Departed Loved Ones.* New York: Ballantine/Villard, 1993. If you're looking for modern "post-mortem apparition" research designed to produce the phenomenon on demand, read this book. If you're brave, try it yourself.

13.

Mediums and Channelers

*"I shall not commit the fashionable stupidity of regarding
everything I cannot explain as a fraud."*
Dr. Carl Jung in a 1919 speech to the Society for Psychical Research

If human consciousness survives death, can we communicate with it? If
so, how? When Thomas Edison tried to invent a machine to communicate with spirits of the dead, he was simply trying to apply modern technology to do a job done over the centuries by mystics, priests, prophets
and shamans specially chosen or trained to act as a "medium" between
the living and the spirit realm.

These mediums communicated with more than just deceased
humans; they also communicated with an amazing variety of good and
evil spirits, ghosts, gods, demigods, angels, demons, sprites, messengers,
guides and assorted, nonphysical intelligent entities—in short, they
acted as an intermediary between humankind and everyone and everything in the "invisible realm." But most information-seekers were probably interested in communicating with a recently deceased, deeply loved
and missed husband, wife, child or friend. That was a job for the local
medium and whatever tools he employed to get the message.

Mediumship done while in a trance can be found in many ancient
cultures ranging from Siberia and Korea to South America, the British

Isles and Finland, from the Chinese and Japanese to the ancient Egyptians and Greeks. We've given mediums a new name, "channelers," but they've been around as long as mankind has. Four thousand years ago, the Chinese were communicating with spirits using a type of Ouija board. Written records in Japan of trance possession and trance communication date back to the 8th century AD. In ancient Greece, the philosopher Plato warned against necromancy, the art of predicting the future by consulting with the dead while Pythagoras, another great Greek philosopher, is recorded as using an Ouija board in séances to gain information from the spirit world.

In addition to divining tools like Ouija boards and oracle bones, mediums used a variety of herbs, drinks and potions, drugs, rituals, prayers and mental and physical exercises to put themselves in a special state of consciousness or trance possession that allowed direct mental contact with the spirit world.

But the rise of monotheistic religions in the West threatened the free-wheeling, polytheistic, direct-contact-with-spirits role of the traditional medium. Both Christianity and Islam frowned on spirit communications and sought to control and suppress unauthorized views of the afterlife that conflicted with the Koran or Bible. Communicating solely with your deceased spouse or relative was not too risky, as long as it was private and discrete, and the dead didn't dabble in theology and put heretical ideas in your head. The church wanted to be the only medium authorized to pass on messages from God. But even limiting your communications to the deceased could put you in jeopardy: if discovered, you could still be accused of communicating with the Devil or evil spirits. Worse yet, a channeler discovered in a trance (spontaneous or self-induced) risked being accused of being possessed by an evil spirit. And the penalty could be death. Eventually, organized religion claimed the right to be the only authorized medium of communication with the spirit world, forcing unorthodox channeling underground.

Christian church leaders continued to receive messages and enlightenment from the "Holy Spirit," as well as various deceased humans (e.g. saints). But the Church jealously guarded its right to control and confirm the validity of any message received by its faithful. Great Christian mystics like Saint Theresa of Avila and St. John of the Cross accepted these restraints, but the Protestant Reformation of the 16th century reopened the doors to direct contact with the Holy Spirit. Messages received direct from God, angels and departed dead from the Other Side multiplied. Mediumship remained risky (Protestants could execute you for heresy as easily as Catholics) but competing messages and visions were now heard.

Exceptional mediums continued to make the case for an afterlife through their reported communications with the dead. In the 18th century, scientist-mystic Emanuel Swedenborg (1688-1772) did much to popularize mediumistic communication among Europe's elite. In one famous instance,[1] Swedenborg reputedly helped a widow hounded by a goldsmith trying to extract double payment for a silver service her husband had ordered before he died. Swedenborg contacted the deceased husband who told him that he had paid for the silver set already and that the receipt would be found in a secret compartment in an upstairs bureau drawer. The lady followed her dead husband's advice and found the receipt.

Unfortunately, shortly after monolithic Christianity began to break up, the Enlightenment also dawned. Doubt about the existence of God and an afterlife began to grow. If there were no God or no afterlife, mediumistic communication with discarnate, deceased humans, or anything else in the spirit world was impossible. The spirit world itself didn't exist. An increasingly confident Science continued to attack established beliefs and pile up successes using logic, reason, careful observation and experimentation. Biblical beliefs crumbled under their assault. Gods, angels, demons, discarnate deceased humans existing in an afterlife—the spirit world itself—were all ridiculed away.

Mediumistic communications were simply a case of the human brain trying to communicate with something that didn't exist. In short, a form of insanity.

By the 19th century, just as Science stood on the verge of consolidating its triumph over the spirit world, the Spiritualism movement swept America. It held that human beings could indeed communicate with the deceased using mediums. The Spiritualists' primary interest in mediums and messages from the Other World—and the general public's main interest as well—was undoubtedly the possibility of proving life after death. Science had declared personal survival a religious myth. Independently validated messages from the dead could perhaps prove Science wrong, and return credibility to humankind's belief in an afterlife.

The movement began in the mid-1800s and eventually spawned innumerable séance parties in living rooms and parlors across the U.S. and Europe. The Spiritualism movement ultimately attracted such prominent persons as Horace Greely, editor of the *New York Times*; England's Sir Arthur Conan Doyle, creator of Sherlock Holmes; Alfred Russell Wallace, who co-developed the theory of evolution with Charles Darwin; American writer James Fenimore Cooper and hundreds of other well-known and socially-respected academics, judges, politicians, physicians, and church leaders.

Even President Abraham Lincoln listened to and followed the advice of a medium, Nettie Colburn, between 1861 and 1863. Based on messages from her spirit guides, she counseled Lincoln not to delay the Emancipation Proclamation that freed the slaves (many of Lincoln's advisers were worried about its effect on the course of the war). On another occasion, Colburn convinced a reluctant Lincoln to visit Union troops on the front lines at Fredericksburg.[2]

The group séance in a darkened room was the principal focus of the movement. During the séance, a medium would call on the spirit of a dead person (often the deceased spouse of one of the attendees) to communicate with him. Some mediums went into a trance and the deceased spoke through them; other mediums would simply pass on messages they received telepathically from the deceased. A son killed in an accident might tell his heart-broken mother that he was happy in the Other World; or a grieving widow might get a chance to talk to her recently deceased spouse. Often, the séance attendee would ask for a sign from the spirit to prove its identity, and the spirit through the medium would provide a private nickname or other piece of knowledge known only to the attendee. In some instances, the information provided was nothing short of astounding; in other instances, the information was so general it could have been produced by an intelligent guess. In addition to messages from the dead, the séance often included a variety of large-scale psychokinesis phenomena—tables tilting and moving, odd noises, and apparitions materializing in the gloomy darkness. With the lights turned off and the curtains closed, obvious opportunities for trickery existed, and many mediums were later proved frauds. Harder to dismiss were the personal experiences of thousands of individuals who themselves successfully channeled in their own homes, experimenting with automatic writing and the Ouija board (or planchette). Among the most famous researchers using these tools was the Frenchman Allan Kardec who attracted thousands in Europe to his Spiritism movement.

Daniel Douglas Home, whom we earlier met in Chapter 7 (psychokinesis), was also a very respected medium.[3] Born into a poor family in Edinburgh, Scotland in 1833, Home was adopted by his mother's sister and immigrated with them to Connecticut in America when he was nine years old. Home had his first spirit encounter at age 13. One night he had a vision of his former playmate and close friend, Edwin, who had moved to another city. Home understood from the apparition that his friend had died. The next morning he told his parents, "I have seen Edwin. He died three days ago." Two days later, a letter came with the news that Edwin had indeed died of a sudden illness.

Home sometimes did as many as seven séances a day. According to channeling researcher Jon Klimo, medium D.D. Home never accepted payment for demonstrating his talents, nor was he ever caught perpetrating a fraud. His skills included full-trance voice channeling as well as clairaudient and clairvoyant light-trance reception. He often conducted his medium work in full daylight; in places chosen by others, and in front of very credible witnesses.

Several of Home's most impressive channeling feats happened early in his life and involved Home providing independently verifiable information unknown and even unsuspected by the people who received it. One famous incident happened in August 1852, at the house of a wealthy silk manufacturer, Mr. Ward Cheney. Home felt ill and, while he was lying in the drawing room, he heard the rustling of a stiff silk dress. At first he couldn't see anyone, but then spied a little old lady in the hallway wearing a gray silk dress. Mr. Cheney next heard the sound, but couldn't see anyone. When he asked "What's that noise?," Home replied that it was the old lady in the gray silk dress. Cheney looked at him oddly but didn't say anything. Home later realized that Cheney hadn't seen anything. Following the dinner, Home heard the rustling noise again and the lady's voice say, "I am annoyed that a coffin should have been placed above mine." He told Cheney. Cheney replied that he had an idea of who the spirit might be, but that the message itself didn't make any sense at all. It was ridiculous. An hour later, Home heard the voice again, this time saying, "What is more, Seth had no right to cut that tree down." He told the astonished Cheney who replied that the lady matched the description of an elderly deceased relative of theirs who wore gray silk dresses. Furthermore, Mr. Cheney's brother Seth had indeed cut down a tree that the old lady would never have allowed to be cut had she been alive. But the coffin comment remained bizarre and nonsensical. A distressed Home went to bed that night convinced he had made a mistake. The next morning Mr. Cheney told Home he could prove that, although the spirit's description seemed correct, the message was most certainly false. He took Home to the local cemetery where they would find the vault containing the remains of several families, including the lady's coffin. As the groundskeeper opened the vault door, he tendered Cheney an apology and a confession. He knew he probably should have asked first, but the day before, since there was some space above the lady's coffin, he had placed the coffin of a baby on top of hers.[4]

Six years before Home died in 1888, a group of prominent English scientists and academics founded the Society for Psychical Research. Their ranks included eight Fellows of the Royal Society and a future British Prime Minister, Arthur Balfour. They set about to systematically and scientifically examine claims for mediumship and other paranormal phenomena. They were determined to be scientific in their investigation, but remain open to all possibilities. As SPR co-founder professor Henry Sidgwick noted in a speech a few years after SPR started its research, there appeared to SPR's early investigators to be a significant "body of evidence—tending prima facie to establish the independence of soul or spirit—which modern science had simply left to one side with ignorant contempt," dishonoring the scientific method of open and fair evaluation of any and all evidence, and thus " had arrived prematurely at her negative conclusion." [5] Indeed, Britain's current Prime Minister at the time, William Gladstone, called psychical research the most important work being done in the world.[6]

Not all SPR members came away convinced of the reality of channeling. But one who did was SPR co-founder F.W.H. Myers, author of the classic two-volume work *Human Personality and Its Survival of Bodily Death*. Myers (who helped introduce the writings of Sigmund Freud to England) believed the evidence supported the argument for life after death as well as communication between the material and discarnate spirits in the Other World.[7]

On the other side of the Atlantic, Harvard psychologist and philosopher William James, author of the famous *Varieties of Religious*

Experience, had established an American branch of the SPR with many prominent members, including future U.S. president Theodore Roosevelt. U.S. medium Leonora Piper was among those investigated by James and the American Society for Psychical Research in cooperation with their British sister organization, the SPR.

Piper was a Boston, Massachusetts medium whom James discovered in 1885. She so impressed James and his colleagues that the Society for Psychical Research (SPR) in England hired her for 200 English pounds sterling a year to give up her career as a professional trance medium, sail to England, and become a test subject for the Society to study.

The SPR assigned Australian Richard Hodgson to conduct their research on Piper. Hodgson, a graduate of Cambridge University like many other SPR leaders, was no wide-eyed, gullible believer in mediums. A few years earlier, he had investigated on SPR's behalf the claims of internationally-famous medium Madame Blavatsky, founder of the popular Theosophical Movement. To Blavatsky's great dismay, he branded her and her messages from her Tibetan master as fakes.

Hodgson took no chances with Piper. He had her tailed by detectives to make sure she wasn't secretly collecting information on those to whom she later channeled for. He arranged for attendees seeking messages via Piper to come to the sitting dressed in disguises and using false names to make sure she knew as little as possible about them before preceding to channel. He eventually sent more than 50 people to Piper as part of this first series of sittings. Hodgson never uncovered a hint of fraud and, with very few exceptions, everyone who participated in the sittings came away convinced of her good faith. Piper's channeled messages weren't always correct; she had misses as well as hits. Indeed, some sittings were total failures. But based on the many verified, evidential messages that were passed on by Piper during her trances—particularly those reported to come from George Pelham (see "Best Evidence" below)—the skeptical Hodgson was ultimately forced to conclude that Paper was sometimes in touch with the deceased and that human consciousness somehow survives death.

Declared Hodgson, "After allowing the widest possible margin for information obtainable under the circumstances by ordinary means, for chance coincidence and remarkable guessing, aided by clues given consciously and unconsciously by the sitters...there remained a large residuum of knowledge displayed in her trance state which could not be accounted for except on the hypothesis that she had some supernormal power..."[8]

Researchers almost uniformly agreed her trance was real, that she was not a fraud or fake, and that something authentic and genuine was happening. They only disagreed on how to explain her. Some saw her mediumistic communications as proof of life after death and the existence of spirits and discarnate entities. Others believed it was some form of super-ESP. Either way, her effect on paranormal research was substantial. The SPR had originally been reluctant to investigate mediums. Piper made medium research respectable to many who once viewed all mediums as frauds and hoaxes.

William James, who investigated Piper's abilities in some depth, concluded that "she had supernormal powers."[9] Parapsychologists are always looking for a "white crow." A single white crow is enough to disprove belief that all crows are black; likewise, one single genuine medium is enough to disprove belief that mediumship is impossible. James called Piper his "white crow."

Unlike many other mediums, Piper did not manifest any psychokinesis effects. She didn't tilt tables, move chairs, or make things appear and disappear. She was simply a channel, a medium for receiving messages from the spiritual world. Like many channels, she worked through a "control," a spirit on the other side who spoke through her while she lay in a trance (Piper's usual control was a spirit personality called Phinuit, who claimed to be a deceased French medical doctor). Later, she passed on messages through an automatic writing process controlled by spirits. Ironically, in one of those later automatic writing sessions Piper reportedly received messages from Hodgson himself, the SPR officer who had studied her so closely before he had died in 1905. One message Hodgson passed on to her came from a fellow spirit in the "other world", F.W.H. Myers, co-founder of the SPR. Hodgson's message from Myers was addressed to physicist Sir Oliver Lodge, yet another prominent SPR member. At the time, 1915, Lodge's son was away in France fighting the Germans in World War I. Lodge interpreted the message from Myers as implying some imminent bad news. Shortly afterwards, on Sept. 15, 1915, Lodge learned that his son had been killed. (World War I with its horrendous loss of life spurred many individuals to seek out mediums to communicate with their dead husbands and sons.) Lodge subsequently received a number of messages from his deceased son via different mediums. They're described in his 1917 book *Raymond, or Life and Death.*

This first golden age of modern mediumship peaked shortly after World War I. Too many mediums were exposed as charlatans and their séances as hoaxes perpetrated on a gullible public. Traditional church leaders threatened by the phenomenon increasingly attacked it from their pulpits as the work of the devil. While a National Spiritualist Association was eventually formed, the movement itself had no rule-enforcing central leadership or required common credo to sustain itself. Like the later American "hippy" movement of the 1960s, the Spiritualism movement was a democratic, freewheeling, heterodox, cultural phenomenon that eventually lost its initial cohesion and momentum.

Science's dismissal of mediums and afterlife studies, the uncovering of embarrassing frauds and hoaxes among Spiritualism's ranks, and alternative explanations from the infant field of psychology left some psychic researchers feeling they had no choice—if they wanted respect instead of scorn, they had to leave the séance parlor. Psychologist Sigmund Freud suggested that mediumship was probably an exercise in wish fulfillment, and the voices and visions were repressed impulses, feelings and thoughts trying to escape from the channeler's subconscious. The Spiritualists' messages from the dead were thus really messages from the living—their own minds. Swiss physician and psychologist Carl Jung offered another source for the messages than the deceased. He suggested that mankind might be accessing a hypothesized collective, shared unconscious—a pool of memories, ideas, thoughts and feelings collected over eons (though he didn't exclude other possibilities, including discarnate spirits).

In the 1930s and 1940s, Duke University parapsychologist J.B. Rhine led his peers away from research on mediums, séances and messages from spirits towards laboratory experimentation on ESP and PK. Interest in survival research (life after death) and mediumship declined among a new generation of psychic researchers. (Before his death, Rhine himself was calling for the abandonment of survival research.)

Psychic researchers began to call themselves parapsychologists (a term Rhine adopted from the German "parapsychologie") to emphasize their affinity to the increasingly respected field of psychology, and psychology itself was now fairly comfortable with the idea of mediumship as a product of overheated imagination, or even mental illness—delusion, schizophrenia, multiple personality disorder—requiring drugs or institutionalization to cure. Ironically, at the turn of the century, before psychology itself became accepted as a science, mediums were suspected of suffering not from a mental disease but from a physical disease. It could be risky believing in channeling at the turn of the century if you fell in the hands of Science. Women were particularly susceptible to Spiritualism, noted one prominent New York doctor, if their menstrual process had been upset, or they had an improperly angled womb. The recommended cure was repeated doses of iron and strychnine, or enemas of turpentine.[10]

Famous channelers continued to appear on the scene—like Americans Edgar Cayce and Arthur Ford[11]—but were left relatively untested and ignored by parapsychology and conventional science. Ford was the first psychic to broadcast a séance over the radio (1937). The American Society for Psychical Research conducted a few laboratory experiments with Ford in 1953, and well-known parapsychologists Dr. William Roll and Dr. Ian Stevenson tried to get Ford into the lab but, for a variety of reasons, it didn't work out.

One who was tested in some depth was British medium Eileen Garrett (1893-1970). The Irish-born Garrett from her early childhood showed herself "sensitive" to invisible spirits and companions. Her clairvoyance and precognition abilities, combined with her ability to channel verifiable information when in a trance, brought her much fame. Among those she counted as her friends were George Bernard Shaw, James Joyce, D.H. Lawrence, Yeats, Aldous Huxley and Arthur Conan Doyle (the creator of detective Sherlock Holmes). But Garrett herself was truly puzzled by her strange abilities. She had not sought them out; they had come to her spontaneously. Consequently, she was determined to find a scientific answer to explain her puzzling talents. She willingly submitted to testing by scientists and academics in England. In 1930, the ASPR invited her to America to do channeling demonstrations and make herself available for scientific testing at Duke and Johns Hopkins universities. Dr. Rhine at Duke was among those who tested her abilities.[12] She particularly wanted to know whether Dr. Rhine could determine whether the "controls" who took over her body and voice while she was in the trance were actually disembodied spirits as they claimed, or whether they were sub-personalities or split-off parts of her own mind. Rhine found Garrett to be a very good ESP subject, but was unable to answer Garrett's question about her "controls."

Garrett viewed her mediumship abilities as unusual and out of the ordinary, but not as a sign of mental illness. While Rhine focused on testing the ESP and PK abilities of average people during a state of normal, waking consciousness, Garrett explored altered states of consciousness. She experimented with LSD in the 1950s, before Timothy

Leary and Richard Alpert studied it at Harvard.[13] Garrett went on to establish the Parapsychology Foundation in New York in 1951 with the financial help of a wealthy U.S. Congresswoman, Frances Bolton. The Foundation pursued a wide variety of interesting psychical research on the survival question and mediumship and disseminated the results in conferences, seminars and publications. It was the Parapsychology Foundation which financially supported the deathbed visions research of Karlis Osis.

In the 1960s, the "hippie" cultural revolution in the U.S. sparked renewed interest in all sorts of paranormal phenomena, including mediumship, altered states of consciousness and life after death speculation. In the early 1970s, American poet and novelist Jane Roberts published the first of several books detailing the messages she received from her source "Seth." The books became national bestsellers and sold millions of copies. (After her death in 1984, Roberts papers and recordings were archived at Yale University.) In 1975, New York psychologist Helen Schucman published her now-famous channeled material *A Course in Miracles.*

While most scientists, including parapsychologists, deliberately kept their distance from this channeling explosion (and the opportunity to study and scientifically test it), the public—as often happens—remained quite open to the possibility of communicating with the deceased. As noted in Chapter 1, the 2001 Gallup Poll found nearly one in three Americans (28%) believe that people can hear from or communicate mentally with someone who has died. Claiming to receive messages from the dead is no longer an automatic ticket to the funny farm.

We are currently in a second "golden age" of mediumship. Klimo has reported estimates of as many as a thousand channelers operating in Southern California alone (particularly Los Angeles). By the 1990s, Great Britain had produced the "Findhorn" channeled material. Canada had the "Hilarion" books of Maurice Cooke. In the U.S., Jane Roberts and "Seth" were joined by other nationally-known New Age mediums include J.Z. Knight ("Ramtha"), Jach Pursel ("Lazaris"), Jessica Lansing ("Michael") and Ken Carey ("The Starseed Transmissions"), among others. There is nothing exceptional about the backgrounds of many channels. Before channeling fame, Roberts was an aspiring poet and novelist; Ryerson a graphic artist; Pursel a Florida insurance supervisor; Carey a postal employee turned farmer. Their messages are distributed through audiotapes and videotapes, direct mail, New Age bookstores, seminars, workshops, private readings and lectures. The better known channels operate regular corporations and undoubtedly earn major incomes. Several national journals are devoted to the channeling phenomenon. Many modern mediums purport to pass on messages from angels, spirit guides, aliens and other non-human entities as well as deceased humans.

Today, psychologists interested in transpersonal psychology, consciousness studies and altered states of consciousness lead the way in examining and philosophically grappling with the channeling phenomenon. Their ranks include researchers like Arthur Hastings and Charles Tart.

Dr. Arthur Hastings, a professor at the Institute of Transpersonal Psychology (www.itp.edu) in Palo Alto, California, authored in 1990 an excellent and highly readable overview on the subject of mediumship, *With the Tongues of Men and Angels: A Study of Channeling.*[14] In it, he neither idealizes channeling like some naïve believers nor discounts it like some rigid skeptics, preferring instead to focus on the richness of the communications themselves. He notes that mediums have channeled health diagnoses and treatments (Edgar Cayce); high-quality literature (poets William Blake and William Butler Yeats); mathematics (modern number theory genius Srinivasa Ramanujan); music and art; valuable practical, therapeutic and psychological advice and insights; important political movements (Joan of Arc); religious revelations and prophecies (Judaism, Christianity, Islam); and even new religions

(Mormonism). According to Hastings, some 15 percent of the U.S. population report having heard at one time or another an inner voice giving them information or guidance.[15] His conclusion as to the source of all these channeled messages? Hastings believes that no single channeling explanation—deceased human beings, non-human discarnate entities, our own subconscious, or some universal consciousness—fits all the evidence.[16]

Hastings' faculty colleague, veteran psychologist and parapsychologist Charles Tart (www.paradigm-sys.com/cttart/), has spent his career studying the nature of consciousness and exploring the limits (if any) of the human mind. He has conducted extensive ESP research, studied Robert Monroe and his OBEs in the laboratory; wrote two classic books in his field, *Altered States of Consciousness* (1969) and *Transpersonal Psychologies* (1975), and wrote the preface to the second modern classic in the field of channeling investigations, Jon Klimo's 1987 book *Channeling: Investigations on Receiving Information from Paranormal Sources*. Tart also remains open to most hypotheses regarding the source of channeled messages, from conventional psychological explanations right up to communication with a disembodied intelligence.[17]

Channeling researcher and author Jon Klimo is himself a poet, artist and former Rutgers University professor who today lives in the San Francisco Bay area, teaching graduate level parapsychology courses. He is also a leading investigator of a relatively new form of mediumship called Electronic Voice Phenomena (EVP), or Instrumental Trans-Communication (ITC). Thomas Edison's failed attempt to invent a machine to communicate with discarnate spirits didn't discourage others from experimenting with the idea, and efforts have increased along with the proliferation of new electronic devices—videotapes, tape recorders, radios, TV, VCRs and computers. To date, however, no EVP-channeled messages have been produced that match the complexity, sophistication and testable veracity of information produced by a human channeler like Eileen Garrett or Leonora Piper.[18]

As we start the 21st century, America's fascination with mediumship shows no sign of waning. John Edward, Sylvia Brown and James Van Praagh are just some of the more recent mediums to emerge on the best-seller lists. *Crossing Over with John Edward* made its debut in June 2000 on the Sci Fi Cable Network, attracting fervent supporters and enraged skeptics in a way not seen since the heyday of medium Arthur Ford a half-century earlier.

Recently, scientists in the psychology department at the University of Arizona conducted some intriguing tests on Edward and some of his fellow well-known mediums. In 1999, Dr. Gary Schwartz and his colleagues at the Human Energy Systems Laboratory there brought in Edward, well-known mediums George Anderson (author of the best-seller *We Don't Die*) and Suzane Northrop (her book *Séance* became a Literary Guild and Doubleday Book Club Selection), and two other skilled mediums to see if any could produce accurate information for a 46 year old Arizona woman (the "sitter") who had lost six close friends and relatives in the preceding decade. None of the five mediums had met the woman before. Each medium met individually with the sitter and provided whatever messages they received under scientifically-controlled test conditions. Schwartz took steps to limit the possibility of fraud or chance (making sure the medium was blind as to the identity of the sitter; keeping the mediums from asking leading questions of the sitter, a technique called "fishing"; separating the mediums from the sitters by a screen to eliminate visual clues; using two videotape cameras to record every second of the sessions; etc.). Despite these controls, the five mediums as a group achieved an average accuracy of 83% in terms of information provided the sitter (e.g. names of deceased people; verified, historical facts; personal descriptions of deceased, etc.). This compared to an average of 36% correct information produced by a control group of 68 male and female undergrad students at the University of Arizona who were challenged to perform the same test with the sitter. Schwartz later conducted a successful replication of the experiment. His conclusion? "The data suggest that highly skilled mediums are able to obtain accurate and replicable information. Since factors of fraud, error and statistical coincidence cannot explain the present findings, other possible mechanisms should be considered in future research. These include telepathy, super psi, and survival of consciousness after death."[19] Skeptics for their part have suggested repeating them with some new test controls.[20]

While American researchers in Arizona test John Edward and other mediums, on the other side of the Atlantic English researchers continue to puzzle over and hotly debate the Scole Experiments. This five-year series of over 500 séances (1993-1998) conducted by a group of amateur English mediums has reportedly produced more than evidential messages from the deceased and various traditional PK effects like raps, table levitations and fights; they have also produced a wide range of physical evidence that can be scientifically examined, including written messages, sophisticated drawings and odd lights captured on sealed, unexposed photographic film or blank videotape in a completely dark room; voices on tape recorders (all sittings were tape-recorded); and several dozen objects which were claimed to have materialized out of thin air ("apports" are a not-unusual phenomena reported in cases involving mediumship and poltergeist manifestations). The scope and range of these physical manifestations of mediumship match those of a century ago at the height of the Spiritualist movement and come at a time when such displays of poltergeist-like, psychokinetic effects have all but disappeared.

During the Scole experiments, a bewildering variety of small, brilliant lights appeared and disappeared, exhibiting extremely rapid movements and high-speed geometrical gyrations, shape changes, and intelligent responses to sitters' requests to move in certain directions, touch their hands, or strike various objects; on some occasions, the lights were also seen and felt to enter the bodies of people present in the room, or enter crystal and plastic objects and make them glow from within. In one session, an audible performance of a part of a Rachmaninoff piano concerto was recorded on a machine that had no microphone. In another session, sitters heard a loud plop in the darkness and, upon turning on the lights at the end of the session, found a copy of the English newspaper the *Daily Mirror*, dated December 16, 1936. Investigators tested the "apport" to see if it was simply a fraudulent copy, but it proved to have been printed by letterpress on genuine wartime paper. Among images mysteriously appearing on sealed, unexposed film were those of St. Paul's Cathedral in London; an image of the River Seine taken from the roof of Notre Dame Cathedral in Paris; and a photo of the late Sir Arthur Conan Doyle, creator of Sherlock Homes and himself a devoted investigator of the paranormal. Meanwhile, a team of a half-dozen spirits on the "other side" reportedly worked together to pass on to attendees at the séances information that convinced many sitters they were in touch with deceased person once known to them in this life.

Prominent member of the venerable Society for Psychic Research in England, along with a dozen other scientists and academics (including a professional magician, James Webster), participated at various times in the séances and/or conducted various scientific investigations.

In December 1999, as the old century expired, the SPR published its official Report on the Scole Experiments.[21] The lengthy, extensively illustrated 300-page report offers one of the most interesting investigations of apparent after death mediumship to appear in the last hundred years. It was authored by three leading members of the SPR with extensive experience in investigating paranormal claims—Montague Keen, Secretary of the SPR's Survival Research Committee; Dr. David Fontana, a former SPR president and professor of psychology; and the late Dr. Arthur Ellison, a former SPR president and professor of electrical engineering. The Report includes comments both pro and con, and concludes by listing the weaknesses in the evidence, but notes the formidable range of talents, knowledge and physical dexterity that would have been required to produce the evidence by trickery, and points to positive features supporting the integrity of the evidence. Fifteen months after the report was issued, the public debate was still continuing unabated. Keen noted that no evidence of fraud had been offered up by critics. "No doubt there may be people who think all or some of the evidence is fraudulent. If so, they have yet to publish or provide authors of the Report with a shred of hard evidence to support that view despite having more than a year (and every opportunity and incentive) to do so."[22]

The mind-boggling, confusing range of evidence produced by the Scole Group has left many observers scratching their heads as they try to sort out the phenomena, the claims and the conditions and controls in place when the events happened. Both supporters and skeptics have something to point to as the controversy continues to rage. Most of the Scole séances were conducted in darkness, and a reasonable request by investigators to use an infra-red camera as a substitute was rejected (con); yet some sessions were held in adequate light, and during the séances held in darkness everyone in the room wore luminous strips of velcro attached to their arms and sometimes legs to allow observers to monitor movements of people during the experiments. Luminous tabs were also attached to the table and other objects (pro). The Scole group generally furnished to the investigators the unexposed film used in the tests, and held it in their custody (con); yet several times the investigators had tight chain of custody from start to finish, and images still appeared on the film (pro). Many sessions had no qualified magician present to protect against clever illusion or fraud (con); yet one magician who did attend sessions came away favorably impressed (pro). Webster, a professional stage magician for many years, a member of the trade's prestigious Magic Circle, and a paranormal investigator for over 50 years, attended three sessions. He is on record as declaring "I discovered no signs of trickery, and in my opinion such conjuring tricks were not possible for the type of phenomena witnessed, under the conditions applied."[23] Taking a page from outspoken skeptic and magician James Randi, who has a standing, famous challenge to believers to produce a paranormal phenomenon under his watchful eye and thus earn a million dollars, Webster issued his own challenge to skeptics: "If any magician can replicate (the Scole phenomena) by complying with the very same rules and conditions as I observed at the cellar of the Scole Group, then let them produce their evidence of proof with myself in attendance." Webster was backed up by the three principal authors of the Scole Report who have noted that no one has successfully taken up Webster's challenge.[24]

Best Scientific Evidence

Leonora Piper-George Pelham Communications (1892-1897)
Leonora Piper had no opportunity, like a lot of mediums, to make a few lucky guesses and quickly move on. Her talent was exhaustively tested and proved remarkably enduring. The SPR conducted *several thousand* sittings over two *decades* with the patient and ever-willing Piper. Details and commentary on these experiments were reported regularly in the *Proceedings of the SPR*, the society's journal. These reports are part of the permanent library of the SPR and available to interested researchers. She is credited with some very impressive hits in terms of verifiable information contained in her channeled messages.

One of the most famous series of evidential messages Piper produced came from George Pelham, an acquaintance of Hodgson before his sudden death in an accidental fall in 1882 at age 32. Pelham, a lawyer, had followed Hodgson's work with Piper and was skeptical about a future life, calling it both incredible and inconceivable. But he told Hodgson that if he died and found himself still alive somehow, he would try to contact Hodgson. Five weeks after his death, while Piper was channeling for John Hart, a close friend of Pelham's, Piper's control

Phinuit announced that a George Pelham was there and wanted to speak.

The spirit of George Pelham began to furnish what would eventually become a wealth of evidential information concerning himself, his friends and his family, together with obscure and confidential details of his former life (unknown to either Hart or Hodgson but later verified as true), to prove that he was indeed George Pelham, still alive on the other side. For example, when George Pelham had died, Pelham's father had sent Hart some shirt studs of George's to keep as a memento. Pelham's spirit not only identified the studs Hart was wearing as formerly his; he also told Hart how his mother had come to choose them and his father to deliver them to Hart.[25]

At this first session, Pelham also talked in detail and at length about other close friends he had while living, including the Howard family and their pretty 15 year-old daughter Katherine. He asked Hart to pass an enigmatic message on to Katherine. "Tell her—'I will solve the problem, Katherine.'—She'll know."[26] When the puzzled Hart inquired, he found out from Mr. Howard that the last time Pelham had stayed with the family before his death, he and Katherine had engaged in a philosophical discussion about the meaning of time, space, God and eternity. Pelham had argued that the commonly accepted beliefs on these topics were unsatisfactory to him, and that he would someday solve the problem and let her know. The message made a major impression on the Howards, who subsequently made arrangements with Hodgson to visit Piper, and talked at length with Pelham's spirit. At their first sitting, each and every reference Pelham made to specific persons and incidents known to the Howards was correct (reading the actual transcript of this session a century later can give you goose bumps).

In another sitting, Pelham announced to Hodgson, "I saw father and he took my photograph and took it to the artist's to have it copied for me." When Hodgson inquired about the claim to Mrs. Pelham, she wrote back, "Some of the things you state are very inexplicable on any other theory than that George himself was the speaker. His father *did*, without my knowledge, take a photograph of George to a photographer here to copy."[27]

Pelham's father eventually wrote to Hodgson, "The letters you have written to my wife giving such extraordinary evidence of the intelligence exercised by George in some incomprehensible manner over the actions of his friends on earth have given food for constant reflection and wonder. (My) preconceived notions about the future state have received a severe shock."

For almost five years, from March 1892 to Sept. 1897, Leonora Piper continued to channel evidential, verified messages from a George Pelham who acted like he was still alive. As Hodgson noted in his 1898 report to the SPR, Pelham's communications "have not been of a fitful and spasmodic nature, they have exhibited the marks of a continuous, living and persistent personality, manifesting itself through a course of years, and showing the characteristics of an independent intelligence."[28] Concluded the formerly skeptical Hodgson: "…many of what were once difficulties to myself in the way of believing that these phenomena (channeled messages in general) were the result of the agency of 'deceased' persons have been removed by the fuller evidence presented by George Pelham…" [29]

Hodgson's exhaustive report on the George Pelham channeled messages runs almost 300 pages, and includes verbatim extracts from the stenographically-reported sessions (written down as they happened), plus specific details on how the sessions were conducted and the controls in place to prevent cheating or fraud. It is difficult to provide, in a few short paragraphs, the sheer detail, richness and complexity of the evidence described in these transcripts. If you're near a large public or university library, you might want to check out the *SPR Proceedings* yourself. You'll be rewarded with some of the best scientific evidence available anywhere suggesting the reality of not only channeling and mediumship but also the survival of consciousness after death.

Eileen Garrett—1930 Airship R101 Case

One of the most scientifically interesting channeling sessions conducted by medium Eileen Garrett happened in 1930. England had developed an expensive, new, 770-foot long dirigible blimp (airship), the R-101, which the Air Ministry believed was the future of aviation. The giant airship was designed to cruise the world, linking Great Britain to all her far-flung colonies. But the airship was over budget and late in completion, and the public and Parliament were beginning to get angry. As a result, the airship was hurriedly completed and poorly tested before setting out on a maiden voyage to India in October 1930. Prior to the ship's departure, Garrett had received several precognitive visions of an airship crash. The R-101 left for India on Oct. 4 and crashed in France in the early morning of Oct. 5th. On Oct. 7th, before any official report on the cause of the crash had been issued by the government, Garrett was in a séance when a spirit identifying itself as Flight Lieutenant H.C. Irwin, recently deceased captain of the R-101, broke in with an urgent message. He preceded to tell Garrett the complete story of the doomed airship's last minutes in great detail. Major Oliver Villiers, of Air Ministry Intelligence, subsequently arranged seven additional channeling sessions with Garrett over the following month which produced further details of the crash which were unknown at the time but subsequently proved accurate.

These channeling sessions involved a wealth of extremely technical terms and comments beyond the comprehension of Garrett (who had no mechanical background). They included a discussion of things like useful lift, gross lift, disposable lift, fuel injection, cruising speed, cruising altitude, trim, volume of structure, etc. The dead Irwin also passed on confidential information unknown to anyone at the time but later proven true. Examples included a hush-hush secret experiment undertaken by the Air Ministry to use a mixture of hydrogen and oil in the airships; the name of a French town the doomed airship passed over which was mentioned by Irwin's spirit but not found on any standard map available to the general public; and the existence of secret diaries of crew members which detailed their fears about the project. As Klimo notes, when authorities studied the session transcripts later, they found the detailed technical information channeled by Garrett to be "completely accurate." In addition, they concluded that Lieutenant Irwin was the only person who could have provided Garrett with the in-flight accident details she channeled.[30] The notes of the sessions with Garrett were later reviewed by the entire executive technical staff at the R-101 base in Cardington who found 40 references to highly technical and confidential details. When they were done, they all agreed that to assume such specialized information could have come from a layman like Garrett was "grotesquely absurd."[31]

Details of the channeled information, taken from the original notes made at the time, can be found in John Fuller's book *The Airmen Who Would Not Die*. It remains one of the most remarkable and fascinating mediumship demonstrations in psychical literature, and has spawned several full-scale attempts to both prove and debunk the story.

Garrett herself was both puzzled about her abilities and open-minded about their ultimate source. She accepted the possibility that the "controls" she tapped when channeling might be split-off parts of her own personality instead of discarnate spirits.[32] Jung, who discussed channeling with Garrett, felt that Garrett might be tapping into humanity's collective unconscious in some instances.[33] But Jung also expressed the opinion that spirits might be the best explanation for some channeled messages. [34]

Highly Recommended Reading

Klimo, Jon. *Channeling: Investigations on Receiving Information from Paranormal Sources* (2nd Ed.). North Atlantic Books, 1998. This is the latest edition of a classic Klimo first published in 1987. It is particularly informative on the history of mediumship/channeling, the methods people use to channel, and the various theories that try to explain channeling.

Solomon, Grant and Jane. *The Scole Experiment: Scientific Evidence for Life After Death.* London: Piatkus Publishers, 1999. This book provides a readable, popular summary of the history of the Scole Experimental Group and its work, as well as photographs of some of the apports that appeared and intriguing images found on the film. The official report and conclusions regarding the Scole experiments produced by the Society for Psychical Research can be ordered directly from the SPR at 49 Marloes Road, London W8 6LA, England (011-44-171-937-8984)

Hastings, Arthur. *With the Tongues of Men and Angels: A Study of Channeling.* Holt, Rinehart and Winston, 1990. Hastings' book focuses a bit more on the rich and complex body of messages delivered by channelers from ancient times to the present and the significant role such channeled messages have played in human history. A harder-to-find book, but well worth looking for. Check out www.abebooks.com if your bookstore doesn't have a copy.

14.

Reincarnation

*"I believe it is better to learn what is probable about
important matters than to be certain about trivial ones."*
Reincarnation researcher Dr. Ian Stevenson

You've undoubtedly read about past life regression in a popular magazine, or browsed through a book on it at your local library or bookstore. Waldenbooks, Barnes & Noble and Borders always carry a
half-dozen titles or more dealing with it. Typically, a hypnotist puts
you in a trance and takes you slowly back in time to your childhood,
then to your infanthood, then to your birth moment, then—beyond
the veil to a past life, one you've lived before this one. You might have
been a farmer in Idaho in 1890, a peasant in 12th century France, a
friend of Julius Caesar, or an Egyptian worker who labored and died
building a pyramid. You describe your daily life during that incarnation
and experience the emotions you felt during that life—joy, anger, fear,
etc.—before re-experiencing the moment of your death in that life.
Eventually, you are brought out of the trance and back to your present
life. When you're done, you're sometimes presented with an audio tape
(or video) of what you said and did during the trance.

Did you actually relive a past life? As we discovered earlier, American
belief in reincarnation is somewhat surprising. Today, one in four

Americans (25%) believes in reincarnation according to a 2001 Gallup Poll, and their ranks in the past have included all sorts of well-known persons from Benjamin Franklin to Henry Ford and General George Patton. Broken down by religion, Gallup found that one in four Catholics (25 percent) and one in five Protestants (21 percent) believe in reincarnation. Divided geographically, the Western states show the highest belief (27 percent) and the Bible Belt South the least belief (16 percent) in reincarnation.[1]

But reincarnation remains a minority belief in the Christianized West, with its religious traditions of resurrection of the physical body, and a permanent, eternal afterlife in either heaven or hell. According to current Christian theology, we only get one chance; we only go around once. This Christian position wasn't universally accepted as dogma in the beginning. The early Christian community debated reincarnation fiercely. Several prominent early Christian theologians and bishops along with various communities within Christianity accepted reincarnation.[2] These apparently included the leading theologian of his age, Origen (185-254 AD) as well as the various Gnostic sects. But the Council of Constantinople in 533 AD finally settled the question by rejecting reincarnation and condemning to hell anyone who professed it. Belief in reincarnation didn't disappear in Christianity; it went underground. But henceforth all who accepted it were considered heretics.

Elsewhere in the world, belief in reincarnation could be found in many different cultures. Hindus and Buddhists throughout the East, Eskimos and native Indian tribes in the Americas, Pacific Islanders, the Yorubas of West Africa and the aborigines of Australia, and even the Teutonic and Celtic tribes threatening Rome professed faith in multiple rebirths of an individual. Even Muslims debated the concept of reincarnation in their religion's early days. Although mainstream Islamic belief today is anti-reincarnation, several Muslim sects accept reincarnation, including the Sufis.

Among people who today believe in reincarnation, this belief takes many different forms. Some believe we are eternally reborn without cease. Others believe the cycle of rebirths eventually ends and reincarnation gives way to permanent, immortal nirvana. Depending on the sect, we are reborn as humans; or animals and bugs (don't squash that cockroach!); some believe when we die our individual identity is mixed with other identities so that the personality reborn is a collection of many individuals, like what happens when two streams of water flow into one; some believe that only fragments or parts of our personality survive and are reborn, not our whole, complete identity; some believe only certain persons are reborn, not everyone.

But most Americans who believe in reincarnation probably envision reincarnation as the rebirth of themselves in another human life. Our soul survives bodily death and is reborn into another human body. Pioneer reincarnation researcher Dr. Ian Stevenson prefers the word "previous personality" to the more religiously charged word "soul" to describe the deceased person who has reincarnated.

Of course, we might be born into a completely different family, in a completely different town or country, come back as a woman instead of a man, a white instead of a black. We probably wouldn't look like our old self in our new incarnation. Which of course raises an interesting question—how could you prove who you once were to someone wanting proof? If you believed you were the reincarnation of someone's grandfather in another town, how would you go about proving it to that family? Stevenson notes that evidence of the persistence of memories provides the best, and perhaps only, indication that a particular person has survived death.[3]

So let's suppose you could tell the family that one July 4th, behind the old Saint Mary's Catholic church on Greenwood Avenue, you stole a kiss from their grandmother, who got so mad she hit you with the buggy whip. And let's say that such a story had indeed been passed down over the years in the family. Then you went on to say that you always hated the way she used to drink her coffee out of a saucer instead of a cup, and never understood why she didn't like the Prince Albert pipe tobacco you smoked when you first were courting her. And again, these things were true and known only within the family. Then the question would arise—how did you know that? How did you end up with his memories? Did you get the information through some natural means—did someone tell you or did you find the information in a book or letter? Did you get the knowledge through some form of telepathy or ESP? Or are you indeed the reincarnation of their grandfather?

Claimed memories, then, are the prime target of modern reincarnation research. And the two most popular research techniques today are 1) the field investigation of spontaneously recalled memories, a case method developed by Dr. Ian Stevenson, and 2) the use of hypnotic regression to put subjects in a trance and induce past life memories, offered by many therapists today.

As we saw, modern scientific research on claims of life after death dates back to 1882 and the foundation in England of the Society for Psychical Research. Reincarnation has always been one possible afterlife scenario, and it was being discussed in Spiritualist circles at the time. Seven years earlier, in 1875 in New York, trance medium Madam Helena Blavatsky had founded the Theosophical Society, an organization that went on to promote and popularize in America many of the ideas now embraced by the New Age, including both channeling and reincarnation.

Channeled messages of reincarnation helped lay the groundwork for the American public's current acceptance of reincarnation as a possible reality. Many well-known American mediums in the 20th century have passed on messages regarding reincarnation, influencing their readers' beliefs.

One of the most influential of these was Edgar Cayce (1877-1945). He is still widely read; go to the New Age section of any major book store and you'll find a half-dozen titles dealing with his life and teachings. Cayce, a photographer by trade, discovered his psychic heal-ing gifts accidentally. Hoping to cure a bad case of laryngitis, he was hypnotized by an amateur hypnotist friend. While in the hypnotic trance, Cayce diagnosed his illness and prescribed a cure that worked. Several years later, a homeopathic physician friend of Cayce's asked Cayce to use his trance gift to help him treat people. Cayce's success in diagnosing illnesses and prescribing cures made him a famous person in the 1920s and '30s.

It also gave credibility to his reincarnation pronouncements. For in addition to providing health advice, America's "sleeping prophet" con-ducted over 2,500 "life readings" on the past lives of people who sought his advice. Though Cayce himself was raised as a Bible Belt Christian to reject reincarnation, during his hypnotic trances he began speaking about reincarnation and eventually incorporated it into his faith. His personal reputation for honesty and his fundamentalist Christian upbringing made him the perfect person to introduce such a strange, "heathen" idea to Christian America.

One of America's most influential channelers in the 1950s was Ruth S. Montgomery, a Washington columnist, friend of clairvoyant and tabloid prophet Jeanne Dixon, and author of a dozen very popular books channeled through "automatic" writing which offered a variety of New Age beliefs, including reincarnation. Like Cayce, Montgomery helped popularize the reincarnation concept among middle-class Americans as well as among some politicians, trend-setting movie stars and society people. Channeled reincarnation messages eventually became part and parcel of the New Age movement which expanded rapidly in the 1960s and 1970s when yogas, Indian sitar music, drugs and esoteric beliefs became fashionable. Actress Shirley MacLaine's 1983 bestseller *Out on a Limb* further popularized the concepts of chan-neling and past lives, and many channeled entities emerging during this period—including Seth, Ramtha, Emmanuel and Michael—all preached reincarnation in some form.

The Eisenhower-era 1950s also saw the publication, in 1956, of Morey Bernstein's phenomenal bestseller *The Search for Bridey Murphy*. The book described how a businessman and amateur hypnotist with an interest in parapsychology hypnotically regressed a Colorado housewife, Virginia Tighe, to a past life in Ireland as a middle-class married woman. The story, published by a major New York book house and replete with vivid remembrances and historical details, captured the imagination of America. Newspapers wrote about the case and reporters scrambled to try and prove or disprove the existence of Bridey Murphy. Many of the details Tighe recalled under hypnosis later were verified by a reporter from the *Denver Post* who visited Ireland and investigated the claims. The *Chicago American* counter-attacked with a series of articles casting doubts on Tighe's memories. Vocal skeptics and die-hard believers continued to battle it out, providing additional publicity to the book. Neither side succeeded in winning a knockout, and the case remains controversial forty years later, but the concept of reincarnation received incredible public exposure.

Bridey Murphy wasn't the only star to emerge from this event. The hypnotic regression technique that produced Murphy's memories also gained tremendous attention and emerged—at least in the public's eye—as *the* way to research reincarnation. Hypnotic regression promised anyone the ability to access their past lives quickly, easily and relatively inexpensively. Today, a whole industry has grown up around hypnotic regression, with therapists around the country offering their services to help people recall past lives. Some therapists accept the recalled information as evidence of a past life; others simply see regression as a tool that can help the patient, whether the information is real or not. The International Association for Regression Research and Therapies (www.aprt.org), founded in 1980, now has almost 1,000 members in 22 countries, including most states in the U.S. Many more hypnotists undoubtedly experiment with past life regression on their friends and neighbors.

But many parapsychologists are concerned about the reliability of hypnosis and the accuracy of the memories it dredges up. Hypnotic regression is not their tool of first choice for reincarnation research.

For many parapsychologists, modern scientific reincarnation research really came of age in 1960 with the publication of a report in the *Journal of the American Society for Psychical Research* entitled "The Evidence for Survival from Claimed Memories of Former Incarnations." The paper offered information on 44 interesting cases of past life recall. The author was U. of Virginia psychiatrist Ian Stevenson, M.D.

Home base for Stevenson is the University of Virginia in Charlottesville where he is Carlson Professor of Psychiatry and Director of the Division of Personality Studies, UVA Health System (www.med.virginia.edu/personality-studies/). Stevenson was born in 1918 in Montreal, Canada and received his M.D. degree from the McGill University School of Medicine there. He trained in psychosomatic medicine at Cornell University, received psychoanalysis training in New Orleans and Washington, and spent eight years teaching psychiatry at Louisiana State University School of Medicine. There he conducted research on hallucinogenic drugs. In 1957, he joined the University of Virginia where he eventually became chairman of the Dept. of Psychiatry at the UVA medical school. Medium Eileen Garrett, President of the Parapsychology Foundation, was among those who encouraged him to investigate an apparent reincarnation case in India, helping launch him on a lifelong investigation of reincarnation claims. Eventually, Chester Carlson, inventor of the Xerox machine, endowed a chair at the university for Stevenson to finance his reincarnation research.

Stevenson's preference for investigating cases of *spontaneous* recall of past life memories (primarily by children) has been overshadowed in recent years by the popularity of inducing past life memories through hypnotic regression techniques. But among many scientists, Stevenson's field study of spontaneous memory cases remains the "gold standard" of scientific reincarnation research.

Stevenson's contributions to the field include defining what would constitute a strong scientific case for the reality of reincarnation.[4] Such a case would have the following elements: 1) the subject under investigation should be able to recall his past life in considerable detail; 2) someone should have made a written record of these claims before any attempt at verification is undertaken; 3) this information should turn out to be accurate upon investigation; 4) the adult or child whose memories are being investigated should display certain behavioral traits apparently inherited from the "donor" personality from whom he claims to have been reborn; 5) he or she should bear a birthmark inherited from a mark or wound on the donor's body; 6) the subject should be able to speak the language (if foreign) spoken by the previous personality during his or her lifetime.

Another of Stevenson's contributions to reincarnation research is the collection of some 2,000 reincarnation case histories (the files are housed today at the U. of Virginia). Stevenson has personally investigated more than half of these cases. Interestingly enough, of the 1,300 cases Stevenson had on file in 1974, the largest number were from the U.S.A. (324). And Great Britain (114 cases) almost matched the total number of cases Stevenson had logged from India (135).[5] Stevenson's research demonstrates that reincarnation is not peculiar to India and other countries with strong belief in reincarnation; modern, Christian, Western nations also have many cases of persons claiming reincarnation.

The subjects studied by Stevenson usually exhibit two basic types of memories: a) "imaged memories" such as knowledge of names, dates, places, scenes they have seen, and other thoughts and feelings associated with his or her previous life; b) "behavioral memories" such as memories of actions, activities and behaviors he or she engaged in during a previous life. A third category of memories, which Stevenson terms "subliminal cognitive memories," includes things the subject has no memory of learning, such as a foreign language. Some subjects have demonstrated the ability to speak fluently a language they don't speak and never studied in their current life. Usually that language is remembered as being the one they spoke in a previous life. This ability, called "xenglossy," can provide evidence supporting a past life claim.

For Stevenson, memories of a previous life are most convincing if they are spontaneous, not induced through hypnosis or deliberately sought out. And he believes the spontaneous experiences of very young children offer the most convincing, available evidence of reincarnation.

One of the biggest problems facing researchers dealing with claimed memories of a deceased person is verifying the information. That done, they also need to establish that the person remembering the information was not consciously or unconsciously exposed to the information by natural means in this life.

The basic research procedures developed by Stevenson include a) personally visiting the town where the case happened; b) interviewing the subject and his family; c) looking for witnesses who can confirm or deny the claims made by the subject and his family; d) independently confirming the claims of the subject, family and witnesses; e) seeing whether it was possible for the subject to have gotten his information normally.

While Stevenson remains by far the preeminent researcher in the field, other people have also made contributions to the field.

The late D. Scott Rogo was not primarily a reincarnation researcher like Stevenson, but did produce some interesting research and commentary on the reincarnation question. A parapsychologist and prolific author, he penned over 27 books and 75 articles on topics ranging from ESP, miracles and out-of-body experiences to poltergeists, hauntings and psychokinesis. The Parapsychology Foundation in New York (www.parapsychology.org) named an annual literary award after him. One of his contributions to reincarnation research is *The Search for*

Yesterday: A Critical Examination of the Evidence for Reincarnation. We've included two past-life regression cases from Rogo's book in "Best Scientific Evidence" (see below).

The late Helen Wambach performed over 2,000 hypnotic regressions in her lengthy career as a clinical psychologist and hypnotherapist. She scientifically analyzed information collected during 1,000 of these regression sessions in a book entitled *Reliving Past Lives: The Evidence Under Hypnosis.*[6] During the sessions, she quizzed her subjects on details of their remembered lives, including the era they lived, their sex, race and social class, and the types of food, clothing and dishes they used. She also catalogued their type of death (natural, accidental, violent). She then set out to see how well this data corresponded to statistical information known about these eras. For example, she found that her thousand-plus subjects lived past lives as women 49.4 percent of the time and as men 50.6 percent—which she argued mirrors biological fact (a roughly equal 50-50 split between male and female births over time). Based on these and other matching data points, Wambach believed the recalled lives were not a product of telepathy, chance or fantasy but truly suggestive of the reincarnation hypothesis. Her 1978 book, which is credited with introducing the concept of past life regression to the field of psychology, was recently re-issued by Barnes & Noble books.

Best Scientific Evidence

As noted, Stevenson believes the best evidence for reincarnation comes from young children who spontaneously remember a past life. No one has suggested to them that they try to remember a previous life, and their very young age reduces the possibility that the story they tell came from a previously read book, or radio or TV program. Among the most interesting cases involving children which Stevenson has researched are the following three. The first two come from his book

Cases of the Reincarnation Type. Volume I: Ten Cases in India (U. Press of Virginia, 1975); the third case, involving Corliss Chotkin, comes from his book *Twenty Cases Suggestive of Reincarnation* (U. Press of Virginia, 1980). As Stevenson notes, none of the cases offer irrefutable proof of reincarnation; but they do suggest this possibility.

Jagdish Chandra, India

This case has been well written about and commented on by other parapsychologists.[7] D. Scott Rogo believes it "may be *the* most evidential that has so far come to light; certainly it is one of Stevenson's best."

Jagdish Chandra was born in Uttar Pradesh, northern India, in 1923. When he was three and a half years old, he began talking of a previous life in Benares, another Indian state. His father, a lawyer, began keeping written notes on the boy's memories. The small boy claimed his "real" father was named Babuji Pandey; said that Pandey had two sons and a wife who had died; that he owned an automobile (a rarity for Indians in India at that time) and would often drive the boy around the town; described his mother and some family relatives; and described in great detail his former home (including where a safe would be found in a wall in an underground room there). Jagdish Chandra's "present" father eventually contacted a newspaper in the Benares area, detailing his son's memories and asking if anyone knew of Mr. Pandey. Babuji Pandey was eventually located and the boy was taken to Benares to visit him. When Jagdish and his father got to Benares, the father tested Jagdish by asking the boy to direct him to his former home as they walked through the maze-like streets of the city. Jagdish did it. He also recognized without apparent prompting some relatives he knew in his previous life, and showed a detailed knowledge of some of the religious and dietary customs of his former family. Jagdish's former family was of the wealthy Brahmin upper class whereas his current family was of a poorer, lower class. But from his earliest years, Jagdish had preferred food prepared the Brahmin way.

The case meets many of Stevenson's criteria in terms of solid evidence suggesting the reality of reincarnation. The memories came from a very young child, reducing the possibility that what he remembered he had learned from books, school or by normal means. His memories were detailed and specific. Written records had been kept of the boy's claims before they were investigated. Most of his claims were, upon investigation, later proven to be true. The boy exhibited behavioral traits from his past life. Many independent witnesses were involved in the case. The boy's former "family" lived at some distance from his current family, and were of another caste, further reducing the chances of collusion between the families involved. It is puzzling indeed.

Kumkum Verma, India

Kumkum Verma, like Jagdish Chandra, was bon in northern India, in Bahera in 1955 to a medical doctor and his wife. The evidence in her case parallels in many ways that of Jagdish Chandra. She first started talking about her previous life when she reached three and a half years old. She claimed to have lived in the neighboring town of Urdu Bazar, was named Sunnary, had married a man of the blacksmith caste, had a son named Misri Lal and a grandson named Gouri Shankar, and had two daughters-in-law, one of whom had poisoned her and caused her death. She described a pond near her home and an iron safe in the house with a pet cobra that was kept near it (little Kumkum herself had no fear of snakes as a little child and had once even stroked a cobra that had fallen from a tree). She also described mango orchards near the house; and said that her father lived in the town of Bajitpur. Though Kumkum's parents dismissed her claims at first, her memories were carefully logged by Kumkum's aunt. Though Kumkum asked repeatedly to return to Urdu Bazar and her former home, her parents refused. In 1959, however, a friend of Dr. Verma, told about the case, followed up on the claims and located in Urdu Bazar Kumkum's "son" from her former life, Misri Lal, and her "grandson" from that life, Gouri Shankar.

Misri was able to confirm most of the claims made by Kumkum about her former life as his mother Sunnary. In addition, he confirmed that Sunnary had died of a sudden illness, and that at the time he had suspected his mother had been poisoned. But relatives had dissuaded him from performing an autopsy.

Corliss Chotkin, Alaska

This case is interesting because it involves two physical scars found in specific locations on the body of the previous personality appearing in the same location on the body of the new personality. A Tlingit Eskimo in Alaska, Victor Vincent was very close to his niece, Mrs. Corliss Chotkin. Before he died in 1946, he told her he would be reborn as her son. He told her she would recognize him because her baby would inherit two scars he had—one on his back from a surgical incision, and one at the base of his nose. Eighteen months after Victor Vincent died, Mrs. Chotkin had a baby boy. The baby had two birthmarks which matched the scars Victor Vincent carried in life (as Stevenson notes, it is extremely unlikely that two people would normally have two specific scars on the same location of their bodies). When he was still a small child, he reportedly asked his mother, "Don't you know me? I'm Kahkody" (Victor Vincent's tribal name). As he grew older he was able to spontaneously recognize people and identify places known to Victor Vincent, apparently without prompting or help from others. He told his parents of incidents in Victor's past life which they had never discussed with him. He also displayed several personality traits of Vincent, including talking with a stutter and a special knack for fixing boat engines.

Based on these three cases and hundreds of other cases he has researched, Stevenson concludes that the evidence suggests that human beings (and perhaps animals too) have minds or souls that survive death and suggests scientists drop some of their assumptions and open-mindedly look at the evidence. He also believes that reincarnation doesn't have to nullify evolution or genetics.[8]

Doris Williams, USA

Cases uncovered under hypnosis during past life regression sessions are more controversial, because the hypnotic technique can cause persons to role-play, imagine events and fantasize details, or gain access to deeply buried subconscious information that can falsely appear to be information he's learned from a past life instead of this life. Stevenson, for example, believes almost all personalities that emerge from hypnosis are imaginary.[9] But the late D. Scott Rogo believed it is a useful tool if not abused. And although most psychologists question the value of hypnotically evoked, past life recall, Rogo felt " the phenomenon bears up surprisingly well when critically examined." [10]

In his book *The Search for Yesterday: A Critical Examination of the Evidence for Reincarnation,* Rogo offered up six cases for consideration that in his opinion were strong enough to justify "some sort of *apriori* belief in reincarnation."[11] Among the six is the Doris Williams hypnotic regression case.

An Ohio native and a registered nurse, Doris Williams moved to California in 1955. She brought with her a life-long fear and overwhelming anxiety of deep water, ocean travel and small boats. Under hypnotic regression, she remembered a former life as Stephen Weart Blackwell, a clerk with the Brown Shipping Co. located at 167 West State Street in Trenton, New Jersey. She recalled his wish to go to medical school, which his mother rejected, and his frequent trips to England on business. Most importantly, she recalled Stephen being a 43-year-old passenger on the *Titanic* on that April 14, 1912 night when it hit an iceberg and sank. She remembered in great detail the clothes he was wearing, the exact place where he stood on the deck as the passengers waited for lifeboats, and the sounds, crying and music that swirled around him as the great ship went down.

Most of the details she provided were later verified by investigation. Some details were relatively common knowledge. The presence of

Stephen Blackwell on the *Titanic* could have been learned by anyone with access to a library since it is found in Walter Lord's bestseller *A Night to Remember*. But other details she provided were apparently quite obscure. For instance, a review of a half-century old U.S. Senate investigative report on the disaster confirmed that Stephen Blackwell had indeed been employed by a Brown Shipley (not "Shipping") Company, once located at the address she remembered. Blackwell, age 43, had been returning to America from a business trip to England when the *Titanic* sank. According to Rogo, Doris Williams herself later lost some of her fear of water and small boats, but had no desire to do any more exploration of her past life memories.

Dr. Arthur Guirdham's "Mrs. Smith"

Robert Almeder, author of *Death & Personal Survival: The Evidence for Life After Death*, offers the reincarnation case of "Mrs. Smith" as among the best scientific evidence available for the reality of reincarnation, in his opinion (though some reasonable criticism has been raised against the case). Smith was a patient in the 1960s of an English psychiatrist, Dr. Arthur Guirdham, who treated her for recurring nightmares and who tells her story in his book *The Cathars and Reincarnation* (Neville Spearman, 1970). As a teenager, Smith had spontaneous memories of an earlier life in medieval France as a Cathar. The Cathars were a Christian sect that was harassed and destroyed by the Inquisition. Smith herself remembered being burned at the stake as a heretic. She provided Guirdham with extensive, detailed information about her former life which she received through dreams and recollections, including specific names and places; complex, intricate religious rituals; social relationships; and other facts and details only known to historians specializing in Cathar history, life and beliefs. She also was able to compose poems and songs in medieval French spoken during the 12th and 13th centuries. Guirdham faithfully collected and recorded her dreams and memories and painstakingly checked them out with experts in the field. In his book, he notes the amazement felt by specialists in the field when presented with Smith's information. In some instances, her information contradicted what historians said—for example, she declared that Cathars didn't always wear black; that some of her friends wore dark blue. Later historical research confirmed that she was right and the historians wrong. Her ability to correctly provide a wealth of obscure but verifiable historical detail on medieval Cathar life and history was exceptional, and compelled Guirdham to conclude that Smith had indeed lived a former life.

Highly Recommended Reading

Shroder, Tom. *Old Souls: The Scientific Evidence for Past Lives*, New York: Fireside, 2001. In 1997, Tom Shroder from the *Washington Post* accompanied Stevenson on trips through India, Lebanon and the United States as Stevenson conducted his reincarnation investigation of children claiming previous lives. A good look at how Stevenson conducts his research.

Stevenson, Ian. *Children Who Remember Previous Lives: A Question of Reincarnation*, McFarland & Co., 2000. This is the revised edition of Dr. Stevenson's 1987 book, summarizing for general readers almost forty years of experience in the study of children who claim to remember previous lives. Stevenson provides updated material relating to birthmarks and birth defects, independent replication studies, and recent developments in genetic study. The book includes an overview of the history of the belief in, and evidence for, reincarnation. He offers representative cases of children and looks at research methods used, analyses of the cases and of variations due to different cultures, and the explanatory value of the idea of reincarnation for some unsolved problems in psychology and medicine. The list includes four cases from the U.S. (from the states of Minnesota, Idaho, Texas and Indiana) Stevenson collected in the 1960s and 1970s. If reincarnation is real,

Stevenson notes, it might help explain a wide variety of early childhood behaviors and conditions, including phobias, unusual talents and interests, temperaments, aggressions, and gender-identity confusion. It might also help explain some birth marks and defects. Currently, our personalities and behavior are explained as being produced by either nature (genetics) or nurture (environment). If reincarnation is real, then we may have to add a third influencing factor—past life experiences.

Stevenson, Ian. *Twenty Cases Suggestive of Reincarnation,* 2nd Rev. Ed., Charlottesville, VA: University Press of Virginia, 1980. A classic first published in 1966 as Vol. 26 of the *Proceedings of the American Society for Psychical Research,* this book offers a good geographical and cultural sample of cases found in Stevenson's database.

Head, Joseph and Cranston, Sylvia. *Reincarnation: The Phoenix Fire Mystery,* Theosophical U. Press, 1994. A good, single volume overview of the history of belief in reincarnation. Every major philosopher, religious leader, politician, artist, author or famous person in the world over the last 3,000 years who has said anything on the topic of reincarnation is listed, along with a short biography and key writings or sayings he or she has made on the subject.

Bernstein, Morey. *The Search For Bridey Murphy,* New York: Doubleday, 1965. The book became a best seller when it first appeared in 1956. It's out-of-print now but can be found in most libraries. One reason to check it out? Stevenson calls it one of the few hypnotic regression stories where the hypnotized person communicated obscure historical and geographical information that she was unlikely to have learned through normal means, as far as Stevenson could discover. [12]

15.

The Future of Science

*"Reality begins to look more like a great thought than a great
machine"*
Astrophysicist Sir James Jeans (1877-1946)

One of the best quotes I came across in my research was from Professor
Henry Sidgwick, co-founder of the Society for Psychical Research.
Speaking a century ago, he noted in a speech that SPR investigators
"believed unreservedly in the methods of modern science and were prepared to accept submissively her reasoned conclusions when sustained
by the agreements of experts; but we were not prepared to bow with
equal docility to the mere prejudices of scientific men."

The paranormal phenomena described in this book are obviously
quirky, unpredictable, and poorly understood. But the scientific evidence for their existence, as we have seen, is substantial and often
impressive. Is it proof? That's your call. But it seems safe to say that the
evidence is good enough to allow an intelligent, educated person to
conclude, without embarrassment or apology, that at least some paranormal phenomena exist, and that their ultimate explanation may
require rewriting science.

How *do* we explain the crisis apparition of Lt. David McConnel, or
the disturbances associated with the Miami poltergeist? The PK

research at Princeton University? Jagdish Chandra's reincarnation claim? Honorton's Ganzfield ESP experiments? Carrel's observation of a faith healing miracle at Lourdes, or Achterberg's cancer visualization study? What is a reasonable explanation for Osis and Haraldssons's collection of death bed visions, or Lady Barrett's account of Dora's dying vision? What do we make of Dr. Michael Sabom's NDE research? The University of Munich's dowsing study? Or medium Eileen Garrett's ability to channel extremely technical details and confidential information regarding the last flight of the doomed airship R-101?

If the evidence doesn't fit current scientific theory, do we toss out the evidence or rethink our theory?

Dr. Dean Radin and many of his fellow ESP researchers at universities in the U.S. and Europe say there is presently available, cumulative statistical databases providing strong, scientifically credible, repeatable evidence for ESP and therefore "ESP exists, precognition exists, telepathy exists and PK exists."[1] I look at their evidence and I tend to agree.

Dr. Robert Jahn, Dean Emeritus of the School of Engineering and Applied Sciences, Princeton University, says that the results of the psychokinesis tests conducted at the PEAR laboratory cannot be explained away by poor equipment, poor experimental protocols, statistical artifacts, pure chance or operator fraud. Unless and until someone can successfully challenge this evidence, it doesn't appear unreasonable to conclude that PK exists.

Professor Hans Bender and Dr. William Roll offer excellent evidence that poltergeists exist. Based on the evidence they present, I find this a reasonable belief.

The dedicated investigators from the Society for Psychical Research collected and scientifically evaluated over 700 ghost and apparition cases for their 1,400 page book *Phantasms of the Living*. What impressed them about the evidence, they said, was "its overwhelming quantity—overwhelming, we mean, to any further doubting of the reality of the class of phenomenon." I agree with them that ghosts and apparitions appear to be a real phenomenon. Based on the evidence, I further find it reasonable to believe that at least some of the reports—like the case of Lt. McConnel—cannot be accounted for by imagination, hallucination, fraud, or other conventional explanation. I don't find it irrational to conclude that the best explanation for the Lt. McConnel case and for the James Chaffin case is the life-after-death hypothesis.

Carlson Professor of Psychiatry Dr. Ian Stevenson, Director of the Division of Personality Studies, Dept. of Behavioral Medicine and Psychiatry, University of Virginia declares that there exists very good evidence suggesting the possibility of reincarnation, and that this evidence should be pursued. I agree.

The celebrated Harvard professor, psychologist and philosopher William James, author of the famous *Varieties of Religious Experience,* said that medium Leonora Piper demonstrated "supernormal powers," as shown during the more than two thousand sittings she did over two decades with the Society for Psychical Research, and consequently that mediumship as a phenomenon exists. I agree, though I have not made up my mind as to what might be the best explanation for it.

Psychology professor Dr. Stanley Krippner declares "There are few medical conditions today that cannot be improved if you know how to trigger the body's tremendous power to heal itself." Dr. Candace Pert argues that the mind is more than the brain. Based on the evidence I've seen, both statements appear reasonable to me.

Solid, random, double-blind scientific research experiments now exist suggesting prayer can heal, and even heal at a distance. I find the evidence worthy of careful consideration, even if its implications make some scientists uncomfortable.

Raymond Moody, M.D., a pioneer in Near-Death Experience research, has concluded that "Death is a separation of the mind from the body, and that mind does pass into other realms at this point." Osis and Haraldsson argue that "death-bed visions, combined with other afterlife research, make possible a fact-based, rational and therefore reasonable belief in life after death." I don't find it irrational or unscientific to hold either belief.

Nobel Laureate Charles Richet studied the evidence for dowsing and declared: "We must accept dowsing as a fact. It is useless to work up experiments to prove its existence. It exists. What is needed is its development." I concur.

We all have our own standard for proof. I have personally concluded from the scientific evidence I have uncovered during my investigation (death-bed visions, ghosts and near-death experiences, in particular) that there probably is life after death; that human consciousness is not confined to our physical body or the brain, and does not die with the body. I wouldn't be overly surprised to find at my death that I move on to another reality where I have a good chance of meeting family, friends and relatives who have passed on before me. Based on NDE reports made by hundreds of apparently sane, normal people, I wouldn't even be surprised to find "God" there (though not the sectarian God and simplistic afterlife taught to me in church as a child).

I'm frankly embarrassed at how close this scientific evidence matches the collective wisdom of the world's many religions and the deepest, traditional spiritual instincts of humans.

Why am I embarrassed? I suspect it's for the same reason millions of people are embarrassed and instinctively balk at accepting any scientific evidence pointing to these conclusions. They contradict modern Science, and no one wants to be considered "unscientific."

But why should we consider these conclusions unscientific? Again, as psychologist Charles Tart reminds us, true science shouldn't be confused with "Scientism," a philosophy of materialism embraced by some scientists. Millions of people today mistakenly believe that one cannot be "modern" and "scientific" without embracing this philosophy. But true science is willing to look at any evidence—and adjust its hypotheses to fit that evidence when necessary. It may turn out that some or all of the "paranormal" phenomena described in this book are simply super-*normal* phenomena—part of a reality ultimately larger and more complex than that currently described by either science or religion.

One of the most interesting efforts to recast science to make room for what the authors call a "compounding constellation of newly inexplicable physical evidence" that threatens science's cultural relevance and ability to accurately describe reality is currently being attempted by Robert Jahn and Brenda Dunne—those two Princeton University scientists who helped demonstrated the reality of PK. In a thought-provoking paper called "Science of the Subjective"[2] they provide the outline for a solution that retains the essence of the scientific method but acknowledges a proactive role for human consciousness in establishing reality itself. Their holistic "super-science" would respect objective science, the ability of humans "to discriminate, to isolate, and to represent elements of reality via precise observation and dispassionate logic." But it would also respect and use "subjective qualities as much as objective, aesthetic sensitivities as much as analytical logic, and mystical insights as much as tangible evidence."

It's a bold proposal, worthy of real Science.

Afterword

Much of the "best evidence" in this book comes from scientific research done in laboratories by academics and scientists who publish their findings in professional journals, papers and books. But most paranormal phenomena happen spontaneously, outside the laboratory. For these events, researchers must seek out the observations, personal experiences or stories of people willing to share them with science and allow them to be examined, investigated and tested. If you have experienced, read about or come across paranormal evidence or research you feel deserves consideration as "best evidence" for the paranormal, I invite you to send a summary of that evidence to me at evidence@aloha.net.

About the Author

Michael Schmicker edits a high-technology industry newsletter covering developments in biotechnology, astronomy, computer software and ocean/earth sciences industries. A veteran journalist and associate member of the national Society for Scientific Exploration, he wrote *Yahoo Internet Life* magazine's guide to the best websites dedicated to "Paranormal Phenomena," and has been a featured guest on national radio talk shows like *Art Bell Coast to Coast AM* and *Uri Geller's Parascience and Beyond.* His interest in investigating the paranormal began as a Peace Corps Volunteer in Thailand where he first encountered a non-Western culture and people who readily accept the reality of a world beyond the five senses—sparking a lifelong curiosity about scientific anomalies unexplainable by current science. He can be reached at evidence@aloha.net.

Index

Footnotes

CHAPTER ONE

[1] *The Gallup Poll, Public Opinion 1990*, Wilmington, DE: Scholarly Resources, 1991, pp. 87-91. Survey on "Psychic and Paranormal Phenomena."

[2] Newport, Frank and Strausberg, Maura. "Americans' Belief in Psychic and Paranormal Phenomena Is Up Over Last Decade," Gallup News Service, June 8, 2001. Story found on Gallup website at www.gallup.com/poll/releases/pr010608.asp.

[3] Polls done in Great Britain by the *Times* (1979), *Daily Mail* (Feb. 2, 1998) and *Sun* (Feb. 4-5, 1998) newspapers are good examples. The national survey done by the *Daily Mail* found the percentage of believers to be 64 percent in "some people have paranormal powers that cannot be explained by science"; 52 percent "that a person's spirit lives on after death"; 47 percent in "thought-reading"; 40 percent in "people can cure illnesses with the power of their mind"; 38 percent in "ghosts"; 34 percent in "objects can be moved by the power of the mind"; 25 percent in "reincarnation" ; and 49 percent "life exists on other planets." According to the 1979 *Times* poll, 81 percent believed that psychic experiences either "certainly" or "probably" exist, and only 2 percent said they "certainly do not exist." The same *Times* survey also found belief levels of 83 percent for ESP; 38 percent for contact with the dead; 54 percent for out-of-body experiences; 53 percent for hauntings; 52 percent for poltergeists; 29 percent for hauntings and a whopping 70 percent for dowsing. Survey results downloaded from the Internet at www.tcom.co.uk/hpnet/survey1.htm. Another good example: 68 percent of 300 students polled at the University of Nice, France agreed that

"mind-induced spoon bending" (psychokinesis) is "scientifically proven, a scientific fact"; and a poll of French beliefs in the paranormal found belief in the paranormal is "directly proportional to the level of education," i.e., the higher their education, the higher their belief in the paranormal. Both polls were cited in Henri Broch. "Save Our Science, The Struggle for Reason at the University," *Skeptical Inquirer*, May-June 2000, pp. 34-39.

[4] Evans, Christopher. "Parapsychology—What the Questionnaire Revealed," *New Scientist*, 1973, 57, p. 209. Wagner, M.W. and Monet, Mary. "Attitudes of College Professors Toward Extra-Sensory Perception" *Zetetic Scholar*, 1979, 5, p. 7-16.

[5] Eisenberg, David, et. al. "Unconventional Medicine in the United States: Prevalence, Costs, and Patterns of Use," *New England Journal of Medicine*, Jan. 28, 1993, pp. 246-252.

[6] Cited in Cochran, Tracy. "The Real Ghost Busters," *Omni* magazine, Aug. 1988, p. 36.

[7] Sturrock, Peter A. *Report on a Survey of the Membership of the American Astronomical Society Concerning the UFO Problem*, Palo Alto, CA: Institute for Plasma Research, Stanford University, 1977. The survey was also later reprinted and serialized in the *Journal of Scientific Exploration*, Vol. 8, No. 1-3, 1994. In 1998, Sturrock took another fascinating look at the UFO phenomenon in his book *The UFO Enigma* (Warner 1998).

[8] *The Gallup Poll: Public Opinion 1991*, Wilmington, DE: Scholarly Resources, 1992, pp. 4-7. Survey on "Fear of Dying."

[9] Gallup, George. *Adventures in Immortality*, New York: McGraw-Hill, 1982, pp. 207-209.

[10] Cox-Chapman, Mally. *The Case for Heaven*, New York: G.P. Putnam's Sons, 1995, p. 179.

[11] Gallup. *Adventures In Immortality*, 210.

[12] Stevenson, Ian. *Children Who Remember Past Lives*, Charlottesville: University Press of Virginia, 1987, p. 26.

[13] Poll done in October 1979. Survey results downloaded from the Internet at www.tcom.co.uk/hpnet/survey1.htm.

[14] Gallup. *Adventures in Immortality*, 190.

[15] Additional data on the paranormal experiences of Americans can be found in Gallup, George. *The Gallup Poll. Public Opinion. 1978*, Wilmington, DE: Scholarly Research, 1979. Also see "Unusual Personal Experiences: Analysis of the Data From Three National Surveys Conducted by the Roper Organization," New York: The Roper Organization, 1991. In addition to the Gallup and Roper poll data, CBS television also conducted, as part of a "48 Hours" program, a nationwide, random sample of 984 adults, interviewed by telephone on Dec. 5-8, 1989. The data showed 64% of Americans believe in the existence of paranormal phenomena; one-fourth of those polled said they had personally experienced such phenomena as ESP and mental telepathy. The poll results are cited in the *American Society for Psychical Research Newsletter*, Spring 1990, XVI, 2, p. 21.

CHAPTER TWO

[1] Forbes, B.C. "Edison Working to Communicate With the Next World," *American Magazine*, Oct. 1920.

[2] The psychokinesis experiment is described in Baldwin, Neil. *Edison: Inventing the Century*, New York: Hyperion, 1995.

[3] What Einstein wrote can be found translated into English in Brian, Denis. *Einstein: A Life*, New York: John Wiley & Sons, 1997, pp. 176-177.

[4] Freud, Sigmund. "Dreams and Telepathy," in George Devereaux, ed., *Psychoanalysis and the Occult*, New York: International Universities Press, 1953, p. 86.

[5] Jones, Ernest. *The Life and Work of Sigmund Freud, Vols. 1-3*, New York: Basic Books, 1957, Vol. 3, pp. 395-396. For a fuller account of

Freud and ESP, read Murphy, Michael. *The Future of the Body*, Los Angeles: Jeremy Tarcher, 1992, pp. 376-378.

[6] Koestler, Arthur. *The Roots of Coincidence*, New York: Random House, 1972, p.101.

[7] Jahn, Robert and Dunne, Brenda. *The Margins of Reality: The Role of Consciousness in the Physical World*, San Diego: Harcourt Brace Jovanovich, 1987, p 41.

[8] Jones, Ernest. *Sigmund Freud: Life and Work*, London: Hogarth Press, 1957, Vol. 3, pp. 419-420.

[9] Jung, C.G. *Synchronicity: An Acausal Connecting Principle*, New Jersey: Princeton University Press, 1973.

[10] Koestler. *The Roots of Coincidence*, 92

[11] Wallace, A.R. *Miracles and Modern Spiritualism*, London: Spiritualist Press, 1878. Cited in Michael Grosso, "The Status of Survival Research: Evidence, Problems, Paradigms." Downloaded from the Internet at www.parapsi.com.

[12] "From Outer Space to Inner Space" in Mitchell, Edgar. *Psychic Exploration: A Challenge for Science*, pp. 25-50.

[13] Broughton. Richard. *Parapsychology: The Controversial Science*, New York: Ballantine Books, 1991, p.105.

[14] Dunne, Brenda J. and Jahn, Robert G. "Experiments in Remote Human/Machine Interaction," *Journal of Scientific Exploration*, Winter 1992, pp. 311-332.

[15] Crichton, Michael. *Travels*, Ballantine Books, 1989

[16] Broughton. *Parapsychology: The Controversial Science*, 66.

[17] Doyle, Sir Arthur Conan. *Wanderings of a Spiritualist*, Berkeley, CA.: Ronin, 1980

[18] Margaret Mead speaking to the members of the AAAS Council, December 30, 1969. Quoted in E. Douglas Dean, "20th Anniversary of the PA and the AAAS, Part I: 1963-1969," *ASPR Newsletter*, Winter 1990, pp. 7-8.

[19] *Phantom Encounters*, Alexandria, VA: Time Life Books, 1988, p.112.

[20] LaGrand, Louis. *Messages and Miracles*, St. Paul, MN: Llewellyn Publications, 1999, p. 168.

[21] "Hilary: Her Imaginary Talks Have D.C. Buzzing," *Honolulu Advertiser*, June 25, 1996, p. A2.

[22] Letter to George Whatley, May 23, 1785, found in Jared Sparks. *The Works of Benjamin Franklin*, Boston: 1856, p. 174.

[23] *San Francisco Examiner*, Aug. 28, 1928.

[24] Fisher, Joe. *The Case for Reincarnation*, New York: Carol Press, 1992. pp. 166-167.

[25] Irwin, Harvey J. "Belief in the Paranormal: A Review of the Empirical Literature," *Journal of the American Society of Psychical Research*, January 1993.

[26] Jones, W.H., Russell, D.W. and Nickel, T.W. "Belief in the Paranormal Scale: An Objective Instrument to Measure Belief in Magical Phenomena and Causes," (1977) Journal Supplement Abstract Service, Catalogue of Selected Documents in Psychology, 7, 100, (MS 1577).

[27] Tobacyk, J.J., Miller, M.J. and Jones, G. (1984), "Paranormal Beliefs of High School Students," *Psychological Reports*, 55, pp. 255-261.

[28] Salter, C.A. and Routledge, L.M. (1971), "Supernatural Beliefs Among Graduate Students at the University of Pennsylvania," *Nature*, 232, pp. 278-279.

[29] Stark, Elizabeth. "Not So-Skeptical Inquirers," *Psychology Today*, Sept. 1984, p. 76.

[30] *Psychology Today* Reader Lifestyle Profile, SMRB, Oct. 1992.

[31] The CBS poll results are cited in *ASPR Newsletter*, Spring 1990, XVI, 2, p. 21.

CHAPTER THREE

[1] *Journal of Scientific Exploration*, Summer 1993, pp. 123-124. Bauer himself has a strong interest in the Nessie mystery and wrote a book on it in 1988 called *The Enigma of Loch Ness: Making Sense of a Mystery.*

[2] Dunne, Brenda J. and Jahn, Robert G. "Experiments in Remote Human/Machine Interaction," *Journal of Scientific Exploration*, Winter 1992, pp. 311-332.

[3] Jahn, Robert and Dunne, Brenda. *Margins of Reality: The Role of Consciousness in the Physical World*, San Diego: Harcourt Brace, 1987

[4] Shroder, Tom. *Old Souls: The Scientific Evidence for Past Lives*, Simon & Schuster, 1999.

[5] See *Omni* magazine, November 1994, p.87 for Radin's expose of a Uri Geller wannabe.

[6] White, Rhea. *Parapsychology: New Sources of Information*, pp. 444-491.

[7] Broughton. *Parapsychology: The Controversial Science*, 125.

[8] Targ, Russell and Puthoff, Harold. *Mind-Reach: Scientists Look at Psychic Ability*, New York: Delacorte Press/Eleanor Friede, 1977.

[9] This story is recounted in Krippner's autobiography, *Song of the Siren: A Parapsychological Odyssey*, New York: Harper and Row, 1975

[10] A link to Greyson's research papers can be found at http://hsc.virginia.edu/personality-studies.

[11] Jahn and Dunne. *Margins of Reality: The Role of Consciousness in the Physical World*, pp. 314-321.

[12] Broughton. *Parapsychology: The Controversial Science*, p. 78-79.

[13] De Beauregard, O. Costa. " Quantum Paradoxes and Aristotle's Twofold Information Concept," in Laura Oteri, (Ed.)*Quantum Physics and Parapsychology*, New York: Parapsychology Foundation, 1975. Also see Puharich, Andrija (Ed.). *The Iceland Papers: Select Papers on Experimental and Theoretical Research on the Physics of Consciousness*, Amherst, WI: Essentia Research Associates, 1979, p. 13 where Costa de

Beauregard "argues that the data and the theory of the physical sciences alone *demands* that ESP and PK exist." In an obituary on Bohm in the *Journal of Scientific Exploration*, Spring 1993, p. 10, it was noted that "Bohm felt that there was room in quantum mechanics—perhaps even a necessity—for psi phenomena, and was not shy about saying so." Bohm earned his Ph.D. from the University of California, Berkeley, and was the last student to study under atom bomb pioneer J. Robert Oppenheimer. From 1961 he served as professor of theoretical physics at Birkbeck College, University of London. He was one of several distinguished scientists to test Uri Geller's PK abilities in the 1970s.

[14] LeShan, Lawrence. "Physicists and Mystics, Similarities in World-View," *Journal of Transpersonal Psychology*, 1, No. 2 (1969), pp. 1-15.

[15] Henry Margenau. "ESP in the Framework of Modern Science" in Smythies, J.R. (Ed.) *Science and ESP*, London: Routledge and Kegan Paul, 1967, p. 213. Cited in Becker, Carl. *Paranormal Experience and Survival of Death*, Albany NY: State University of New York Press, 1993, p. 124.

CHAPTER FOUR

[1] Hartmann, William K. *Moons and Planets*, Wadsworth Publishing, 1983.

[2] Feldman, Anthony. *Scientists and Inventors*, New York: Facts on File, 1979. Also, Truzzi, Marcello. "Reflections on the Reception of Unconventional Claims in Science," *Frontier Perspectives*, Vol. 1, No. 2 (Fall/Winter 1990), Center for Frontier Sciences, Temple University. Downloaded from Internet. Also, Wooley quote from Clark, Jerome. *High Strangeness*, Detroit: Omnigraphics, 1996, p.185.

[3] Broughton. *Parapsychology: The Controversial Science*, 5.

[4] Milton, Richard. *Alternative Science: Challenging the Myths of the Scientific Establishment*, Vermont: Park Street Press, 1996, pp. 11-12.

[5] From the website "It'll Never Work!," a funny list of negative and pessimistic comments about new ideas.

[6] Milton. *Alternative Science: Challenging the Myths of the Scientific Establishment*, 11.

[7] *The New Columbia Encyclopedia*, New York: Columbia University Press, 1975. See reference to "continental drift."

[8] Truzzi, Marcello. "Reflections on the Reception of Unconventional Claims in Science," *Frontier Perspectives*, Vol. 1, No. 2 (Fall/Winter 1990), Center for Frontier Sciences, Temple University. Downloaded from Internet.

[9] C.E.M. Hansel. *ESP: A Scientific Evaluation*, New York: Scribners, 1966. Cited in Russell Targ and Harold Puthoff. *Mind Reach*, Delacorte Press, 1977, p. 167.

[10] Editorial. "Scanning the Issue," *Proceedings of the IEEE*, March 1976, No. 3, p. 291. Cited in Russell Targ and Harold Puthoff. *Mind Reach*, Delacorte Press, 1977, p. 169.

[11] *USA Today*, June 1988, pp. 1-2. The magazine is published by the Society for the Advancement of Education.

[12] Kuhn, Thomas. *The Structure of Scientific Revolution*, University of Chicago Press, 1970.

[13] For a good explanation of the limits of scientific "truth," read Dr. Henry Bauer's book *Scientific Literacy and the Myth of the Scientific Method* (University of Illinois Press, 1994).

[14] Jung. *Synchronicity*, 6.

[15] Braude, Stephen E. The *Limits of Influence: Psychokinesis and the Philosophy of Science*, New York: Routledge & Kegan Paul, 1986, pp. 26-54.

[16] *Ibid*, 29

[17] Tart, Charles. "Altered States of Consciousness and Psi Phenomena," *ASPR Newsletter*, XX, No. 1, p. 3.

[18] Truzzi. "Reflections on the Reception of Unconventional Claims in Science".

[19] For a brief history of CSICOP's foundation and early days, see Melton, J. Gordon, Clark, Jerome, and Kelly, Aidan. "Anti-Paranormal: Skeptics and the New Age," *New Age Almanac*, Detroit: Visible Ink Press/Gale Research Inc., 1991, pp. 105-114; See also Broughton, *Parapsychology: The Controversial Science*, pp. 81-86

[20] See Hansen, George P. "CSICOP and the Skeptics: An Overview," *Journal of the American Society for Psychical Research*, Vol. 88, No. 1, Jan. 1992, pp. 19-63. A copy of the paper can be found on Hansen's website at www.tricksterbook.com/ArticlesOnline/CSICOPoverview.htm.

[21] Rawlins, Dennis. "sTARBABY," *Fate*, October 1981.

[22] Truzzi. "Reflections on the Reception of Unconventional Claims in Science."

[23] Hyman, Ray. "Proper Criticism," *The New York Skeptic*, Spring 1988. Cited in Melton et al. *New Age Almanac*, 113.

[24] Matt Nisbet. "The Best Case for ESP?" Article of July 28,2000 found on the CSICOP website at www.csicop.org/genx/ganzfield/. Some criticisms can also appear surprisingly weak when analyzed carefully. See for example "Debunking Common Skeptical Arguments Against Paranormal and Psychic Phenomena," by Winston Wu (found on the Internet at www.angelfire.com/realm/psyzone/winston.htm).

[25] Siano, Brian. "Culture Wars: Skeptics, Parapsychologists and New Agers: Has the 'Good Guys Vs. Bad Guys' Rhetoric Hindered the Quest for Truth?," *Skeptic*, Vol. 3, No. 2, 1995, pp. 98-101.

[26] Truzzi, Marcello. "Zetetic Ruminations on Skepticism and Anomalies in Science," *Zetetic Scholar*, 12/13 (1987), 7-20.

[27] Lyons, Arthur and Marcello Truzzi.. *The Blue Sense: Psychic Detectives and Crime*, New York: Warner Books/Mysterious Press, 1991.

[28] Milton. *Alternative Science*, 155.

CHAPTER FIVE

[1] Broughton. *Parapsychology: The Controversial Science,* 72

[2] Evans, Christopher. "Parapsychology—What the Questionnaire Revealed," *New Scientist,* 1973, 57, p. 209.

[3] "Brian Inglis on answers to the *Times* questionnaire on the paranormal," downloaded from the Internet at www.tcom.co.uk/hpnet/survey.htm.

[4] For the latest edition (13th) see: Atkinson, Rita L., Atkinson, Richard C., Smith, Edward E., Bem, Daryl, Nolen-Hoeksema, Susan. *Hilgard's Introduction to Psychology,* Harcourt College Publishers, 1999.

[5] For a good lay discussion of some of the rule-bending realities of quantum physics, try Talbot, Michael. *The Holographic Universe,* Harper/Perennial, 1992; or Goswami, Amit. *The Self-Aware Universe,* New York: Tarcher/Putnam, 1995. For a shorter but equally thought-provoking read, try Apollo 14 astronaut Dr. Edgar Mitchell's paper "Nature's Mind: The Quantum Hologram" found under "Consciousness Studies" on the Web at www.nidsci.org.

[6] Swords, Michael. "Look It Up: Parapsychology," *Journal of Scientific Exploration,* Vol. 6, No. 1, 1992, pp. 85-86.

[7] Jones, Lewis. "A Tabloid Encyclopedia? The Americana Disappoints," *Skeptical Inquirer,* Summer 1992, p. 130-132.

[8] *The American Dowser,* Summer 1993, pp. 9-11, quoting an article in the Sept./Oct. 1992 issue of *John Harvard's Journal.*

[9] Raloff, Janet. "Dowsing Expectations: New Reports Reawaken Scientific Controversy Over Water Witching," *Science News.* Vol. 148, Aug. 5, 1995, pp. 90-91.

[10] "They Fly Through the Air with the Greatest of...*ki?*" *Business Week,* Jan. 23, 1995, p. 60.

[11] "U.S. Sicced Psychic Spies on Gadhafi," Associated Press, *Honolulu Advertiser,* Nov. 20, 1995, p. A6. For a detailed discussion of the program, see Chapter 6 of this book.

[12] "Levitating Frogs," *Popular Science*, November 1997, p. 39.

[13] *Science*, Oct. 23, 1998.

[14] Yankelovich Partners, "Belief in the Beyond" poll published April 20, 1997 in *USA Today*.

[15] Krippner, Stanley. "Four Models of Healing: A Cross- Cultural Comparison," *ASPR Newsletter*, Vol. XIX, No. 4, p. 9.

[16] Cardena, Etzel, Lynn, Steven Jay, Krippner, Stanley. *Varieties of Anomalous Experience: Examining the Scientific Evidence*. American Psychological Association, 2000.

[17] Knaster, Mirka. "Dolores Krieger's Therapeutic Touch," *East West Magazine*, August 1989, p. 56.

[18] Dossey, Larry. "Guest Column: NIH Creates the Office of Alternative Medicine," *Journal of Scientific Exploration*, Summer 1993, p. 119. He references research by M. Cooper and M. Aygen: "Effect of Meditation on Blood Cholesterol and Blood Pressure," *Journal of the Israel Medical Association*, 95:1, July 2, 1978.

[19] *Honolulu Star Bulletin*, July 28, 1993, p. A7 quoting a *New York Times* story by Molly O'Neill. Since then, Highmark Blue Cross Blue Shield of Pennsylvania has added the program (1997).

[20] "Federal Panel Says Acupuncture Valid as Pain Treatment," *Honolulu Advertiser*, Nov. 7, 1997, p. E1 quoting *Los Angeles Times* story.

[21] "*Living Right*, American Cancer Society, Hawaii Pacific Division, Summer 1995, p. 38.

[22] "High Impact Serenity," *Time*, Aug. 7. 1995 p. 50.

[23] White. *Parapsychology: New Sources of Information*, pp. 551-579.

[24] Fort, Charles. *The Complete Books of Charles Fort*, New York: Dover Publications, 1974. This 1125-page compendium includes all four of his books: *Book of the Damned; New Lands; Lo!;* and *Wild Talents*. It is found in many local libraries.

[25] Clark, Jerome. *Unexplained! 347 Strange Sightings, Incredible Occurrences and Puzzling Physical Phenomena*, Visible Ink Press, 1993.

CHAPTER SIX

[1] Weibel, Fr. E.J. *Forty Years Missionary in Arkansas*. St. Meinrad, IN.: Abbey Press, 1968.

[2] Moore, R. Laurence. *In Search of White Crows: Spiritualism, Parapsychology and American Culture*, New York: Oxford University Press, 1977, p. 204.

[3] Rhine, J.B. *Extra-Sensory Perception*, Boston: Branden Press, 1973, p. 147.

[4] Rhine, J.B. and Pratt, J.G. "A Review of the Pearce-Pratt Distance Series of ESP Tests," *Journal of Parapsychology*, 1954, 18, 165-177.

[5] Rhine. *Extra-Sensory Perception*, 147.

[6] Rhine, Louisa E. *PSI, What Is It?: The Story of ESP and PK*, New York: Harper & Row, 1975, p. 39.

[7] Rhine. *Extra-Sensory Perception*, p. xxxvii.

[8] Rhine. *PSI, What Is It?: The Story of ESP and PK*, 41-42.

[9] Honorton, Charles and Ferrari, Diane. "Future Telling: A Meta-Analysis of Forced Choice Precognition Experiments, 1935-1987," *Journal of Parapsychology*, 35, 1989, pp. 281-308. Cited in Gruber, Elmar. *Psychic Wars: Parapsychology in Espionage—and Beyond*, London: Blandford Books, 1997, pp. 227-228.

[10] Rhine. *Extra-Sensory Perception.*, p. xxxv.

[11] A Harvard professor and president of the Institute of Mathematical Statistics, B.H. Camp, gave his imprimatur to Rhine's work in the late 1930s. See Moore. *In Search of White Crows: Spiritualism, Parapsychology and American Culture*, 195.

[12] Moore. *In Search of White Crows: Spiritualism, Parapsychology and American Culture*, 192. Rhine's rebuttal of the sloppy research criticism is found in Chapter IX of *Extra-Sensory Perception*.

[13] Rhine. *Extra-Sensory Perception*, 155.

[14] Broughton. *Parapsychology: The Controversial Science*, 10.

[15] *Ibid*, 18.

[16] *Ibid*, 20.

[17] From the L.E. Rhine Collection of Spontaneous Psi Experiences, Institute for Parapsychology, Durham, N.C.

[18] Wagner, M.W. and Monnet, M. "Attitudes of College Professors Toward Extra-Sensory Perception," (1979) *Zetetic Scholar*, 5, 7-17. Cited in Bem, Daryl and Honorton, Charles. "Does Psi Exist?," *Psychological Bulletin*, 1994, Vol. 115, No. 1, pp. 4-18.

[19] *Ibid*.

[20] For a good explanation of meta-analysis, see Broughton. *Parapsychology: The Controversial Science*, pp. 279-284

[21] Broughton. *Parapsychology: The Controversial Science*, pp. 100-101

[22] Rhine. *Extra-Sensory Perception*, p. xxxv.

[23] Atkinson, R., Atkinson, R.C., Smith, E.E., Bem, D.J. *Introduction To Psychology* (10th Ed.), San Diego: Harcourt, Brace Jovanovich, 1990.

[24] White, Rhea. "Without Vision A Discipline Can Perish: Myers, Rhine and Murphy," *ASPR Newsletter*, Vol. XIX, No. 1, pp. 8-10.

[25] Harary, Keith. "The Call of the Wild in Transformative Experiences," *ASPR Newsletter* Vol. XIX, No. 2, p. 2.

[26] See Gruber, *Psychic Wars: Parapsychology in Espionage—and Beyond*.

[27] "Report on Government-Sponsored Remote Viewing Programs," *Journal Of Scientific Exploration*, Vol. 10, No. 1, Spring 1996, pp. 1-109. Some of the papers from this journal can be found on the web at www.lfr.org/csl, home of the Cognitive Sciences Laboratory website run by Dr. Edwin May, a later director of the Star Gate program.

[28] Schnabel, Jim. *Remote Viewers: The Secret History of America's Psychic Spies*, New York: Dell Publishing, 1997.

[29] According to Hal Puthoff. See "Report on Government-Sponsored Remote Viewing Programs," *Journal Of Scientific Exploration*, Vol. 10, No. 1, Spring 1996, p. 64.

[30] For the actual, entire transcript of the remote viewing session, see Puthoff, Harold E. and Russell Targ (1975). "Perceptual Augmentation Techniques" *SRI Progress Report No. 3* (31 Oct. 1974) and *Final Report*

(1 Dec. 1975) to the CIA. An excellent summary is found in Schnabel's book, pp. 104-112.

[31] See the paper "Operation Anomalous Cognition" found on the web site of Dr. Ed May's Cognitive Sciences Laboratory, www.lfr.org/csl.; Also found in Schnabel's book, p. 113.

[32] To appreciate how amazingly close his drawing was to the actual crane, see Targ, Russell and Katra, Jane. *Miracles of Mind: Exploring Non-Local Consciousness and Spiritual Healing*. Novato, CA.: New World Library, p. 48.

[33] *Ibid*, pp. 45-50.

[34] *Ibid*, 74.

[35] *Ibid*, 44.

[36] For an account of the operation, see Schnabel. *Remote Viewers: The Secret History of America's Psychic Spies*, pp. 285-286.

[37] Gruber. *Psychic Wars: Parapsychology in Espionage—and Beyond*, p.79

[38] For Price's sketch of the site and the later discovered 1913 photo, see Targ and Katra. *Miracles of Mind: Exploring Non-Local Consciousness and Spiritual Healing*, pp. 42-44.

[39] May, Edwin C. et al (1988). "Review of the Psychoenergetic Research Conducted at SRI International (1973-1988)," *SRI International Technical Report*, March 1989.

[40] For May's ESP theory, see his comments found on the web site of the Cognitive Sciences Laboratory, www.lfr.org/csl.

[41] Utts, Jessica. "The American Institutes for Research Review of the Department of Defense's STAR GATE Program: An Assessment of the Evidence for Psychic Functioning," University of California, Davis, 1995. A copy of the paper can be found on May's website www.lfr.org/csl.

[42] Hyman, Ray and Honorton, Charles. "A Joint Communique: The Psi Ganzfield Controversy," *Journal of Parapsychology*, 50, 1986, pp. 351-364.

[43] Bem, Daryl and Honorton, Charles. "Does Psi Exist?: Replicable Evidence for an Anomalous Process of Information Transfer," *Psychological Bulletin*, pp. 4-18.

[44] Hyman, Ray. "Comment," *Statistical Science*, 6, 1991, pp. 389-392.

[45] Psychologists Julie Milton and Richard Wiseman, for example, found no consistent evidence for psi in their 1999 study. But Milton subsequently acknowledged that, if their analysis were updated to include nine additional Ganzfield studies done after they had published their research, the psi effect would indeed be statistically significant. See *Science News Online*, July 31, 1999, Vol. 156, No. 5. Also see "Tales of the Paranormal," *New Scientist*, March 3, 2001.

[46] Utts, Jessica. "An Assessment of the Evidence for Psychic Functioning" (1995).

[47] Cited in Gruber. *Psychic Wars: Parapsychology in Espionage—and Beyond*, p. 128

[48] Broughton. *Parapsychology: The Controversial Science*, 288.

[49] See the *Journal of Scientific Exploration* (Vol. 10, No. 1) for a fairly complete discussion of the 24-year long government sponsored remote viewing experiments at SAIC and SRI, and the subsequent official evaluation reports. It also includes the in-depth comments of former program directors Hal Puthoff and Ed May, and their colleague, SRI researcher Russell Targ.

[50] Mumford, M. D., Rose, A. M., and Goslin, D. A. (1995). "An Evaluation of Remote Viewing: Research and Applications." The American Institutes for Research report. September 29.

[51] Utts, Jessica. "An Assessment of the Evidence for Psychic Functioning," (1995).

[52] Hyman, Ray. "The American Institutes for Research Review of the Dept. of Defense's Star Gate Program: Evaluation of Program on Anomalous Mental Phenomena," 1995. A copy of the paper can be found on May's website www.lfr.org/csl. The same site includes a paper detailing Utts' subsequent response to Hyman's report.

[53] May, Edwin C. "The American Institutes for Research Review of the Dept. of Defense's STAR GATE Program: A Commentary," *Journal of Parapsychology*, 60, 3-23. March 1996. A copy of the paper can be found on May's website www.lfr.org/csl. See also Gruber. *Psychic Wars: Parapsychology in Espionage—and Beyond*, pp. 89-90.

[54] Puthoff, H.E. "CIA-Initiated Remote Viewing Program at Stanford Research Institute," *Journal Of Scientific Exploration*, Vol. 10, No. 1, Spring 1996, p. 75.

[55] Gruber. *Psychic Wars: Parapsychology in Espionage—and Beyond*, p. 74.

[56] Weiner, Debra and Haight, JoMarie. "Charting Hidden Channels: A Review and Analysis of Louisa E. Rhine's Case Collection Project," *Journal of Parapsychology*, Vol. 47, Dec. 1983, pp. 303-321.

CHAPTER SEVEN

[1] See his paper "Researching Remote Viewing and Psychokinesis," found on the Web at http://www.tcom.co.uk/hpnet/houck1.htm

[2] Francis Bacon. *Sylva Sylvarum*, 1639, p. 210.

[3] As the Society for Psychical Research noted regarding Home and Palladino, "…a mass of material exists from authorities of competence and integrity, of such a kind as to place their case in a wholly different category." E. Fielding, W.W. Baggally and H. Carrington. "Report on a Series of Sittings With Eusapia Palladino," *Proceedings of the Society for Psychical Research*, 1909, p.311.

[4] Braude, Stephen. *The Limits of Influence: Psychokinesis and the Philosophy of Science*. New York: Routledge and Kegan Paul, 1986, pp.73-74 (A revised edition came out in 1997).

[5] Crookes, William. "Notes of Séances with D.D. Home," *Proceedings of the Society for Psychical Research*, Vol. 6, 1889-90, pp.101-103.

[6] Crookes, William. *Journal of the Society for Psychical Research*. Vol. VI, pp.341-342.

[7] For a fascinating and detailed, 38-page overview of Home's feats, see Braude. *The Limits of Influence: Psychokinesis and the Philosophy of Science*, 70-108.

[8] Stein, Gordon. *The Sorcerer of Kings: The Case of Daniel Douglas Home and William Crookes*, Buffalo, NY: Prometheus Books, 1993. For a less critical but somewhat questioning review of Home's career, see "Some Thoughts on D.D. Home" by Count Perovsky Petrovo Solovovo in the *Proceedings for the Society for Psychical Research*, Part 114, 1930, pp. 247-263.

[9] See parapsychologist John Beloff's review of Gordon Stein's book in *The Journal of Parapsychology*, Sept. 1994, pp. 331-337.

[10] Fodor, Nandor. *Encyclopedia of Psychic Science*, Hyde Park, NY: University Books, 1966. Cited in Spraggett, Allen. *Arthur Ford: The Man Who Talked With The Dead*, New York: Signet Books, 1974, p. 168.

[11] Lodge, Sir Oliver. "Introduction to the Earl of Dunraven's Record of Experiences with D.D. Home," *Proceedings of the Society for Psychical Research*, Part XCIII, June 1924, pp. 11-12.

[12] Richet, Charles. *Thirty Years of Psychical Research*, New York: Macmillan, 1923, pp. 496-97.

[13] Hurwic, Anna. *Pierre Curie*, Paris: Flammarion, pp. 263-264. Cited in Cremo, Michael. "Famous Scientists and the Paranormal: Implications for Consciousness Research." Paper presented at an April 27-May 2, 1998 conference in Tucson Arizona entitled "Toward a Science of Consciousness (Tucson 3)". Incidentally, Cremo himself is the author of an intriguing book of archeological anomalies entitled *The Hidden History of the Human Race* (Torchlight Publications, 1999).

[14] E. Fielding, W.W. Baggally and H. Carrington. "Report on a Series of Sittings With Eusapia Palladino," *Proceedings of the Society for Psychical Research*, 1909, pp. 306-589. For a summary, see Braude. *The Limits of Influence: Psychokinesis and the Philosophy of Science*, 128-141

[15] A number of magicians well-known to the magicians' fraternity are on record as accepting the reality of the paranormal. A good list is

found in Hansen, George. "Magicians Who Endorsed Psychic Phenomena," *The Linking Ring*, Aug. 1990, Vol. 70, No. 8, pp. 52-54. The publication is the monthly magazine of the International Brotherhood of Magicians. Their ranks include Howard Thurston, Jean Robert-Houdin, Samri Baldwin and Will Goldston. Hansen's article also cites one poll of magicians that showed 82% of them expressed a positive view of ESP.

[16] See Spraggett, Allen. *Arthur Ford: The Man Who Talked With The Dead*. New York: Signet Books, 1974, p. 99.

[17] Milbourne, Christopher. *Seers, Psychics and ESP*. London: Cassell & Co. 1970. Cited in Spraggett. *Arthur Ford: The Man Who Talked With The Dead*, p. 168.

[18] Besterman, Theodore. "The Mediumship of Rudi Schneider," *Proceedings of the Society for Psychical Research*, 46, 1931-32, pp. 433-436. This paper provides a good summary of all the tests conducted by scientists on Rudi between 1924-1930.

[19] Gissurarson, Loftur. "The Psychokinesis Effect: Geomagnetic Influence, Age and Sex Differences," *Journal of Scientific Exploration*, Vol. 6, No. 2, 1992.

[20] Panati, Charles. *The Geller Papers*. Boston: Houghton Mifflin, 1976, pp. 153-155.

[21] Professional magic's suspicious attitude towards paranormal phenomena has deep historical roots. For an interesting and highly readable discussion of that relationship over the last century, see Chapter 8 of Allen Spraggett's book *Arthur Ford: The Man Who Talked With The Dead*.

[22] Puthoff, H.E. "CIA-Initiated Remote Viewing Program at Stanford Research Institute," *Journal of Scientific Exploration*, Vol. 10, No. 1, Spring 1996, p. 65.

[23] Watkins, Graham and Anita. "Apparent Psychokinesis on Static Objects by a 'Gifted Subject': A Laboratory Demonstration" in W.G.

Roll, R.L. Morris and J.D. Morris, (Eds.). *Research in Parapsychology 1973*, Metuchen, N.J.: Scarecrow Press, 1974, pp. 128-134.

24 Braud, William. "Allobiofeedback: Immediate Feedback for a Psychokinetic Influence upon Another Person's Physiology," *Research in Parapsychology 1977*, Metuchen: Scarecrow Press, 1978, pp. 123-124. Cited in Gruber. *Psychic Wars: Parapsychology in Espionage—and Beyond*, pp. 157-161.

25 Owen, Iris M. *Conjuring Up Philip*, New York: Harper and Row, 1976.

26 Overall, PK effects observed during REG experiments have ranged from less than 1 percent up to 3-4 percent above what is expected by chance. It is for this reason that Jahn talks of our ability using PK to affect the "margins of reality." But the odds against achieving even this little 1 percent variation are enormous.

27 Jahn and Dunne. *The Margins of Reality: The Role of Consciousness in the Physical World, 139.*

28 *Ibid*, 148.

29 Radin, Dean and Nelson, Roger. "Evidence for Consciousness-Related Anomalies in Random Physical Systems," *Foundations of Physics*, 19 (12), 1989, pp. 1499-1514. Cited in Gruber. *Psychic Wars: Parapsychology in Espionage—and Beyond*, p 184.

30 Panati. *The Geller Papers*, 190.

31 Rhine, J.B. *The Reach of the Mind*, New York: William Sloan Associates, 1972 (originally printed 1947), pp. 143-144.

32 Braude, Stephen E. "The Fear of Psi Revisited...or It's the Thought That Counts," *ASPR Newsletter*, Vol. XVIII, No. 1, p. 10.

33 Batcheldor, K.J. "Report on a Case of Table Levitation and Associated Phenomena," *Journal of the Society for Psychical Research, 1966*, 43, pp. 339-356. Also, Batcheldor, Kenneth J. "Contributions to the Theory of PK Induction from Sitter Group-Work," *Journal of the American Society for Psychical Research*, 1984, 78, pp. 105-122.

[34] Brookes-Smith, Colin and Hunt, D.W. "Some Experiments in Psychokinesis," *Journal of the Society for Psychical Research*, 1970, 45, pp. 265-281. Also, "Data-Tape Recorded Experimental PK Phenomena," *Journal of the Society for Psychical Research*, 1973, 47, pp. 69-89.

[35] Moody, Raymond, M.D. *Reunions: Visionary Encounters With Departed Loved Ones*, New York: Villard Books, 1993, p. 24.

[36] R.G. Jahn, B.J. Dunne, R.D. Nelson, Y.H. Dobyns and G.J. Bradish. "Correlations of Random Binary Sequences with Pre-Stated Operator Intention: A Review of a 12-Year Program," *Journal of the Society for Scientific Exploration*, 1997, Vol. 11, No. 3, pp. 345-367.

[37] Jahn and Dunne. *The Margins of Reality: The Role of Consciousness in the Physical World*, 306.

[38] Radin, Dean and Nelson, Roger. "Meta-Analysis of Mind-Matter Interaction Experiments: 1959 to 2000." Paper can be downloaded from www.boundaryinstitute.org/experiments.htm

[39] Fielding, Baggally and Carrington. "Report on a Series of Sittings With Eusapia Palladino," *Proceedings of the Society for Psychical Research*, p. 317.

[40] *Ibid*, p. 462.

[41] *Ibid*, p. 566.

[42] Braude. *The Limits of Influence: Psychokinesis and the Philosophy of Science*, pp. 92-94

[43] Crookes. "Notes of Séances with D.D. Home," *Proceedings of the Society for Psychical Research*, p 99.

[44] Braude. *The Limits of Influence: Psychokinesis and the Philosophy of Science*, 94.

[45] *Ibid*, 92-93.

[46] G. Zorab. "Tests Settings With D.D. Home in Amsterdam," *Journal of Parapsychology*, 34, 1970, pp. 47-63. Zorab concludes his report on the Amsterdam sittings by reviewing four hypotheses modern skeptics might raise to try and explain the events normally. He concludes that none of them work. His conclusion: "Stated in modern parapsycholog-

ical terms, the above would mean: probably the phenomena were paranormally produced." See also comments on the event by John Beloff in a book review in the *Journal of Parapsychology*, Sept. 1994, pp. 335-336.

[47] Barrett, W.F. and Myers, F.W. H. (1889). "Review of D.D. Home, His Life and Mission," *Journal of the Society for Psychical Research*, 4, pp. 133-4.

[48] Braude *The Limits of Influence: Psychokinesis and the Philosophy of Science, 65*. The late Dr. Karl Osis, famous for his investigation of death-bed visions and other life after death questions also called just before his death for parapsychology to return to its roots and again start looking at the "big stuff." See Osis, Karlis. "Core Visions of Psychical Research: Is There Life After Death? A Cross-Cultural Search for the Evidence," *Journal of the American Society for Psychical Research*, Vol. 92, July 1998, p. 251.

[49] If you enjoy theoretical speculation on how paranormal phenomena might work, make sure you read Michael Talbot's book *The Holographic Universe*. It's a delightful, lay-oriented explanation of one interesting hypothesis—that the universe we exist in and perceive with our five senses is really a hologram.

CHAPTER EIGHT

[1] See *New York Times* story by Hanson Baldwin, Oct. 11, 1967. For a detailed account of the Marine's involvement with dowsing during the war, see Chapter 11 of Bird, Christopher. *The Divining Hand: The 500-Year-Old Mystery of Dowsing*, Atglen, PA: Schiffer Publishing, 1993.

[2] Bird. *The Divining Hand: The 500-Year-Old Mystery of Dowsing*, 217.

[3] For a detailed history of Brown's successes, see Chapter 10 of Bird's book.

[4] Bird. *The Divining Hand; The 500-Year-Old Mystery of Dowsing*, 106.

[5] *Ibid*, 117.

[6] *Ibid*, pp. 44-50.

[7] *Ibid*, pp. 329-334.

[8] Hansen, George. "Dowsing: A Review of Experimental Research," *Journal of the Society for Psychical Research*, Vol. 51, No. 792, Oct. 1982, pp. 343-367. The paper needs updating, but provides a good review of some credible scientific tests conducted on dowsing. Hansen, a professional parapsychologist and member of the International Brotherhood of Magicians, is author of several books, including *The Trickster and the Paranormal* (Xlibris Publishers, 2001).

[9] Bird. *The Divining Hand: The 500-Year-Old Mystery of Dowsing*, pp. 253-266.

[10] In the appendix to *The Divining Hand: The 500-Year-Old Mystery of Dowsing*, pp. 313-350, Bird offers up his evidence for the reality of dowsing.

[11] *Ibid*, pp. 321-322.

[12] For a skeptical critique of the German experiments, see J.T. Enright. "The Failure of the Munich Experiments," in the Jan./Feb. 1999 issue of the *Skeptical Inquirer*. The article can be accessed on the web at www.csicop.org/si/9901/dowsing.html.

[13] Betz, Hans-Dieter. "Unconventional Water Detection: Field Test of the Dowsing Technique in Dry Zones," *Journal of Scientific Exploration*, Vol. 9, No. 1, p. 1 ff, 1995 and Vol. 9, No. 2, p. 159 ff, 1995.

[14] "Raloff, Janet. "Dowsing Expectations: New Reports Reawaken Scientific Controversy Over Water Witching," *Science News*, Vol. 148, Aug. 5, 1995, pp. 90-91.

[15] Randi, James. "Help Stamp Out Absurd Beliefs," *Time*, April 13, 1992, p. 80.

[16] Bird. *The Divining Hand; The 500-Year-Old Mystery of Dowsing*, p. 11.

[17] *Ibid*, 14.

[18] Barrett, Sir William and Besterman, Theodore. *The Divining Rod: An Experimental and Psychological Investigation.* New Hyde Park, NY: University Books, 1968, pp. 86-102.

[19] *Ibid,* 102.

[20] Bird. *The Divining Hand; The 500-Year-Old Mystery of Dowsing,* p.318.

[21] *Ibid,* pp. 19-26.

[22] *Ibid,* p.187.

CHAPTER NINE

[1] Gordon, Richard. *The Alarming History of Medicine,* New York: St. Martin's Press, 1995, p. 49.

[2] Dossey, Larry, M.D. *Healing Words: The Power of Prayer and the Practice of Medicine,* San Francisco: HarperSanFrancisco, 1993, p.29.

[3] Krippner, Stanley. "Exceptional Human Experiences in the Field of Healing," *ASPR Newsletter,* Vol. XIX, No. 1 (1994), p.5.

[4] *Ibid,* 5.

[5] Murphy, Michael. *The Future of the Body: Explorations into the Further Evolution of Human Nature,* Los Angeles: Jeremy Tarcher, 1992. (Chapter 12 "Placebo Effects.")

[6] Beecher, H.K. "The Powerful Placebo," *Journal of the American Medical Association,* 1955, 159: 1603-4.

[7] Allington, H.V. "Sulpharsphenamine in the Treatment of Warts," *Archives of Dermatology and Syphilology,* 29, 1943, pp. 687-690.

[8] Murphy. *The Future of the Body: Explorations into the Further Evolution of Human Nature,* p.247.

[9] Thomas, K.B. "General Practice Consultation: Is There Any Point in Being Positive?" *British Medical Journal,* 294 (1987): 1200-1201. Quote from Molly Cox-Chapman. *The Case For Heaven,* New York: G.P. Putnam's Sons, 1995, p. 124.

[10] Krippner. "Exceptional Human Experiences in the Field of Healing," p.5.

[11] See two studies cited in Murphy. *The Future of the Body: Explorations into the Further Evolution of Human Nature*, 310.

[12] Michael Nash. "You Will Buy This Magazine: Shattering Myths About Hypnosis," *Scientific American*, July 2001, pp. 46-55. Six magazine staffers who had never been hypnotized before were hypnotized by the author of the article. Afterward, they concluded that seeing was believing when it came to hypnosis. "Here at *Scientific American* we pride ourselves on our skepticism towards pseudo-science and our hard-nosed insistence on solid research….What we found surprised us." (page 54).

[13] See many studies cited in Murphy. *The Future of the Body: Explorations into the Further Evolution of Human Nature*, pp. 332-339.

[14] Esdaile, J. (1846). *Mesmerism in India and its Practical Application in Surgery and Medicine.* Longman, Brown, Green, and Longmans. Reprinted in 1975, Arno Press.

[15] Hilgard, J. *Personality and Hypnosis: a Study of Imaginative Involvement,* University of Chicago Press, 1979.

[16] Nash. "You Will Buy This Magazine: Shattering Myths About Hypnosis," p 55.

[17] See five studies cited in Murphy. *The Future of the Body: Explorations into the Further Evolution of Human Nature*, 333-334.

[18] Ullman, M. "On the Psyche and Warts. I. Suggestion and Warts: A Review and Comments," *Psychosomatic Medicine*, 1959, 21: 473-488.

[19] Krippner. "Exceptional Human Experiences in the Field of Healing," pp. 1-7.

[20] Achterberg, Jeanne. "Mind Medicine: The Role of Imagery in Medicine," *ASPR Newsletter*, Vol. XVII, No. 4, pp. 5-9.

[21] Achterberg, Jeanne. *Imagery in Healing: Shamanism and Modern Medicine*, Boston: Shambala, 1985.; *Rituals of Healing: Using Imagery for Health and Wellness*, Bantam Books, 1994.

[22] See seven clinical studies cited in Murphy. *The Future of the Body: Explorations into the Further Evolution of Human Nature*, 360.

[23] See five clinical studies cited in Murphy. *The Future of the Body: Explorations into the Further Evolution of Human Nature*, 361.

[24] Green, E. and Green, A. 1986. "Biofeedback and States of Consciousness," in B. Wolman and M. Ullman (Eds.), *Handbook of States of Consciousness*, 1986: Van Nostrand Reinhold.

[25] See many studies cited in Murphy. *The Future of the Body: Explorations into the Further Evolution of Human Nature*. pp.354-355.

[26] Murphy. *The Future of the Body: Explorations into the Further Evolution of Human Nature*, p.368.

[27] Green, E. and Green, A. *Beyond Feedback*, Dell Publishers, 1977.

[28] McClure, C.M. "Cardiac Arrest through Volition," *California Medicine* 1959, 90:440-441.

[29] Benson, H. et al. (1982}. "Body Temperature Changes During the Practice of g Tum-mo Yoga," *Nature*, No. 295. See also Krippner. "Exceptional Human Experiences in the Field of Healing," p. 6.

[30] Achterberg. *Imagery in Healing*, p.78.

[31] *Ibid*, p.79.

[32] *Ibid*, pp. 79-81.

[33] Epstein, Gerald, M.D. *Healing Visualizations*, New York: Bantam Books, 1989, pp. 116-118.

[34] Achterberg. "Mind Medicine: The Role of Imagery in Medicine," p.8.

[35] Epstein. *Healing Visualizations*.

[36] Moyers, Bill. *Healing and the Mind*, New York: Doubleday, 1995, pp. 71-72.

[37] *Ibid*, 233.

[38] *Ibid*, 218.

[39] Spiegel, David, Bloom, J.R. and Kraemer, H.C. "The Effect of Psychosocial Treatment on Survival of Patients With Metastatic Breast Cancer," *Lancet*, Oct. 14, 1989, Vol. 2, No. 8668, p. 888.

[40] Moyers. *Healing and the Mind*, 68.

[41] *Ibid*, 107.

[42] *Ibid*, 220-221.

[43] "Study Finds Churchgoers Healthier," Karen Garloch, (Knight-Ridder News Service), *Honolulu Advertiser*, Nov. 8, 1997 p. B3.

[44] Moyers. *Healing and the Mind*, p. 220.

[45] *Ibid*, 230.

[46] "Neglect Shown to Affect Infant Brain," *Honolulu Advertiser* Tuesday Oct. 28, 1997, p. A10.

47 Tanner, Lindsey. "Researchers Are Exploring Laughter as the Best Medicine," *Honolulu Star-Bulletin*, Sept. 2, 2001, A5. (Associated Press story).

[48] Moyers. *Healing and the Mind*, p. 221.

[49] *Ibid*, 219.

[50] *Ibid*, 203.

[51] *Ibid*, 191.

[52] *Ibid*, 332.

[53] *Ibid*, 178.

[54] *Ibid*, 173-237.

[55] Pert, Candace. *Molecules of Emotion: Why You Feel the Way You Feel*, New York: Scribner, 1997.

[56] Braud, William. "Mental Techniques for Self-Healing and for Remote Influence," *ASPR Newsletter*, Vol. XVIII, No. 1, pp. 4-8.

[57] Moyers. *Healing and the Mind*, pp.188-189. The British scientist Sir Oliver Lodge, who earned his knighthood from his research on radio waves and electrons, also argued that the mind and brain were not the same. When doctors would point out that consciousness disappeared with damage or death of the brain, Lodge argued that it was equally possible that what was missing was the *display* of consciousness, not consciousness itself. The analogy would be a TV turned off. Although the TV is off, the programs are still in the airwaves and still exist; they just can't be displayed on the equipment. Likewise, a damaged brain

can't display consciousness, but it doesn't mean consciousness doesn't continue to exist. Lodge's analogy is reported in John Fuller's book *The Airmen Who Would Not Die* (New York: Putnam, 1980, pp. 58-59)

58 Dossey. *Healing Words: The Power of Prayer and the Practice of Medicine*, p. xv.

59 *Journal of Reproductive Medicine*, Sept. 1999.

60 Murphy. *The Future of the Body*, pp. 267-271.

61 Murphy. *The Future of the Body: Explorations into the Further Evolution of Human Nature*. (Chapter 12 "Placebo Effects.")

62 Hilgard, J. *Personality and Hypnosis: a Study of Imaginative Involvement*. University of Chicago Press, 1979.

63 See seven clinical studies cited in Murphy. *The Future of the Body: Explorations into the Further Evolution of Human Nature*, 360.

64 See many studies cited in Murphy. *The Future of the Body: Explorations into the Further Evolution of Human Nature*. pp.354-355.

65 Murphy. *The Future of the Body: Explorations into the Further Evolution of Human Nature*, 368.

66 Moyers. *Healing and the Mind*, p.196. Also, in the introduction to Norman Cousin's book *Anatomy of An Illness*, Rene DuBos cites studies showing the ability of the mind under hypnosis to obliterate vascular manifestations of a tuberculin test. "The tuberculin Mantoux reaction pertains to the kind of body response that immunologists designate 'cell-mediated immunity'," explains Dubos. "Since this form of the immune response plays an essential role in resistance to important infectious diseases such as tuberculosis, and probably also in resistance to cancer, there is good reason to believe that the patient's state of mind can affect the course of all pathological processes that involve immunological reactions."

67 Epstein. *Healing Visualizations*, pp. 116-118.

68 See studies cited in Murphy. *The Future of the Body: Explorations into the Further Evolution of Human Nature*, pp. 333-334.

[69] Klein, K. and Spiegel, D. "Modulation of Gastric Acid Secretion by Hypnosis," *Gastroenterology*, 1989, 96: 1383-7.

[70] See studies cited in Murphy. *The Future of the Body: Explorations into the Further Evolution of Human Nature*, 361.

[71] Fred Sicher, Elisabeth Targ, Dan Moore and Helene Smith. "A Randomized Double-Blind Study of the Effect of Distant Healing in a Population with Advanced AIDS," *Western Journal of Medicine*, 169 (December 1998), pp.353-363.

[72] Byrd, Randolph. "Positive Therapeutic Effects of Intercessory Prayer in a Coronary Care Unit Population," *Southern Medical Journal*, 81, No. 7 (July 1988), pp. 826-829.

[73] Harris, William. "A Randomized, Controlled Trial of the Effects of Remote, Intercessory Prayer on Outcomes in Patients Admitted to the Coronary Care Unit," *Archives of Internal Medicine*, 159: 2273-2278, Oct. 1999.

[74] Moyers. *Healing and the Mind*, p.200.

[75] *Ibid*, 196.

[76] Krippner. "Exceptional Human Experiences in the Field of Healing." For details, see Achterberg, Jeanne. *Imagery in Healing*, pp. 185-190.

[77] Carrel, Alexis. *Voyage to Lourdes*, New York: Harper, 1950. Cited in Murphy. *The Future of the Body*, pp. 268-269.

[78] Carrel. *Voyage to Lourdes*, pp.50-51.

CHAPTER TEN

[1] One well-written book offering some scientific evidence for life after death is Robert Almeder's *Death and Personal Survival: The Evidence for Life After Death* (Rowman & Littlefield, 1992). In it, he offers up his own intriguing list of "Best Scientific Evidence" cases that suggest the possibility of life after death.

[2] Osis, Karl and Haraldsson, Erlendur. *At the Hour of Death, (Rev. Ed.)*, Mamaroneck, N.Y: Hastings House, 1990, p. 3.

3 Barrett, William. *Death-Bed Visions: Psychical Experiences of the Dying,* London: Methuen, 1926.

4 Barrett. *Death-Bed Visions: Psychical Experiences of the Dying* (Aquarian Press, 1986 reprint), pp. 10-12.

5 Bozzano, E. *Dei Fenomeni di Telecinesia in Rapporto Con Eventi di Morti.* Verona (Italy): Casa Editrice Europa, 1948.

6 Osis, Karl. "Core Visions of Psychical Research: Is There Life After Death? A Cross-Cultural Search for the Evidence," *Journal of the American Society for Psychical Research,* Vol. 92, July 1998, p. 252.

7 Osis and Haraldsson. *At the Hour of Death, (Rev. Ed.),* pp. 82-83.

8 *Ibid,* 69.

9 *Ibid,* 42.

10 *Ibid,* 66.

11 Osis. "Core Visions of Psychical Research: Is There Life After Death? A Cross-Cultural Search for the Evidence," *Journal of the American Society for Psychical Research,* p. 247.

12 Morse, Melvin, M.D. *Parting Visions: Uses and Meanings of Pre-Death, Psychic, and Spiritual Experiences,* New York: Villard Books, 1994.

13 Osis and Haraldsson. *At the Hour of Death, (Rev. Ed.),* p.3.

14 Hart, Hornell and Hart, Ella. "Visions and Apparitions Collectively and Reciprocally Perceived," *Proceedings of the Society for Psychical Research,* Vol. XLI, 1932-33, pp. 218-219.

CHAPTER ELEVEN

1 Plato. *The Republic.* Edited by Alan Bloom. New York: Basic Books, 1968, p. 298.

2 For the full story, visit the copyrighted (1998) Capt. David Perry Website created by Denise Jones at http://homepages.rootsweb.com/~dagjones/captdavidperry/

3 Jaffe, Anelia, (Ed). *Memories, Dreams, Reflections* New York: 1965, p. 291. Cited in Cox-Chapman, Mally. *The Case for Heaven,* p. 187-188.

According to Cox-Chapman, when the BBC interviewed Jung in the 1970s and asked him if he believed in God, he reportedly answered, "I don't believe—I know."

[4] Ritchie, George. *My Life After Dying,* Norfolk Virginia: Hampton Roads Publishing, 1991.

[5] Ring suggested the NDE be broken into 5 separate stages; Sabom preferred 10 elements to the NDE. See Gibbs, John. "Moody's Versus Siegel's Interpretation of the Near-Death Experience: An Evaluation Based on Recent Research," *Anabiosis—the Journal for Near Death Studies,* Vol. 5, No. 2. p. 69.

[6] Cox-Chapman. *The Case for Heaven,* 180.

[7] *Ibid,* 179.

[8] Greyson, Bruce and Charles Flynn, (Eds.). *The Near Death Experience; Problems, Prospects, Prospectives,* Charles C. Thomas Publishers, 1984, Chapter 19.

[9] See Cox-Chapman. *The Case For Heaven,* Chapter 8: "What Happens When People Who Don't Believe In Heaven Have NDEs?" As Cox-Chapman notes, however, an older mystical tradition within Judaism does hold belief in an afterlife. The Kabbalah text paints a specific picture of what happens at the moment of death in terms very close to the modern NDE experience.

[10] As much as 18 percent according to one study. See Rommer M.D., Barbara. *Blessing In Disguise: Another Side of the Near Death Experience,* Llewellyn Publications, 2000.

[11] Atwater, P.H.M. "Is There a Hell? Surprising Observations About the Near-Death Experience," *Journal of Near-Death Studies,* Spring 1992, Vol. 10, No. 3. Atwater's findings are based on interviews from 105 such negative NDE cases discovered among some 700 NDE experiencers she interviewed The paper is also available on the author's website at www.cinemind.com/atwater/hell.html.

[12] Gallup, Jr. George. *Adventures in Immortality,* New York: McGraw Hill, 1982.

[13] Gibbs. "Moody's Versus Siegel's Interpretation of the Near-Death Experience: An Evaluation Based on Recent Research," pp. 68-73.

[14] Sabom, Michael, M.D. *Recollections of Death: A Medical Investigation*, New York: Harper & Row, 1982, p. 83.

[15] *Ibid*, 87.

[16] *Ibid*, 114.

[17] *Ibid*, 169.

[18] Gibbs. "Moody's Versus Siegel's Interpretation of the Near-Death Experience: An Evaluation Based on Recent Research," p. 77.

[19] Visit the Near Death Experience Research Foundation (www.nderf.org) to review the largest current online collection of personal accounts of NDEs. The site also carries reviews of NDE books written by experiencers. The site was created and is run by IANDS Director Dr. Jeff Long, M.D.

[20] Sabom, Michael. *Light and Death: One Doctor's Fascinating Account of Near-Death Experiences*, Zondervan Publishing, 1998.

[21] Ring, Kenneth and Cooper, Sharon. *Mindsight: Near-Death and Out-of-Body Experiences in the Blind*, The William James Center for Consciousness Studies, 1999.

[22] Dr. Emily Williams Cook, Dr. Bruce Greyson, and Dr. Ian Stevenson. "Do Any Near-Death Experiences Provide Evidence for the Survival of Human Personality After Death? Relevant Features and Illustrative Case Reports," *Journal of Scientific Exploration* 12:377-406, 1998.

[23] Sarah Tippit, *"Mind Continues After Brain Dies, Scientist Says."* Reuters news service, June 28, 2001

[24] Lommel MD, Pim van, et al. "Near Death Experience in Survivors of Cardiac Arrest: A Prospective Study in the Netherlands," *The Lancet*, Vol. 358, No. 9298, 15, Dec. 2001. It also includes a list of medical journal articles dealing with NDEs for serious investigators of the NDE phenomenon.

[25] Shiels. D. "A Cross-Cultural Study of Beliefs in Out of the Body Experiences," *Journal of the American Society for Psychical Research*, 49: 697-741, 1978.

[26] Twemlow et al. *The Out-of-Body Experience: Phenomenology*, 1980. Paper presented at the annual meeting of the American Psychiatric Association.

[27] Hart, Hornell and Hart, Ella. "Visions and Apparitions Collectively and Reciprocally Perceived," *Proceedings of the Society for Psychical Research*, Vol. XLI, 1932-33, pp. 205-249.

[28] Monroe, Robert A. *Journeys Out of the Body*, New York: Dolphin/Doubleday, 1971, pp. 46-47.

[29] "The OBE Psychophysiology of Robert A. Monroe," from *With the Eyes of the Mind* by Glen O. Gabbard and Stuart W. Twemlow. Praeger Publishers, 1984. Also reprinted in Monroe, Robert. *Far Journeys*, Dolphin Books, 1985, pp. 271-274.

[30] Charles Tart. "A Second Psychophysiological Study of Out-of-the-Body Experiences in a Gifted Subject," *International Journal of Parapsychology*," 1967, Vol. 9, 251-258. A copy of this paper can also be found on the web at www.paradigm-sys.com/cttart/sci-docs/ctt67-aspso.html.

[31] Charles Tart. "Six Studies of Out-of-the-Body Experiences." Paper found on Tart's website at www.paradigm-sys.com/cttart/sci-docs/ctt97-ssooo.html

[32] Rogo, D. Scott. "Researching the Out-of-Body Experience: The State of the Art," *Anabiosis - The Journal of Near Death Studies*, Spring 1984, Vol. 4, No. 1, pp. 22-49.

[33] Letter of April 5, 1999 from Dr. Sabom to radio program host Art Bell.

[34] Sabom. *Recollections of Death: A Medical Investigation*, pp. 99-105.

[35] Lawrence, Madelaine and Ring, Kenneth. "Further Evidence for Veridical Perception During Near-Death Experiences," *Journal of Near Death Studies*, 11, No. 4: 223-229.

[36] Hart and Hart. "Visions and Apparitions Collectively and Reciprocally Perceived," *Proceedings of the Society for Psychical Research,* pp. 222-224. Original found in *Phantasms of the Living* (1886), written by Edmund Gurney, Frederic Myers and Frank Podmore and published by the Society for Psychical Research.

[37] Morse, Melvin, M.D. *Parting Visions: Uses and Meanings of Pre-Death, Psychic, and Spiritual Experiences,* 37.

[38] Moody, Raymond. *Life After Life,* Covington, GA: Mockingbird, 1975, p. 151.

CHAPTER TWELVE

[1] Becker, Carl. *Paranormal Experience and Survival of Death,* Albany NY: State University of New York Press, 1993, p. 44.

[2] Cited in *Phantom Encounters,* Alexandria, VA: Time-Life Books, 1988, p. 21

[3] *Ibid,* 23.

[4] Morse, Melvin. *Parting Visions: Uses and Meanings of Pre-Death, Psychic, and Spiritual Experiences.*

[5] Prince, Walter F. *The Enchanted Boundary,* Boston: Boston Society for Psychical Research, 1930, pp. 165-167.

[6] Hart, Hornell and Hart, Ella. "Visions and Apparitions Collectively and Reciprocally Perceived," *Proceedings of the Society for Psychical Research,* Vol. XLI, 1932-33, pp. 205-249.

[7] Duncan. Lois and Roll, William George. *Psychic Connections: A Journey into the Mysterious World of Psi,* Delacorte, 1995.

[8] Stevenson, Ian. "Six Modern Apparitional Experiences," *Journal of Scientific Exploration,* 1995, Vol. 9, No. 3, pp. 351-366.

[9] Moody, Raymond, M.D. *Reunions: Visionary Encounters With Departed Loved Ones,* New York: Villard Books, 1993, p. 181.

[10] "Case of the Will of James L. Chaffin," *Proceedings of the Society for Psychical Research,* Vol. XXXVI, 1926-28, pp. 517-524.

[11] Sidgwick, Eleanor. *Proceedings of the Society for Psychical Research,* Vol. XXXIII, 1923.

[12] Underwood, Peter. *Hauntings: New Light on 10 Famous Cases,* London: 1977.

[13] Roll, William G. *The Poltergeist,* New American Library, 1983, pp. 91-93.

[14] Bender, Hans. "An Investigation of 'Poltergeist' Occurrences," *Proceedings of the Parapsychological Association,* No. 5, 1968, pp. 31-33. Also see Vol. No. 6, 1969.

[15] Gauld, Alan and Cornell, A.D. *Poltergeists,* Boston: Routledge & Kegan Paul, 1979.

[16] Mischo, John, Timm, Ulrich and Vilhjalmsson, Geir. "A Psychokinetic Effect Personally Observed," *Proceedings of the Parapsychological Association,* No. 5, 1968, pp. 33-35.

[17] Roll. *The Poltergeist,* pp. 92-93.

[18] Gauld and Cornell. *Poltergeists,* p. 89.

[19] *Ibid,* 91.

[20] Roll, W.G. and Pratt, J.G. "The Miami Disturbances," New York: *Journal of the American Society for Psychical Research,* 1971

CHAPTER THIRTEEN

[1] Berger, Arthur S. *Aristocracy of the Dead: New Findings in Postmortem Survival,* Jefferson, N.C.: McFarland & Co., 1987, p.7.

[2] Klimo, Jon. *Channeling: Investigations on Receiving Information from Paranormal Sources,* Los Angeles: Jeremy Tarcher, 1987, pp. 100-101. Klimo cites as his source an article by Nettie Colburn entitled "Séances With Abraham Lincoln" in David Knight's book *The ESP Reader,* New York: Grosset & Dunlop, 1969, pp. 31-46.

[3] Klimo. *Channeling: Investigations on Receiving Information from Paranormal Sources,* p. 101.

[4] Jenkins, Elizabeth. *The Shadow and the Light: A Defense of Daniel Douglas Home, the Medium,* London: Hamish Hamilton, 1982, pp. 16-18.

[5] *Presidential Addresses to the SPR, 1882-1911.* Glasgow: Robert Maclehose, 1912, p. 35.

[6] Moore. *In Search of White Crows: Spiritualism, Parapsychology and American Culture,* 139.

[7] Myers, F.W.H. *Human Personality and Its Survival of Bodily Death.* (Suzy Smith, Ed.; abridged edition), New Hyde Park, NY: University Books, 1961, p.407.

[8] Hodgson, Richard. "A Further Record of Observations of Certain Phenomena of a Trance," *Proceedings of the Society for Psychical Research,* Vol. 13, 1897-1898, p 285.

[9] James, William. "Certain Phenomena of Trance," *Proceedings of the SPR,* 6 (1890), p. 652.

[10] Moore. *In Search of White Crows: Spiritualism, Parapsychology, and American Culture,* pp. 136-137.

[11] For a good biography of Ford, try Allen Spraggett's book *Arthur Ford: The Man Who Talked With the Dead* (New York: Signet, 1973).

[12] See Chap. 25 of Rhine, Louisa. *Psi, What is It? The Story of ESP and PK,* New York: Harper & Row, 1975.

[13] Moore. *In Search of White Crows: Spiritualism, Parapsychology and American Culture,* pp. 205-206.

[14] Hastings, Arthur. *With the Tongues of Men and Angels: A Study of Channeling,* Holt, Rinehart and Winston, 1990.

[15] *Ibid,* 1.

[16] *Ibid,* 183-184.

[17] Klimo. *Channeling: Investigations on Receiving Information from Paranormal Sources,* p. 253.

[18] Very few controlled experiments have been attempted on EVP phenomena. For a recent attempt, read Imants Baruss, "Failure to

Replicate Electronic Voice Phenomenon," *Journal of Scientific Exploration,* Vol. 15, No. 3, 2001, pp. 355-367.

[19] Gary E.R. Schwartz, Linda G.S. Russek, Lonnie Nelson, and Christopher Barentsen, "Accuracy and Replicability of Anomalous After-Death Communication Across Highly Skilled Mediums," *Journal of the Society for Psychical Research,* Jan. 2001.

[20] Richard Wiseman and Ciaran O'Keefe, "A Critique of Schwartz et al.'s After Death Communication Studies," *Skeptical Inquirer,* November/December 2001, pp. 26-30.

[21] The full report appears in the *Proceedings of the Society for Psychical Research.*

[22] Letter of March 10, 2001 from Montague Keen to *Psychic World.*

[23] *Psychic World,* No. 90, June 2001, p. 10.

[24] *Psychic World,* No. 88, April 2001, p. 9.

[25] Hodgson, Richard. "A Further Record of Observations of Certain Phenomena of a Trance," *Proceedings of the Society for Psychical Research,* Vol. 13, 1897-1898, pp. 297.

[26] Hodgson. "A Further Record of Observations of Certain Phenomena of a Trance," *Proceedings of the Society for Psychical Research,* pp. 297-298.

[27] Hodgson. "A Further Record of Observations of Certain Phenomena of a Trance," *Proceedings of the Society for Psychical Research,* p. 304.

[28] Hodgson. "A Further Record of Observations of Certain Phenomena of a Trance," *Proceedings of the Society for Psychical Research,* p.330.

[29] Hodgson. "A Further Record of Observations of Certain Phenomena of a Trance," *Proceedings of the Society for Psychical Research,* p. 405.

[30] Klimo. *Channeling: Investigations on Receiving Information from Paranormal Sources,* pp. 116-117.

31 Fuller, John. *The Airmen Who Would Not Die*, New York: Berkeley, 1980, p. 269.

32 Garrett, Eileen. *My Life as a Search for the Meaning of Mediumship*, London: Rider and Co., 1939, pp. 163-225.

33 *Psychics: In-Depth Interviews*, New York: Harper & Row, 1972, pp. 44-45.

34 Jung, Carl. *Collected Letters, Vol. 1, 1906-1950.* Princeton, N.J. Bollingen #45/Princeton University Press, 1973, p. 43.

CHAPTER FOURTEEN
1 Gallup. *Adventures in Immortality*, New York: McGraw-Hill, 1982,

2 Head, Joseph and Cranston, S.L. *Reincarnation: The Phoenix Fire Mystery*, New York: Julian Press, 1977, pp. 134-160.

3 Stevenson, Ian. *Children Who Remember Previous Lives: A Question of Reincarnation*, McFarland & Co., 2000, p.3.

4 Criteria presented by Stevenson at a summer 1972 conference on parapsychology at the U. of Edinburgh as cited in Rogo, D. Scott. *The Search for Yesterday: A Critical Examination of the Evidence for Reincarnation.* Englewood Cliffs, NJ: Prentice-Hall, 1985, p. 42

5 Becker. *Paranormal Experience and the Survival of Death*, p.18.

6 Wambach, Helen. *Reliving Past Lives: The Evidence Under Hypnosis.* Barnes & Noble Books, 2000.

7 The story was originally told in a 1927 book by the boy's father, K.K. N. Sahay, entitled *Reincarnation: Verified Cases of Rebirth After Death*. Stevenson researched the case in the 1960s. A good summary and commentary on the case can also be found in D. Scott Rogo's book *The Search for Yesterday: A Critical Examination of the Evidence for Reincarnation*, pp. 46-49.

8 Stevenson. *Children Who Remember Previous Lives: A Question of Reincarnation*, p. 4.

[9] Stevenson believes that "nearly all such hypnotically evoked 'previous personalities' are entirely imaginary," thus he is "not in favor of serious research with hypnotic regression." See his statement "Hypnotic Regression to 'Previous Lives' " found on the website of the Division of Personality Studies, University of Virginia (www.med.virginia.edu/personality-studies/regression.html)

[10] Rogo. *The Search for Yesterday: A Critical Examination of the Evidence for Reincarnation,* p.116

[11] *Ibid,* 115.

[12] Stevenson. *Children Who Remember Previous Lives: A Question of Reincarnation,* p. 45

CHAPTER FIFTEEN

[1] See FAQ "What is the state-of-the-evidence for psi?" stored on his website at www.psiresearch.org.

[2] Jahn, Robert and Dunne, Brenda. "Science of the Subjective," *Journal of Scientific Exploration.* Vol. 11, No. 2, pp. 201-224, 1997.